Praise for
The Keystone Advantage

"Building on a perceptive biological metaphor, Iansiti and Levien develop a thoughtful analytic framework for business ecosystems operating in our networked economy. With elucidative case studies, they identify alternative, role-based technology and operations strategies that companies can execute in the context of the dynamics and health of their ecosystem. *The Keystone Advantage* is a valuable contribution to business and technology strategy."

—Dr. Robert Martin, former Chief Technology Officer, Bell Labs

"Today's business climate requires ongoing innovation and rapid time to market—companies cannot get there on their own. AT&T is a real-life example of a "keystone" company integrating our in-house-owned and -controlled services with products and services from best-of-breed partners and suppliers. The authors show the imperative, and the method, for operating successfully within complex business ecosystems."

—David Krantz, Vice President, Product Management,
Strategy, & Business Development, AT&T Consumer Services

"Iansiti and Levien present a wealth of biological system analogs and extensive industry casework to provide a powerful and compelling new lens for analyzing enterprise growth. The authors not only provide

new frameworks, but also strategies and detailed approaches for suc-
ceeding in this new 'networked' era."

—Eric Pelander, Partner and Global Leader,
Strategy and Change Services, IBM

"No company is an island, and sustained success depends on embracing and leveraging business ecosystems. In *The Keystone Advantage,*
Iansiti and Levien vividly illuminate the importance of business networks. Companies can no longer dwell within their own walls if they
want to cultivate new capabilities and stay competitive. This book
shows better than ever before how webs of vital external relationships
profoundly impact the fortunes of companies large and small."

—David Aronoff, General Partner, Greylock Partners

"After reading *The Keystone Advantage,* business executives and strategic
planners will never again view long-term success in a traditional way,
i.e., based solely on strategic positioning and operational efficiency
vis-à-vis customers, suppliers, and competitors. Using biological ecosystems as an analogy and real business examples from diverse industries, Iansiti and Levien present a compelling case that identifying your
ecosystem and determining its health will ultimately determine your
company's fate. More than just a neat idea, the book provides quantita-
tive tools for companies to gauge the health of their current ecosystem
and develop strategies to enhance their position."

—Lou Tomasetta, President and Chief Executive Officer,
Vitesse Semiconductor Corporation

The Keystone Advantage

The Keystone Advantage

What the New Dynamics of
Business Ecosystems Mean
for Strategy, Innovation,
and Sustainability

Marco Iansiti
Roy Levien

Harvard Business School Press
Boston, Massachusetts

Library of Congress Cataloging-in-Publication Data
Iansiti, Marco, 1961–
    The keystone advantage : what the new dynamics of business ecosystems
    mean for strategy, innovation, and sustainability / Marco Iansiti. Roy Levien.
        p. cm.
    ISBN 1-59139-307-8
    1. Strategic planning. 2. Business enterprises—Technological innovations.
    3. Organizational effectiveness. I. Levien, Roy. II. Title.
    HD30.28.I26 2004
    658.4—dc22

                                                                    2004002105

This book is dedicated
to our children,
Alexander, Ethan, Isaac,
Julia, and Shira.

Contents

Acknowledgments

This book would not have been possible without the help and inspiration provided by an enormous number of people. The work is founded on a number of research projects and consulting assignments, and a large number of collaborators, research participants, and clients have had a major impact on its evolution.

First of all, without the help of many colleagues and Ph.D. students at Harvard University, this project could not have been accomplished. We would first like to mention Warren McFarlan, George Westerman, and Alan MacCormack. Much of the research for this book was done in collaboration with them and draws in major ways from their work. Warren was instrumental in exposing us to fascinating examples from Li & Fung, Merrill Lynch, and Charles Schwab and deserves much credit for extending our insights into new contexts. Similarly, George Westerman greatly expanded our understanding with his study of innovation in Internet retailing, which included brilliant insights on the importance and nature of integration in that context. Alan is a long-time collaborator and deserves much credit for our understanding of platforms and organizational adaptation. We also drew considerable insights and inspiration from our collaborations with H. T. Kung, and from many of the students in the Ph.D. program for Information Technology and Management, including Marcin Strojwas, Jason Woodard, and Feng Zhu, among many others. Many other colleagues, including Carliss Baldwin, Saikat Chaudhuri, Kim Clark, Lee Fleming, Frances Frei, Rob Huckman, Edward Jung, Mark Malamud, Andy McAfee, Gary Pisano, Jan Rivkin, Roy Shapiro, and Jonathan West, also had a major impact on this research by providing crucial insights and advice.

Many of the ideas and examples were drawn from work performed in real firms. We would like to thank Henry Liu, Greg Richards, Gregg

Rotenberg, and Jeremy Schneider at Keystone (see www.key-inc.com), whose insights were fundamental to this book. Their work on projects for a variety of Global 1000 clients was invaluable in defining, framing, and grounding the ideas around keystone, dominator, and niche strategies. This work captured much of their thinking.

The book would also not have been done without the help of David Evans, who provided ongoing encouragement and many important insights, particularly around the concept of N-sided markets, and the network dynamics of the Visa platform. David's NERA colleagues, including Richard Bergin, John Scalf, and Jay Wynn, also contributed greatly.

We are also thankful to a number of clients, specifically Microsoft and IBM. Much of this work was performed during engagements with them, and their insights were extraordinarily valuable. A number of executives, including Tom Burt, Tom Button, Joel Cawley, Drew Clark, Dan Hay, David Heiner, Gerry Mooney, Claudia Fan Munce, Joe Nastasi, Steven Sinofsky, Jim Spohrer, and Dee Dee Walsh, added greatly to our understanding of these phenomena. John Herr and Patrick Jabal from eBay, as well as Tim Brady and Katie Burke from Yahoo!, also provided invaluable contributions.

The Keystone Advantage

CHAPTER ONE

Rethinking Networks

Strategy is becoming, to an increasing extent, the art of managing assets that one does not own.

For many years, Kmart and Wal-Mart reigned as the flagships of the U.S. retail industry, with little to distinguish them in the eyes of most consumers and practitioners but matters of style. But Kmart filed for Chapter 11 protection in January 2002, whereas Wal-Mart continues to thrive as the most successful retailer of all time. Colorful and sinister theories accounting for Wal-Mart's spectacular success abound: Accounts have mentioned everything from predatory pricing to employee culture and from Sam Walton's overalls to his knack for identifying productive store locations. However, an examination of Wal-Mart's relationship with its vast network of business partners highlights a very different driver of its success: Wal-Mart, like Microsoft, is successful because it figured out how to create, manage, and evolve an incredibly powerful business ecosystem.

Over the years, Wal-Mart took advantage of its ability to gather consumer information to coordinate the distributed assets of its vast network of suppliers. You can almost think of it as a single enormous operation, made up of thousands of companies. Through a combination of technology, capabilities, and policies, Wal-Mart wove the fabric that organized this massive network of organizations into a collective force that worked to provide customers with the products they needed at the time they needed them, at the lowest possible cost. This strategy proved remarkably effective, resulting in dramatic performance advantages in cost, operating margin, and sales per square foot—a gap that Wal-Mart has sustained and even widened over time.

Wal-Mart's approach evolved over a long period. But even early in its history, Wal-Mart made a point of tracking demand information in real time. The key was that it decided to share this information with its supplier network. It introduced Retail Link, the system that still delivers the most accurate real-time sales information in the industry to Wal-Mart partners. Wal-Mart was unique in the retail space in offering this kind of service, turning Retail Link into a critical supply chain hub that now connects the information systems of thousands of manufacturers, including the likes of Tyson Foods, Gillette, and Procter & Gamble. Moreover, through the software and hardware it disseminated, Wal-Mart provided the tools and technological components that enabled its network partners to make Retail Link an integral element in their respective supply chains, further amplifying the impact of the consumer information it provided. In this way, thousands of individual firms have been able to share in the value created by Wal-Mart's information infrastructure, and have built their own technology and business processes to leverage Wal-Mart's information assets.

By sharing sales data, as well as through other contributions, such as sharing the massive scale economies of its stores and centralizing the structure of its supply network, Wal-Mart effectively provided a low-cost, high-efficiency, and information-rich platform for the distribution of an enormous variety of products. This was valuable to Wal-Mart's many suppliers, which in turn reflected on Wal-Mart's own position and advantage. Ultimately, Wal-Mart was successful because it made use of its unique position in its network of suppliers and shared the value that was created by being a network hub.

Like Wal-Mart, the dramatic success of Microsoft is also frequently ascribed to simplistic theories, ranging from conspiracy to luck. But looking carefully at how Microsoft managed its network of business partners over time yields an intriguing explanation: that like Wal-Mart, Microsoft created and actively maintained a platform that a vast number of firms could leverage to increase productivity, enhance stability, and use as the building blocks for innovation.

From the earliest days of the microcomputer industry, Microsoft focused on designing programming tools and technologies that were used by thousands of organizations and millions of developers. Indeed, Microsoft's first product was not an application or an operating system, but the first popular version of BASIC to run on microcomputers—effectively a tool that enabled developers to more easily create software that would run on a large number of machines. Since the early 1980s, Microsoft has been offering operating systems, such as MS-DOS and Windows, that included standard interfaces for writing application programs. These technologies evolved further during the late 1980s and 1990s to include a powerful combination of operating systems, reusable programming components, and tools. These elements increased developer productivity and innovation, enabling this community to create a variety of applications without having to worry about hardware-specific details. Thus, like Wal-Mart, Microsoft simplified the challenge of connecting a very large and distributed network of companies for its customers. Like Wal-Mart, Microsoft acted as a crucial hub in a vast and diverse business ecosystem.

Both Wal-Mart and Microsoft deliberately chose to shape the collective performance of the networks of firms that depend on them by offering *platforms* on which others could build. Both firms were successful because they appreciated the impact these platforms could have on these business networks and took steps to realize this impact by creating real opportunities for other firms. These firms in turn made investments in leveraging these platforms and began to depend on them for their success. This created a virtuous cycle in their respective industries through which a broad variety of firms achieved high levels of productivity, stability, and innovativeness. This in turn led to outstanding operating performance for both Microsoft and Wal-Mart, sustained over decades.

Despite their drastically different settings, the two firms' success stories share a number of critical factors. Like Wal-Mart, Microsoft's performance is linked to that of its vast network of business partners, numbering in the tens of thousands. Like Wal-Mart, Microsoft has worked hard to organize the behavior of these business partners, creating opportunities for growth and innovation. And like Wal-Mart, Microsoft is only strong if this business community is large, healthy, and growing. This does not mean that all members of these communities are always happy with Microsoft's or Wal-Mart's behavior, since both firms frequently adopt aggressive positions in negotiations. Regardless of the intensity of *individual* encounters, however, both firms understand that they can only win if they continue to sustain the *collective* health of their vast networks of business partners.

In essence, both of these firms understand that their fate is shared with that of the other members of their business network. Rather than focusing primarily on their internal capabilities (as many of their competitors did), they emphasize the collective properties of the business networks in which they participate, and treat these more like organic *ecosystems* than traditional supply chain partners. They understand their individual impact on the health of these ecosystems and the respective impact of ecosystem health on their own performance.

Ultimately Wal-Mart and Microsoft were successful because they played the role of a *keystone* in their respective ecosystems. Drawn from biology, the term describes a pattern of behavior that improves the performance of an ecosystem and, in doing so, improves individual performance. This kind of keystone strategy is the focus of this book. As will become increasingly clear, this approach to strategy challenges many prevailing views about how critical firms such as Wal-Mart and Microsoft work, and calls into question much conventional wisdom about the management practices of firms as diverse and varied as eBay, Enron, Charles Schwab, and IBM.

Business Networks

Wal-Mart and Microsoft are by no means alone in operating within business networks. Business networks are ubiquitous in our economy. Dozens of organizations collaborate to bring electricity into our homes. Hundreds of organizations join forces to manufacture and distribute a personal computer. Thousands of companies coordinate with each other to provide the rich foundation of applications necessary to make a software operating system successful. This pervasive networked nature of our business environment has triggered a significant evolution in the design of business operations and in the role of managers. For an increasing portion of our business leaders, the fundamental challenge they now face is the management of assets that are not directly owned by their own firms.

Business networks did not start with the Internet. Networks are now more widespread in our economy than ever before, but their pervasiveness is the result of an evolution in social, economic, political, and technological systems that has stretched over the last few centuries. For hundreds of years, the Italian apparel industry (originating in the Prato region) has been organized as a loosely connected network of many organizations, many as small as one person. The local autonomy of this system enabled the kind of focus, flexibility, and quick reaction that ensured strong performance in a highly turbulent environment. At the same time, organizations evolved to coordinate the network. Starting with the *impannatore* of Renaissance Italy, these organizations orchestrated an integrated production and distribution system from the individual parts of the distributed network. To do this, they developed a range of processes and technologies connecting their network partners to each other and coordinating their collective response. This combination of autonomy and coordination enabled the Italian apparel network to become robust enough to survive hundreds of years of technology and market changes, achieving enough productivity and innovation to triumph over competitive systems. Even now, the Italian apparel network is a remarkably distributed operation in which a small number of organizations, such as Benetton, function as keystones to help coordinate network behavior.

Despite the rich and deep roots of our networked economy, the nature of business challenges evolved significantly during the second half of the twentieth century. During much of the 1900s, the mantra of most modern businesses was still vertical integration, as organizations such as DuPont, Ford, and IBM evolved as juggernauts that directly owned the vast majority of the assets necessary for their daily operation. Creating distributed business networks was too difficult and costly, and the advantages of vertical integration dominated in most environments. But during the last decades of the twentieth century significant changes in our legal, managerial, and technological capabilities made it much easier for companies to collaborate and distribute operations over many organizations. In industries as different as personal computers and personal care products, companies leveraged multiple organizations in distributed supply chains, integrated technological components from a variety of business alliances, collaborated with a number of channel partners to distribute their products, and leveraged complementary services from banks, insurance providers, or retailers. This pushed many of our industries toward a fully networked structure, in which even the simplest product or service is now the result of collaboration among many different organizations.

Business networks thus emerged in industries as different as automobiles and fast foods. The auto industry evolved to exhibit a widely distributed structure, with more than half of the value of any individual car being contributed by an increasingly extensive supplier base. Companies such as Ford and Chrysler found themselves at the hubs of increasingly complex and global networks, which motivated the development of new capabilities, processes, and technologies. During the same time period, food service institutions such as McDonald's and Burger King were built on top of extensive supplier bases and developed massive networks of franchisees.

During the second half of the twentieth century, large, distributed business networks became *the* established way of doing business in the modern economy. They can be identified in industries ranging from biotechnology to insurance, and from banking to software. Just because they are ubiquitous, however, does not mean that they are easy to manage.

Network Challenges

In the last ten years, the combination of readily available technology and capital has made the creation of business networks easy. Despite being simple to create, business networks are still poorly understood and most often poorly managed. In the boom years of the Internet, there was an almost universal euphoria about the power of networks. Business networks would enable unforeseen efficiencies in operations and innovation. New network technologies would disrupt traditional companies and create unprecedented opportunities for new company growth and innovation. Network "effects" would create enormous value and large barriers to entry in businesses as different as enterprise software and grocery delivery. But things were not so easy.

The implosion of the Internet bubble made it obvious that network members share a common fate, which means that they can both rise *and* fall together. And although many had predicted that the bubble could not last, the sharpness, suddenness, and violence of the fall surprised a lot of people. The stunning reversal of the virtuous cycle that seemed to automatically drive endless growth left many questioning the very foundation of their faith in the power of business networks. But the Internet was by no means alone in generating business network failures. The effective coordination of distributed operating assets has eluded managers in organizations as different as Enron and the State of California, and in industries as different as electricity and software.

Behind these failures is a school of management thinking that focuses primarily on the internal operations of the firm and tells us little about how to manage vast networks of firms. The majority of books on our management bookshelves tell us to build internal capabilities, focus on our core competencies, create small, dedicated teams, and ward off disruptive technologies by spinning off small, focused, dedicated ventures. Prevailing management theories all too often advise the operating manager to create small, isolated units to fight problems and leverage opportunity. Given their emphasis on understanding focused, tightly coupled systems, these theories have a difficult time dealing with a huge, unfocused, unbounded, amorphous, and constantly evolving network like the Internet. They can't tell us how to manage a network of business partners that is one thousand times the size of the firm, as is the case in industries as different as apparel and software. They don't tell us why IBM's innovation strategy is more dependent on influencing the behavior of the millions of free software developers scattered outside its organizational boundaries than on the hundreds located in its internal Thomas J. Watson Research Center. And they can't explain why Microsoft and Wal-Mart have been able to sustain unprecedented growth in revenues and profits by leveraging their networks of business partners.

When the Internet took off and business networks became ubiquitous, our understanding of management and strategy simply did not keep up. Consultants and academics rushed to propound new theories, but often without a solid foundation in research or experience. The executives who ran new Internet ventures or attempted to modify the operating models of established firms were thus often flying blind, attempting new business models and structures without solid foundations. The results are now all too obvious.

As our economy recovers and evolves, it is essential that we finally develop a solid understanding of how networks and key firms within them support or inhibit innovation, how they can enhance or damage operational productivity, and how they can provide healthy, sustainable environments for the creation of new firms and products. This, in essence, is the objective of this book.

Business Networks as Ecosystems

The collapse of the Internet economy—the few successes, the many failures, and the many lessons drawn from the evolution of traditional firms—provides the perfect opportunity to reflect on, research, and finally learn how to manage complex networks of firms. This motivated us to launch research programs involving dozens of firms across a variety of industry sectors. Over the last few years, we examined a massive number of public sources, interviewed hundreds of managers, and analyzed more than a hundred projects performed by diverse companies scattered across different industries.

Our approach integrated a deep foundation of managerial research with a broader understanding of networks drawn from a variety of other academic fields. The problems faced in business networks are not unique: Similar networks are found in a wide range of domains. The good news is that in fields as different as physics, biology, and social psychology, the study of networks has advanced dramatically in recent years. These advances helped us fill some of the voids in management theory and practice.

We found that perhaps more than any other type of network, a biological ecosystem provides a powerful analogy for understanding a business network.[1] Like business networks, biological ecosystems are characterized by a large number of loosely interconnected participants who depend on each other for their mutual effectiveness and survival. And like business network participants, biological species in ecosystems share their fate with each other. If the ecosystem is healthy, individual species thrive. If the ecosystem is unhealthy, individual species suffer deeply. And as with business ecosystems, reversals in overall ecosystem health can happen very quickly.

Like business networks, evolved biological ecosystems, from the Atlantic Ocean to the Amazon, are essentially communities of entities with differing interests bound together in a collective whole. The robustness and long-term dynamism achieved by these networks in nature highlight their power. Moreover, the specific features of these ecosystems—their structure, the relationships among members, the kinds of connections among them, and the differing roles played by their members—suggest important analogies for understanding business networks. Perhaps the most important one is that the structure of biological networks is not homogenous: In the majority of these networks the appearance of richly connected "hubs," at all scales, is almost inevitable. Naturally, the behavior of these hubs can have profound effects on the health of the entire network.

Looking more deeply into the ecosystem metaphor reveals that in almost all ecosystems these hubs take the form of active keystones whose interests are aligned with those of the ecosystem as a whole and who serve as critical regulators of ecosystem health. Extending this observation to other evolved biological systems, one finds that keystones are in fact quite common; almost all of these systems possess some kind of keystone—either embodied in a special member of the system or encoded in universally agreed-to protocols, rules, and goals—that enhances stability, predictability, and other measures of system health by regulating connections and creating stable and predictable platforms on which other network members can rely.

It is important to state at the outset what will become clear as we proceed: We are not arguing here that industries *are* ecosystems or even that it makes sense to organize them *as if they were,* but that biological ecosystems can serve as a source of vivid and useful terminology as well as provide specific and powerful insights into the different roles played by firms.[2] Most critically, when we viewed our research observations across industrial sectors through the lens of the ecosystem metaphor, it rapidly became clear that almost all healthy business ecosystems were characterized by some kind of keystone function—and that the efficiency, innovativeness, and robustness of the members of these ecosystems were fundamentally linked to keystone behavior.

Close examination of the structure of industries with this in mind reveals that there are generally a relatively small number of network hubs (and thus potential keystones). This does not mean that the large number of other firms do not have a critical role to play in regulating the health and stability of the ecosystem. These firms constitute the bulk of the ecosystem and are responsible for the lion's share of value creation and innovation. These firms need, for their own good as well as the good of the entire system, to learn to effectively manage what the network provides. The implications of our ideas therefore extend to all firms in an ecosystem.

Implications

In this book, we put forth a holistic view of strategy that fits the world of business ecosystems. We draw from biology and complexity theory and articulate this view by describing different strategic modes. We differentiate between keystone, dominator, and niche strategies. Keystone and dominator strategies can be pursued by firms that occupy important hubs in their business networks. Keystone strategies shape and coordinate the ecosystem, largely by the dissemination of platforms that form a foundation for ecosystem innovation and operations. These contrast with dominator strategies, which attack the ecosystem, absorbing and integrating external assets into internal operations. Niche strategies can be pursued by the much larger number of firms that make up the bulk of the ecosystem. These firms emphasize differentiation by focusing on unique capabilities and leveraging key assets provided by others.

Traditional models of strategy that emphasize *internal* competencies fail to account for these dynamics because they focus on the evolution of firm capabilities and business models instead of on the relationship between the firm and its *external* ecosystem. Our shelves are full of books that talk about how companies will be distinguished by the internal competencies they develop and will be disrupted by the next generation of technology or business model that makes their internal assets and capabilities obsolete. We argue, however, that the crucial battle is not between individual firms but between networks of firms. Innovation and operations have become a collective activity. Ecosystems will share in a common fate, and firms will be distinguished by the way they manage the massive web of dependencies that is created between them and the rest of the world. Keystones will win by virtue of the powerful platforms they create and by the processes and assets they share with their ecosystems. Keystones will lose if their ecosystem fails by becoming unhealthy or if the ecosystem abandons the keystones' architectures for different platforms. Niche firms will win if they leverage powerful and well-run platforms and manage the dependencies that are created. Niche firms will lose if they misread the complex dynamics of their surroundings, if they associate with a weak keystone, if they are overrun by an aggressive dominator, or if they become dependent on outdated or unsustainable platforms.

The following chapters explore these implications in detail as we elaborate a framework for shaping technology and operations strategies which acknowledges the realities of business ecosystems. Effective firms, from large influential platform-defining keystones such as Microsoft, Wal-Mart, or Taiwan Semiconductor Manufacturing Corporation (TSMC) to smaller platform-leveraging niche firms such as Intuit or NVIDIA, have all succeeded in large part because they appreciate that they are bound to business networks with which they share a common fate. These firms balance a concern for their internal capabilities with an appreciation of the opportunities and challenges created by their dependence on the collective health of their ecosystem. In what follows we elaborate a comprehensive ecosystem-inspired view of how firms can operate most effectively in business networks by looking closely at what these firms and many others do right—and wrong—as they strive to face the challenges and exploit the opportunities that they encounter as a consequence of being embedded in a business network.

Although not the main focus of this book, it is also useful to highlight some of the broader implications of our ideas. Implications for policy makers are particularly interesting. Existing policy does not always appear to address the realities of modern networked industries. The Clinton administration exploited the idea that "network effects" could inhibit challenges to entrenched technology as a means of rationalizing antitrust action against Microsoft and other players. It does, of course, make sense to think about modern corporations as part of interdependent systems. But it is now clear that the network economics frameworks used by the Justice Department had significant problems—many of the same misconceptions that undermined the lawsuits were also behind the misinterpretations that caused the Internet bubble.

Whether we are talking about networks of people, firms, or countries and whether we are debating antitrust law or the future of the United Nations, our approach is to focus on the economic health of these systems. Whether we are talking about antitrust law or foreign policy, our view would argue that the presence of different entities that control key hubs in an ecosystem is not *necessarily* bad for the health of the ecosystem as a whole. Like their biological counterparts, leading firms in business ecosystems, or leading countries in international settings, can play the role either of dominators that reduce productivity and make their partners more vulnerable to external shocks or of keystones that nourish diversity and stabilize their environments even as they vigorously pursue their own ends. Although dominator strategies, when selectively applied, can serve to stabilize or simplify an ecosystem, in many cases they should be a red flag for policy makers, whereas keystone strategies should most often not be. Indeed, we believe that public policy could be designed to *reinforce* keystonelike behavior and avoid harming critical network hubs, considering that the associated damage could paralyze vast numbers of ecosystem participants.

Book Structure

This book is designed to reveal the dynamics and implications of a business ecosystem perspective to business leaders and policy makers. It is organized into three parts and eleven chapters. Part I introduces and motivates our ecosystem framework. Part II continues by discussing implications for strategy. Part III focuses on operating implications by discussing three foundations of competition in a networked world. As much as possible, we use detailed cases and examples to illustrate our findings.

Part I, "The Ecosystem Framework," begins with chapter 2, "Shared Fate." This chapter sets the stage for our analysis by taking a look at the evolution of business ecosystems, drawing a number of analogies with their biological counterparts and focusing on the software industry in detail. We then expand our analysis to frame the networked properties of other industries. This chapter also briefly traces the emergence of shared fate by summarizing the stages of ecosystem evolution as illustrated by the computing industry in its transition from an integrated to a networked structure over the past several decades. Chapter 3, "Collective Behavior," focuses on the fundamental idea that the behavior of a community of organizations in a business ecosystem is inextricably intertwined. The performance of any individual organization is tied to the performance of the whole. We introduce three cardinal measures of ecosystem performance or health: productivity, robustness, and niche creation.

Part II of this book, "Ecosystem Strategies," develops the strategic implications of our ideas. Chapter 4, "Operating Strategies," frames these implications as three foundational strategies—keystone, dominator, and niche player—that describe characteristic patterns in the behavior of organizations competing in a business network. Chapter 5, "Keystones," details the characteristics of a keystone strategy. It draws from a variety of analogies and examples to show how keystones improve ecosystem health and, in doing so, increase their own operational performance. It goes on to describe in some detail the two components of a keystone strategy: value creation and value sharing. Chapter 6, "Landlords and Dominators," covers other types of network operating strategies that organizations occupying a network hub may deploy. Taking examples from history and current business, the chapter describes a number of striking failures in organizations and draws some important lessons. Chapter 7, "Niche Players," discusses in some detail the nature of operating strategy for the bulk of the ecosystem—the organizations that do not occupy one of the network hubs. It speaks to the challenges of managing the dependencies between niche players and ecosystem hubs, and describes the most critical capabilities.

Part III, "Foundations for Competition," delves into operating implications by exploring three foundations of sustainable performance in a business ecosystem. The first foundation is discussed in chapter 8,

"Architecture, Platforms, and Standards," which defines how companies draw boundaries between technologies, products, and organizations, thereby shaping the ecosystem in which they compete. The second foundation is the subject of chapter 9, "Integration, Innovation, and Adaptation," which discusses how organizations work across these ecosystem boundaries, leveraging the ecosystem's distributed capabilities for operations, innovation, and adaptation. The third foundation is covered in chapter 10, "Market Design, Operation, and Competition," which discusses how organizations operate within the complex market dynamics that govern their ecosystem.

Chapter 11, "Business Ecology," concludes this book by reflecting on some of its broader implications for the evolution of firms. It addresses the fundamental challenge of sustainability in business and argues that a new, holistic approach to strategy is critical to an increasingly broad range of firms in our economy as they face the new set of challenges and responsibilities created by competing in business ecosystems.

I

The Ecosystem Framework

CHAPTER TWO

Shared Fate

It has become an axiom of news coverage and opinion pieces in the wake of the terrorist attacks of September 11, 2001, that we live in a highly interconnected world. We are repeatedly reminded—often with urgency bordering on panic-mongering—that just about everything is connected to just about everything else. As the head of the Energy Department's energy infrastructure assurance program warned shortly after the attacks, "What you have is a complex system of systems on which the U.S. depends. Everything's hooked to everything."[1] The conclusions drawn from this observation are typically that this inter-connectedness makes us all more vulnerable than we might otherwise be; that because "physically isolated events ripple through everyday lives thousands of miles away," being interconnected puts us at greater risk.[2] Although this is disputable (as we shall discuss at some length later), and claims about the nature of this interconnectedness are often inaccurate or overstated (as we shall see), the basic observation is not: The ability of individuals to search across the country or the world for a competitive price on a favorite or hard-to-find product from the comfort of their dens in the middle of the night, or of firms to build supply chains that stretch from vast distribution facilities in the middle of the United States to small-scale family clothing manufacturers in remote locations in China or Palestine, is based on the fact that we live in a networked world.

Although the threat of terrorist attacks has newly focused our attention on some of its potential dangers, the phenomenon of intercon-nectedness is, of course, not new: It has evolved steadily over human history and has accelerated dramatically with each new wave of social transformation or enabling technology, most recently driven by the spread of capitalist market systems and of computing and communications technology. Increasingly, through recent decades, we have been living with—and taking for granted—the benefits of living in a networked world. Our current concern with the extent of our dependence on each other and on the consequences of this interconnectedness is appropriate, however: We live embedded in a system, and, more than ever before, *our* fates depend on *its* fate.

This fact has important consequences that reach far beyond the scope of this book, but in the context of business practice, it raises important questions:

- How can we as practitioners and managers act to take advantage of our interconnectedness?

- The fact that firms increasingly build products that depend on the products and technologies produced by other firms demands explicit management focus: The network of which a firm is a part is more than just a threat to be warded off or a source of raw materials to be harvested. It is a dynamic system in which each firm is embedded and which demands active and informed management. Can we characterize the kinds of management stances that exhibit this kind of informed approach?

- How can we avoid making mistakes that will damage the networks of which we are a part?

- Because firms' fates are bound together, they must take special care to avoid actions that undermine the health of those networks. These can be as sinister as Enron's manipulation of power distribution in California or as ultimately naïve as Yahoo!'s past traffic-sharing and advertising strategy.[3] Can we identify specific mistakes or modes of thinking that can cause damage—perhaps widespread and indirect—to our networks?

- Are there specific actions we can take that enhance the health of our networks? Are there things we need to be aware of in light of the fact that our actions may have indirect and widespread effects throughout the system?

- As the examples of Wal-Mart and Microsoft illustrate, it is clear that some firms are particularly effective at following strategies that achieve sustainable business performance while contributing to the health of their networks. Can these approaches be generalized? What can we learn from them?

We will turn to these questions in chapter 3. First, however, we need to develop a better understanding of just what it means to be part of a networked system and to understand how networked business systems arose.

Shared Fate in Nature

A compelling place to turn for a better appreciation of what it means to be a part of a richly networked system is the study of biological systems. Although we rarely appreciate the fact, just about every interesting accomplishment of the natural world is the product of the collective interactions of many richly interconnected players. From the networks of energy flow and predation in ecosystems to the feedback loops that control gene expression to the checks and balances that regulate the efficient distribution of foraging honeybees among patches of flowers or set the thermostat in a termite colony, webs of interdependence shape collective success and drive the achievements of biological systems from genes to societies. Interconnectedness is a rule in biological systems. Not only in the complex inner workings of a cell and the regulatory interactions among genes, but also in the delicate balance of populations in natural ecosystems, the common theme is the profound extent to which each member of the system—gene, protein, organ, species, or individual—is dependent on others. Since these systems are, in a very real sense, our predecessors and are thus stunningly accomplished pioneers in the successful management of networked systems, there is potentially much we can learn from them.

This interdependence is the foundation of the stability, productivity, and creativity of biological systems. Because species in an ecosystem, for example, can consume one another's outputs (waste, shelter, structure, or other by-products), they can exploit these as a foundation for their own activity. In effect, their ability to *leverage* these elements from their network allows them to avoid having to create them themselves, which allows them to save energy and frees them to focus on other things and to specialize and do things they otherwise would not be able to do. In fact, it is because of these positive dependencies that all individuals are so sensitive to the health of the whole: Their fate is bound to the fate of the entire network of other species in the ecosystem—to the structure of that network, and the roles played by its members.

A variety of fig species serve, for example, as critical foundations for communities in the neotropics, where their complex aseasonal fruiting patterns provide a reliable source of food for a wide variety of animal species even in times of fruit scarcity and where they additionally provide a source of specific important nutrients that are not readily available elsewhere.[4] Such species essentially serve as a kind of foundation or platform on which other species can depend for a variety of essentials.

Such species thus illustrate the central feature of ecosystems that accounts for the potentially catastrophic effects of their removal: Each member of the ecosystem depends to some degree on the presence of every other for the simple reason that they are adapted to each other's presence. Essential "inputs" to the survival and health of every member of an ecosystem are provided by the other members of the system. Whereas removal or displacement of these members results in the loss of important food sources, destruction of essential microhabitats, or loss of protection from a predator or competitor, their continued presence sustains the health of the system and helps to shape and maintain a system that provides benefits to the entire ecosystem.

We humans, as external manipulators of natural systems, especially ecosystems, all too often take their remarkable stability and complexity for granted, while paying little heed to the complex and subtle nature of the networks that are the foundation of their achievements. Thus, while the ultimate implications are positive and enabling, we are most aware of this dependence when these systems fail. The tragic consequences of changes or damage to even a single gene are all too well known, and the effects on ecosystems of the removal of key species or the introduction of foreign species can be catastrophic. The feature of these examples that has relevance to understanding interdependencies in business networks is that even apparently localized disruptions can result in widespread and cascading consequences throughout the system: Many or even all members of the system may be adversely affected.

Natural systems that have endured and evolved over thousands or even millions of years—that have survived countless shocks and exhibited continuous "innovation" and adaptation—can experience catastrophic failure when subjected to careless manipulation by humans. Far too often the effects of actions are like a surgeon cutting an artery, and the contrast between the initial disruption and the scope of its consequences can be stunning.[5] At some point in the late 1980s, for example, a small Russian mollusk, the zebra mussel (*Dreissena polymorpha*), was inadvertently introduced into one of the Great Lakes (Lake St. Clair, between Lakes Huron and Erie) when it was dumped along with the bilge water from a visiting cargo ship. Biologists believe that only a small number of larvae were involved in this accidental introduction, but today consequences of that single event cost Ontario Hydro an estimated $376,000 per generating power station and cost the power industry alone over $3 billion from 1993 to 1999. In the United States, congressional researchers estimate the mussel will cost businesses and communities over $5 billion by the end of 2004. Even these huge sums only scratch the surface of the total impact of these biological invaders, for they only represent the direct measurable impact on human economic activity. Lurking beneath these already significant costs are incalculable damages to entire ecological webs. Indeed, it is critical to appreciate that it is not the zebra mussel per se that causes such havoc but the destruction of entire ecosystems triggered by the zebra mussel's presence.

The magnitude of damage caused by the introduction of invasive species like the zebra mussel is so great because these species either break key connections that are essential for the healthy functioning of the system (often by eliminating or dominating them itself) or turn those connections into amplifiers of negative or detrimental effects (such as toxin accumulation). Other species that depend on the presence and proper functioning of these connections are adversely affected, as are those that depend in turn on them. As a result, the fate of organisms can hinge on the fate of others remote from the introduced species in the web of ecosystem interactions.

What is going on in ecosystems, and indeed in all natural systems (at all scales, from the genome to entire ecological communities), is that the members of the system have coevolved mutual dependencies that work to their benefit. Each member, in effect, leverages the network of interactions in the system to its advantage. When these connections are compromised, the species that depend on them suffer. The health of each depends on the health of the whole: All are bound by these leveraging relationships to a common fate. Thus, although the most spectacular examples of shared fate are negative—the collapse triggered by the removal of critical species or the destruction caused by an invasion by foreign species—it is important to keep in mind that shared fate, in the absence of careless external disruptions, is almost always empowering and enabling.

Shared Fate in Business

This pattern of interconnectedness and shared fate enabling stability and innovation can be seen in a variety of industries today. The most striking example is perhaps found in the computing sector.

Computing

Today's computing firms are highly specialized and compete fiercely within narrow domains of expertise. From companies that specialize in customer relationship management (such as Siebel and Onyx) to microprocessor manufacturers such as Intel and AMD, firms in this environment focus on doing a relatively small number of things well. Indeed, the fraction of the industry's market capitalization captured by Microsoft, today's leader, is very small relative to the fraction that was captured by IBM in the mid-1960s.[6]

Firms in the computing ecosystem are specialized to such an extent that a single product is often the result of the collective efforts of many firms, with a significant proportion of those firms' contributions taking the form of offerings that would have no value on their own outside the context of the collective effort. "Fabless" semiconductor design companies such as Broadcom and NVIDIA, for example, possess no substantial manufacturing assets and rely instead on third-party foundries such as TSMC and UMC. In this environment, traditional R&D is focused on improving performance in narrow domains. This results in rapid parallel advances in many areas because each is propelled by highly focused domain-specific innovation. The goal is no longer to lock out entire vertical stacks with proprietary advantage, but to be the best in a chosen area of specialization.[7] The destinies of many organizations are therefore now linked, and interaction among firms has become an increasingly critical and complex phenomenon, sharing elements of both cooperation and competition through a rich network of interrelated products, services, and technologies.[8] Crucially, this interaction is not along traditional industry boundaries, but connects the destinies, strategies, and operational capabilities of customers and suppliers and partners and competitors, and reshapes competitive and operational dynamics at the most fundamental level.

Apparel: Deep Roots in a Traditional Industry

The computing industry is, of course, not alone in having evolved a network structure. Complex networks of firms and products have become an increasingly common feature of the business landscape in general, and the implications of shared fate reach well beyond the computing industry.[9] Networks with many of the same features seen in technology-heavy domains such as computing and chip manufacture have evolved even in surprisingly low-tech traditional domains.

An example is the apparel industry, which has leveraged networks of firms for hundreds of years.[10] The industry consists of tens of thousands of specialized companies that provide materials and manufacturing capabilities, ranging in size from single-person operations to multibillion-dollar textile firms such as Levi Strauss & Co. Companies in the apparel network form a massive, distributed business ecosystem, in which the delivery of a single line of products may frequently leverage the assets of dozens of organizations.

The industry is composed of four major segments: fiber producers, textile mills, apparel manufacturers and other textile users, and apparel and other soft goods retailers. Agricultural and chemical suppliers produce natural or synthetic fibers. Textile mills then convert this fiber to fabric. Once finished, the fabric is sold to apparel manufacturers, who turn fabric into finished goods. The finished goods are then sold to retailers and become available to customers.[11] Thousands of firms worldwide are involved in these four stages. The industry is also fragmented, with over 300,000 distributors in the United States alone, the top five of which make up less than 20 percent of total sales.

As with biological networks, business ecosystems usually evolve hubs, which play an essential part in shaping the stability and capabilities of the network. In the apparel industry, Li & Fung, a hundred-year-old Hong Kong–based trading company, is a clear hub for its ecosystem. Li & Fung has relationships with more than 8,000 specialized companies in over forty countries. The company customizes supply chain services to fit the needs of individual retailers such as the Gap or the Limited. In doing so, it orchestrates the production assets of thousands of manufacturers, including more than a million total employees. Although it only employs a few thousand people, Li & Fung reaches, influences, and affects more people than live in a number of significant countries.

Li & Fung connects multiple organizations even in the supply of a single line of products. To produce a line of garments for an American retailer, Li & Fung might purchase Chinese yarn that was woven and dyed in Thailand, send the fabric to be cut in Bangladesh, ship the pieces for final assembly to South Korea (where the garments would be matched with Japanese zippers), and finally deliver the finished product to various geographically dispersed retailers at the appointed time. Whether to meet the specific needs of a customer or simply to construct a particular product, Li & Fung can configure activities as though they were modules in a process. A South Korean yarn provider might be appropriate for one product line, but an Indonesian supplier that uses a different raw material or production technology might be the better choice for another. One product might require three additional steps in the supply chain, whereas another requires two fewer steps. For each customer and product, Li & Fung assembles the right modules for the job.

Li & Fung adds tremendous value to its retail customers, delivering a flexible supply chain that has much faster delivery times, lower costs, and superior innovative capabilities. Moreover, Li & Fung increases the network's robustness against exogenous shocks. Through load balancing and reallocation, it can shift resources to different members of the network when faced with changes in technology, consumer preferences, or government regulation, or with other unforeseen events. Having a wide network—and thus more options—provides for considerable flexibility when faced with industry challenges. Following the September 2001 terrorist attacks in New York and Washington, Li & Fung quickly shifted production from high-risk countries to lower-risk ones. Companies with tightly coupled processes can also re-source production, but not quickly—and only at considerable expense. Li & Fung, on the contrary, moved production locations affecting hundreds of millions of dollars in merchandise in just seven days.

As this example shows, the apparel community is well represented by a large, loosely connected network of firms. This network exhibits clear hubs, such as Li & Fung, that have an enormous impact on its dynamics. As a result of these connections, firms in the ecosystem are dependent on each other. There are small apparel manufacturers in Bangladesh whose only access to the Gap is provided by Li & Fung. If Li & Fung went out of business and disappeared overnight, a vast community of manufacturers would be isolated. Conversely, Li & Fung is dependent on its manufacturers for the quality and timeliness of any delivery. If significant parts of its manufacturing network were shut down or became inaccessible (say, by some sort of economic or political shock), Li & Fung and its customers would suffer deeply.

These operational interactions imply that the economic well-being of organizations in the apparel ecosystem is also interconnected. If Li & Fung were to extract too much value from its network, its suppliers would gradually switch to other hubs (say, Japanese trading companies) or go out of business. As this happened, Li & Fung would suffer and eventually fail.

The enormous constellation of organizations in the apparel sector therefore share fate in a way that bears a striking similarity to a biological ecosystem. The system thrives when everyone is healthy. At the same time, the system becomes unsustainable if significant assets get hurt or if significant segments of the system are out of balance.

Telecommunications: Overcapacity and Broad Collapse

The consequences of shared fate can be seen dramatically in business networks where interconnections among communities can cause errors and miscalculations in one to spread catastrophically to others. Mistakes in a single community—even simple overinvestment or over-heated expectations—can lead to collapses from which not only that community but also a much broader network to which it is connected can find it hard to recover.

In the late 1990s, for example, telecommunications companies collectively made huge overinvestments in fiber-optic cable, believing that Internet traffic would experience sustained explosive growth.[12] The statistic often repeated was that Internet traffic doubled every 100 days, and the race was on to bury millions of miles of fiber-optic lines beneath streets and oceans. But this annual growth rate of over 1,000 percent never materialized—instead, Internet traffic grew at a rate closer to 100 percent a year. This growth rate was "not nearly fast enough to use all [capacity built in the] late-1990s frenzy. Nationwide, only 2.7 percent of the installed fiber is actually being used, according to Telegeography Inc. Much of the remaining fiber—called 'dark fiber' in industry parlance—may remain dormant forever."[13] This overcapacity has caused bandwidth prices to decline "an average of 65 percent each of the last two years. It also has led most of the long-haul data-transmission companies to file for Chapter 11 bankruptcy protection."[14] While prices were declining, the telecom industry was struggling with huge debts it had incurred to pay for its building binge. "Since 1996, telecoms . . . borrowed more than $1.5 trillion from banks and issued more than $630 billion of bonds."[15] Because of this excess capacity and enormous debt, telecom stock prices dropped some 95 percent or more from their highs, resulting in investor losses of some $2 trillion. Within two years, half a million workers had lost their jobs, and debt-laden telecommunications companies had collapsed, with over sixty telecom carriers filing for bankruptcy protection.[16]

When network dynamics work to drive a downward spiral, as they have in the telecommunications industry, it can be extraordinarily difficult to reverse the process. Overcapacity, price wars, and slowing usage are causing a continued slowdown in telecom growth:

Consumers and businesses are taking longer to soak up the capacity built up in the last decade. Offers of free wireless minutes on nights and weekends are prompting many consumers to cancel their traditional long-distance plans. Meanwhile, data traffic, once thought to be the savior of the industry, is growing more slowly than originally forecast, and it isn't nearly as profitable as old-fashioned voice calls. That's because users pay for data in bulk instead of per minute. This is why e-mail, which is replacing millions of calls a day, is considerably less profitable for telecoms than phone calls.[17]

In effect, by overreacting to the near-term potential for growth and transformation represented by the Internet, the telecom sector of the network of firms and technologies that make up the broader "communications ecosystem" trapped itself in a corner from which it is unlikely to be able to emerge for quite some time. Firms are now too cash-strapped and focused on the bottom line to be able to entertain the kinds of transformations that once seemed an inevitable part of the endless growth of new communications technologies. Until they are healthier, telecoms are thus likely to hold up the broader advance of the communications ecosystem to which they are bound.

Ecosystem Evolution

It is important to appreciate that although the trend toward interconnectedness has always existed, the highly distributed and highly networked structure we see in many industries today is a relatively recent phenomenon, and thus the critical importance of shared fate is a new reality that requires a new framework for thinking about industry health and, indeed, about what constitutes an industry in the first place.

Even in the computing industry, where high degrees of interconnectedness and various forms of "modularity" have long been characteristic of much of the underlying technologies, the emergence of a true networked structure is a phenomenon of only the past decade and a half. In deep contrast with the vertically integrated nature of the computer industry of thirty years ago, today's industry is divided into a large number of distinct segments producing specialized products. It is characterized by many organizations involved in the design, production, or distribution of even a single product, which thus share a common fate that in many cases is tied to the fate of that product. As a result, this complex industry and the broad community of organizations that interact with it bear many important similarities to a biological ecosystem: Each of the different players in the industry is dependent on the others, and the interactions among them are critical for the evolution of the whole. This has not always been the case, however.

Integrated, Independent Technology Stacks

In the computing industry of the 1960s and 1970s, complete suites of products fought head-to-head for dominance, and competitors could lose market share and be displaced if they did not keep up with technological developments in a broad spectrum of domains. Interoperability between competing product suites was not a design goal—the objective was to create distinct integrated offerings that delivered the complete functionality desired in a computer system. Firms in this industry focused on creating and owning a proprietary "stack" of hardware and software products.[18]

In this climate, firms fought to keep ahead by generating innovations internally in a vast collection of areas, while generally viewing external "change" as a threat to firm survival. Leading firms in this climate actively pursued innovations designed specifically to enhance a firm's suite of offerings, and thus often narrowly applicable to that firm's products. This objective was reflected in these firms' broad approach to R&D. Companies typically supported deep R&D programs in both software and hardware technologies. IBM's R&D was potentially the most striking example, as it was focused on virtually every technological driver of computing performance, from research on glass ceramics to the design of efficient software algorithms.

Moreover, much R&D was focused on creating costly "fundamental" innovations in an effort to provide dramatic and visible advantage to an entire stack and to counteract the effect of dilution throughout that stack. Again, IBM provides the most striking examples, with efforts such as the introduction of its first transistor mainframe during the late 1950s and the introduction of the first commercial magnetic core memories in the 1960s. The impact of these developments was largely constrained within IBM. Solid Logic Technology, for example, introduced by IBM in 1964, provided a technological breakthrough that created the technology foundation for a generation of mainframes, but it was never commercialized to any other company (indeed, IBM limited its production of integrated circuits to captive use until 1993). Although some of the ideas behind Solid Logic Technology were leveraged by other firms, no other company ever adopted a similar set of technological components, and its impact was therefore largely limited to IBM products.

Platforms, Design Rules, and Fragmentation

In the mid-1960s, the vertically integrated stacks of computer companies began to disintegrate into the computer industry that we see today. The introduction of the IBM System 360 in 1966 was important in establishing this trend.[19] Originally motivated by the need to reduce internal project complexity, the 360's design followed an architectural approach that was profoundly different from that of other mainframes. For the first time, an IBM mainframe system defined a clear, modular interface between software and hardware, which guaranteed compatibility between models. This clear interface had an unintended but crucial effect—it set in motion a process to fragment the industry into a wide variety of diverse organizations, each providing different product and service components and focusing on different capabilities.

The gradual trend that began in the 1960s was dramatically stepped up during the late 1970s and 1980s with the birth of microcomputers and the success of the DOS/ISA architecture. The combination of Microsoft DOS and the IBM personal computer (PC) defined a clear platform that enabled a vast number of software providers to design general-purpose applications that would run on a wide variety of hardware combinations. This architecture thus formed a powerful hub in the network of computing firms, connecting a large number of hardware and software providers and leading to the industry structure we see today, in which a large number of firms operate in many distinct segments. Each of these firms is highly specialized and competes fiercely within a narrow domain of expertise. Firms focus on doing a relatively small number of things well. This helps to explain the patterns mentioned earlier: The industry's market capitalization has decreased (even Microsoft's share today is a small fraction of that captured by IBM in the mid-1960s); many firms (such as fabless semiconductor companies) possess no substantial manufacturing assets of their own; and R&D is focused not on building broad exclusive portfolios, but on narrow areas of specialization. Critically, this distribution of activity brings the opportunity to innovate closer to the loci of innovative thinking and problem solving—to specialists and users— thus enhancing the quality and relevance of innovations.[20]

The industry thus fragmented into a number of clusters of firms, each supported by a different type of computing platform. Each platform had well-defined interfaces, or "design rules," defining a standard way that different products could connect with each other to support and extend the underlying infrastructure.[21] MS-DOS/ISA thus defined one of the first truly popular and widespread computing platforms, with many others, including Apple Macintosh, Microsoft Windows, and Linux, following a similar path.[22] Each of these platforms had published interfaces (application programming interfaces, or APIs) that enabled a variety of organizations to build system components that worked effectively together, ranging from integrated circuits to software applications.

In each individual platform, components were tightly integrated with each other, defined by rich sets of APIs. On the other hand, when this model first evolved, the connections across platforms were extremely weak. This meant that each platform was largely independent, with the challenge of sharing data between different systems (say, an IBM mainframe and a Macintosh computer) extremely difficult. Information technology (IT) organizations were thus plagued by the challenge of integrating across maddeningly different platform infrastructures, such as IBM mainframe, Novell client-server, Sun Solaris, Apple Macintosh, and Microsoft Windows, among many others. In essence, components were either tightly integrated with each other or completely separate, virtually islands in an ocean.

This period in the history of the computer industry was thus characterized by fierce competition among completely separate platforms.

Each of the platforms had created what was in essence a separate ecosystem of business partners, each including different component suppliers, system vendors, and software developers (independent software vendors, or ISVs). In the mid-1980s, for example, Intel, IBM, and Microsoft were in one ecosystem, and Motorola, Apple, and Claris were in a separate ecosystem. Each organization had a close affiliation with the "mother" platform, which in some cases became something akin to a religion for its devoted disciples. This naturally gave rise to fierce competitiveness between platforms, such as the battles between Apple's Macintosh computer and IBM's PC, or those between Sun and Apollo.

Loosely Coupled Systems and Networks

Both the Apple Macintosh and the DOS/ISA architecture embodied the beginnings of a new trend in the evolution of business network structure: Compared with their mainframe ancestors, both these platforms were significantly more accessible to outside software developers (the DOS/ISA platform was also more open to hardware developers). DOS and Windows, in particular, saw striking growth in the numbers of independent software developers during the 1980s, starting from a mere handful in 1981 and rising to millions of people during the 1990s. These developers leveraged the simple but surprisingly sophisticated and rapidly evolving development tools and increasingly powerful operating system provided by Microsoft to build what were effectively enhancements to the basic PC's functionality. They grew into a network with Microsoft at its hub: a hub to which they were connected not by conformance to a strict modular hierarchy, but simply by virtue of the tools they used and the technology they exploited.

This trend accelerated later in the 1980s (and continued aggressively during the 1990s), as some events began to unfold that would deeply influence both computing architectures and the structure of the industry. A new, looser type of interface had begun to emerge that enabled connections across disparate computer systems. Rather than a set of restrictive "design rules" that clearly defined and constrained interactions among system components, what some call "loosely coupled" integration methodologies started to emerge.[23] The idea is simple—enable different computer systems, components, or applications to interact with each other, while specifying or constraining as little as possible (ideally nothing at all) about their design.

Loose coupling achieves integration in a way that is quite different from traditional modular design. Obtaining true design modularity in a system requires the interchangeability of design components (as in designing muskets with interchangeable parts or designing personal computers with different plug-compatible components). This is very challenging to do, and typically causes substantial constraints on the designers, requiring the definition of and adherence to extensive and cumbersome design guidelines. Loosely coupled systems, in contrast, require only interoperability and extensibility based on satisfying just-sufficient protocols for interaction and leveraging. These are much easier to define and follow, and result only in minimal constraints on the system's components. Loosely coupled integration therefore requires only standardization at the "thinnest" possible point of interaction and lends itself much better to the design of widely distributed systems, or networks.

One of the first truly widespread applications of loosely coupled networks in enterprise computing was the emergence of standards for electronic data interchange (EDI) during the 1980s, which provided a broadly used infrastructure for connecting business processes such as procurement and order management in disparate enterprises.[24] It was the implementation of EDI that enabled Wal-Mart to coordinate its powerful network of suppliers, exchanging market demand information with them in real time. EDI was useful and thus widely implemented, although its semantics were relatively inflexible and thus largely limited to supply chain applications.[25]

Loose coupling standards enjoyed rapid adoption rates during the late 1980s and 1990s, with the evolution of the TCP/IP and HTTP protocols (key components of the Internet and the World Wide Web), which provided a broad-based communications infrastructure that could be used for sharing information. This infrastructure took off when coupled with the widespread adoption of HTML (Hypertext Markup Language, used in defining Web pages), which made possible a standard way to display simple information across most existing platforms, thus making that information accessible and useful.

However, as evidenced by the failure of many Internet companies, this infrastructure still did not provide the value expected. Critically, it did not yet solve the integration problem. True, the same data could be viewed by users using a variety of different computer systems. However, different systems still could not share information: Data buried in an outdated legacy database system had little hope of being linked with data stored in a recently installed Oracle or SQL database. The first generation of Internet applications thus failed to integrate with the more traditional legacy systems (e.g., IBM mainframe applications) and client/server systems (e.g., SAP and other enterprise resource planning systems), which still contained the vast majority of corporate data and enabled most corporate business processes.

During the late 1990s, however, the birth of XML (Extensible Markup Language) and its critical evolution from a data presentation standard to a machine-to-machine data interchange format began to finally resolve this crucial problem. Hailed by both Bill Gates and Scott McNealy as the solution to data interchange problems, XML (and related standards such as SOAP, UDDI, and WSDL, all of which are used to help locate and describe functionality or "services" that produce results in XML) is finally providing the needed framework for connecting the many existing disparate computer platforms. Using this framework, a wide variety of data (including the masses still buried in traditional enterprise systems) is finally being surfaced and exposed to other network participants through what some are calling "Web services," enabling new levels of business networking and collaboration. Moreover, unlike EDI, XML is a very general framework for capturing data. It is therefore not limited to business collaboration, or even to integration between different databases, but is even being used as a standard for connecting clients and servers (with HTTP-based remote procedure calls) and is being investigated as a standard for internal communications within computer clients themselves.

The result of the broad adoption of standards such as EDI, HTML, and XML is the creation of a truly interconnected ecosystem in which organizations are integrating both technology infrastructure and business processes.[26] Sun systems programmed in Java can easily exchange information with Microsoft systems programmed in C++ or C#, and corporate networks can manage a greater diversity of platforms at a much lower cost. Each segment of the computer industry is (or can easily be) connected with every other segment, and the environment has truly become a single, massively interconnected ecosystem.

This interconnection transcends the boundaries of computing, shaping not only new technology-heavy industries such as chip manufacture but also ancient labor-intensive ones such as apparel, merging them into a single interdependent ecosystem. Li & Fung, for example, launched an intranet in 1995 that linked offices and manufacturing sites around the world and streamlined internal communications: "The progress of orders and shipments could be tracked in real time and digital imagery allowed for online inspection and troubleshooting."[27] Li & Fung furthered its Internet initiative with the launch of secure extranet sites in 1997. Each of these secure customized extranet sites linked Li & Fung directly with a key customer:

> Through each Internet site, Li & Fung could carry out online product development as well as order tracking, obviating much of the cost and time necessary to send hard copies of documents back and forth. Furthermore, with Li & Fung as the key link between manufacturers and retailers, the extranet provided a platform for the two to interface, thus streamlining communications as the order moved through the supply chain. Customers could track an order online just as it was possible to track a UPS delivery. This monitoring of production also enables quick response manufacturing. Until the fabric is dyed, the customer can change the color; until the fabric is cut, the customer can change the styles or sizes offered, whether a pocket or a cuff is to be added, and a number of other product specifications.[28]

By 2002, Li & Fung would rank IT as its "second greatest" investment and extend its commitment to open standards such as XML through a partnership with Microsoft.[29] Li & Fung is extending the reach of its web and improving its efficiency by taking advantage of the openness and flexibility of standards such as XML and HTML. The boundary between the computing and apparel "industries" is thus becoming blurred, making it more accurate to think of an integrated apparel supply-chain and clothing design and distribution ecosystem that spans traditional industrial domains.

The brief history of business ecosystem evolution just presented has illustrated some clear, relentless trends. These show the inexorable fragmentation of the industry into a broad variety of interconnected industry segments. These segments are all linked to each other, and interaction among firms has become an increasingly complex phenomenon, sharing elements of both cooperation and competition. Additionally, with the emergence of a variety of standards like EDI, HTML, and XML, switching costs between different platform affiliations have become significantly lower.

Despite much finger pointing in the popular press by competitors accusing each other of "controlling" various standards, it is important not to lose sight of the forest for the trees: Over the long term, the computing industry has become increasingly open, which has given rise both to increased competition and increased opportunity for a growing variety of firms supplying an increasing range of functionality, and has extended its reach into a wide range of other industries, which effectively form a collection of broadly overlapping ecosystems.

Formalizing Business Ecosystems

As we have suggested in many examples in this chapter, we believe that a particularly powerful way to conceptualize business networks is to compare them to biological ecosystems. Like biological ecosystems, business ecosystems are formed by large, loosely connected networks of entities. Like species in biological ecosystems, firms interact with each other in complex ways, and the health and performance of each firm is dependent on the health and performance of the whole. Firms and species are therefore simultaneously influenced by their internal capabilities and by their complex interactions with the rest of the ecosystem.

This analogy operates at many levels: Firms, business units, technologies, and products all exhibit networks of interdependencies and ecosystem-like dynamics. Moreover, the details of the interactions at one level are often crucial for shaping the interactions at others. The kinds of information that Wal-Mart's Retail Link provides to vendors shape the interactions between Wal-Mart and its partners. Similarly, the architectural decisions that determine the boundary between the operating system and the hardware of a personal computer go a long way toward defining the interactions among Microsoft, Intel, PC hardware manufacturers, and system builders such as Dell or Hewlett-Packard. Conversely, defining the architecture of a technology, the interfaces between components of a product, and the way that functionality is packaged—all important elements of, for example, the design of Microsoft's Windows APIs—are important strategic tools for a firm in a networked environment. Although we will often point out these connections as we develop our argument in later chapters, our focus will be on the general classes of operational decisions that managers can make; thus, we will concentrate on the *strategic business units* where these decisions are implemented.

Ultimately, our interest lies in the operational decisions made by managers. Our focus will therefore not be on the business units themselves, but on the patterns of behaviors that characterize those business units: the operational strategies of business units. The key analogy we draw is between the characteristic behavior of a species in an ecosystem and the operating strategy of a strategic business unit. It is important to keep this in mind when we refer to a firm as "being" a dominator, for example: This should be understood as shorthand for the fact that a firm has business units that are pursuing dominator strategies.

To the extent that the comparison of business networks to ecosystems is a valid one, it suggests that some of the lessons from biological networks can fruitfully be applied to business networks. Specifically, because they are governed by shared fate, we should expect that many of the features that enable stability, longevity, and productivity in these biological systems will be found in business networks.

- **We should expect to see far more robustness in the face of external shocks than is generally assumed in existing frameworks for thinking about business networks.**
  Ecosystems, and indeed almost all naturally occurring networks, show highly discontinuous responses to external input. Although certain kinds of targeted damage, or damage to critical members, produces widespread collapse, the vast majority of perturbations are absorbed by these systems. Critically, the

extent of the damage is not determined by some external feature of the shock (technology, business models, etc.), but by whether it directly affects and damages a hub in the network.

- **We should expect to see a capability for creation of novelty, linked with a specialization of network members.** Naturally occurring systems are, of course, the consummate creators of novelty. Evolution is driven by novelty creation, and the capacity for natural systems to combine robustness and persistence with the creation of novelty is the driving force behind the creative process of evolution.

- **We should expect a heterogeneous structure, with different firms adopting dramatically different roles that influence different aspects of the stability and productivity of the network.** Natural systems achieve their stability and productivity partly because they lack any externally imposed notions of a level playing field or of parity among network members. These systems almost invariably evolve a structure in which some members acquire highly influential positions, whereas many others do not.

The following chapters explore the validity of these predictions and develop their implications for management practice as we shift to a view that the network can be a source of firm renewal rather than being the external threat that is often the focus of existing frameworks in management practice.

Finally, we would like to emphasize that analogies can be dangerous things, so it behooves us to use them with care. Throughout this book we argue that important insights about the way networked industries function can be gained by transferring lessons and observations learned in the study of biological ecosystems to the context of business networks. It should be clear that we are not claiming that business networks *are* ecosystems. Instead, we seek to develop a view that borrows terminology and insights from our understanding of biological ecosystems. In fact, in many ways the biological ecosystems are simply a point of departure for a search for analogies and metaphors as well as theoretical foundations for an understanding of the challenges and opportunities we face in formulating strategies in a networked world.

It is best then to think of our ecosystem view as specifically pertaining to business ecosystems, which differ in critical ways from their biological counterparts:

- **Innovation.** Ecological ecosystems do not compete with each other for the attention of some outside observer, nor do they have an audience to please. As a result, they emphasize stability and durability in the face of external shocks—important goals for industries and firms as well—but they are less concerned with innovation. They are not under pressure to grow and to serve new functions or satisfy new demands. Ecosystems that do this will, of course, tend to spread and be more successful, but it is not a primary focus of their dynamics, nor of the literature about them. We can overcome this limitation easily, however, by extending our metaphorical foundation from ecosystems as narrowly defined in ecology to the much wider universe of evolved biological systems such as genomes and cellular machinery, which *do* routinely exhibit novelty creation and about which there is an extensive literature that focuses on the process.

- **Competition for members.** As we shall discuss at greater length in the following chapters, networks of firms and technologies are in constant competition for members. To grow, firms need to attract new customers and partners; as a consequence, their imperative for growth translates into a growth imperative for the entire ecosystem. Indeed, our argument about the incentives that shape the health of ecosystems hinges on the fact that firms are mobile and that they have and exercise the freedom to move from one ecosystem to another.

- **Intelligent actors.** Finally, unlike the members of biological ecosystems—even the most broadly defined—the members of business ecosystems are capable of some degree of forethought and planning. Although in much of what follows we argue that the choices available to managers and other ecosystem decision makers are limited and shaped by the forces governing the dynamics of their ecosystems, this in no way diminishes the importance of their responsibility for informed decision making.

In short, then, we ask the reader to keep in mind that we are developing a new concept of ecosystem, the *business ecosystem,* which is a descendant of its biological ancestor but with significant modifications derived largely from a broadened view of evolved biological systems in general.

Beyond Firms and Industries

One of the more interesting differences between the approach that we suggest here and more traditional analyses of technological transitions is that the unit of analysis is not the industry, but the particular part of an ecosystem in which an organization finds itself. The "boundary" of the relevant ecosystem or part of an ecosystem need not (and typically does not) correspond to traditional industry boundaries, but is instead defined by the strength and type of organizational interactions that occur. For example, ecosystems may be defined by the sharing of tools and technological components, as in the Microsoft developer network, or by buyer/supplier interactions, as in Wal-Mart's supplier network. Organizations in these communities are driven in large part by the collective health of these networks. Because of this, ecosystems may span several traditional industries. The computing ecosystem, for example, includes not only the software industry and significant segments of the hardware industry but also many other industries that rely on computing and information technology and devote resources to adapting them to their needs.

Because of these factors, the effects of ecosystem health and dynamics easily breach traditional industry boundaries. A dramatic recent example is computing, in which advances in the computing *industry* have resulted in widely distributed productivity gains in a wide variety of industries throughout the computing *ecosystem.* This crossing of traditional industry boundaries can work in the opposite direction as well. When many unrelated industries in an ecosystem experience simultaneous disruption or contraction, these effects can propagate back to the "core" of the ecosystem, as they have in the case of the computing ecosystem in the last several years. This definition of business ecosystems, although it contrasts with traditional industry definitions, is in the same spirit as the definitions used in biology, where what matters is the strength and nature of interactions rather than any preconceived categorizations.

Moreover, as with biological ecosystems, the boundary of a given ecosystem is often difficult to establish. Organisms may interact with each other through many indirect connections even if they are separated in space or time (e.g., through their influence on ambient factors such as temperature, or through intermediary species). Similarly, firms may interact with each other even if they appear distant at first glance. Therefore, rather than establishing a static and clear boundary between ecosystems, as we often do for the boundary between industries, it is better to gauge the *degree* of interaction between different firms and to depict ecosystems as communities of firms characterized by a given level and type of interaction (e.g., market relationships, technology-sharing and licensing agreements). This is essentially the approach followed in the analysis of social networks, which conceptualizes structure as lasting patterns of relationships among actors.[30]

Most important, like their biological counterparts, business ecosystems are characterized by a large number of loosely interconnected participants who depend on each other for their mutual effectiveness and survival. In the following chapter, we argue that because the health of individual firms and the utility of individual products in such highly interconnected networks depend so much on the health of *other* firms and products in the network, it is especially important to develop ways to characterize the *collective* health of entire business ecosystems and to understand the ways in which firms can influence and respond to this collective health.

CHAPTER THREE

Collective Behavior

Collective Collapse

Yahoo! hit the wall in December 2000. It happened almost overnight. One quarter, the firm was growing profitably; the next, it was losing vast amounts of money and shrinking. Cisco hit the wall one month later and wrote off close to two billion dollars in inventory. Why, and more interestingly, why so suddenly? Yahoo! and Cisco failed because their vast business ecosystem slowly became increasingly unhealthy, and finally collapsed. Even though their downfall was sudden, no sudden actions triggered it. The violence of their collapse was instead a testament to the frequently bewildering collective behavior of distributed networks of organizations.

As with species in a biological ecosystem, the performance of firms in a networked industry is heavily dependent on each other. NVIDIA's value and financial performance is highly correlated with that of TSMC, the Taiwanese manufacturing platform it leverages. NVIDIA is in turn coupled with Microsoft through its Xbox relationship, which also creates linkages to Flextronics, the Xbox circuit board assembler, and to Electronic Arts, which produces a number of Xbox games. The many dependencies among these firms can lead to subtle but strong correlations among the results they experience, even if the companies appear unrelated at first glance. It is not immediately obvious that the performance of a video game producer and a circuit board assembler, operating in different industries, should have anything to do with each other, but because the community of video game–producing firms and the community of circuit board assemblers are both part of a larger business ecosystem, they do.

Very often, the relevant boundaries for understanding the behavior of a business ecosystem will extend way beyond obvious industry definitions. Crucial players in the Yahoo! ecosystem were not limited to other Internet firms, or even related software or Internet retail companies, but extended to a number of other business communities, even into the financial sector, encompassing venture capital firms, investment banks, and pension funds. As we will see later in this chapter, many of Yahoo!'s Internet business partners had chronic problems, which may have been exacerbated by Yahoo!'s behavior. But the participants in the various financial communities were strong enough to prop up Yahoo!'s Internet partners for an extended period of time. Money flowed from a pension fund in Michigan to a venture capital firm in Silicon Valley, to a business-to-consumer (B2C) company in South of Market, to Yahoo!, and to Cisco's massive Internet equipment business. When this cash flow could no longer mask inherent problems with the business models of many of Yahoo!'s partners, the shock reverberated through the entire network.

Yahoo! and Cisco did well when their business partners could attract cash. They could charge more for sophisticated telecommunications equipment, advertising, and traffic-sharing agreements despite the deep-rooted operational problems that characterized the Internet business community. As many companies would have done, Yahoo! and Cisco exploited their position and extracted as much financial benefit as they could. This optimized their immediate profit but hurt their long-term prospects by creating dependencies on unhealthy business communities. Gradually, this cycle of dependencies turned south as the markets began to readjust and the collective expectations of the financial community came back to reality. As financial support dried up, the inherent problems in the B2C community surfaced, and the whole system collapsed.

Because the performance of several organizations in a domain of interdependent industry segments is correlated, the business ecosystem domains surrounding Xbox, Cisco, and Yahoo! acquired shared or "collective" properties. These can be thought of as unifying characteristics that describe the behavior of the domain as a whole. This idea then scales to establish collective properties for an entire ecosystem. As with a biological ecosystem, which either appears to thrive or to become polluted and endangered, we suggest that the "health" of a business ecosystem (and of its various communities) is a crucial collective property to define, understand, and analyze. In the cases of Yahoo! and Cisco, the poor health of their business ecosystem should have raised enormous red flags, despite the significant profit.

This chapter focuses on understanding the collective health of a business ecosystem. To do this, we extend our discussion of biological ecosystems and use it as a metaphor, while also borrowing heavily from the broader literature on the evolution of complex systems. This leads to measures of ecosystem health and highlights their implications for firms' strategy.

Ecosystem Health

In a networked environment, no firm's actions can be viewed in isolation. The performance of a firm is a function not only of its own capabilities or of its static position with respect to its competitors, customers, partners, and suppliers, but also of its dynamic interactions with the ecosystem as a whole. Therefore, before looking at specific approaches that a firm can take to enhance its own performance, it is critical to develop ways of understanding and assessing the impact that firm-level strategies can have on the networks of products, technologies, and other firms that characterize its ecosystem.

How do we simplify the vast complexity of an ecosystem? It is often useful to subdivide an ecosystem into a number of related business *domains* as a matter of convenience for performing analysis. These domains can be thought of as groups of organizations engaged in similar activities, and may sometimes be similar to conventional industries. Each ecosystem thus encompasses several domains, which it may share with other ecosystems. Figure 3-1 depicts some of the more crucial domains in the software ecosystem and is drawn from the perspective of one of its essential hubs, Microsoft. For the ecosystem to function well, *each* domain that is critical in the delivery of a product or service should be healthy. The fragility of any single domain can undermine the performance of the whole. This means that Microsoft's performance is dependent on the individual health of the independent software vendor (ISV) and systems integrator domains, for example.

A firm that takes an action that defines its strategy without understanding its impact on its many neighboring business domains, or on the ecosystem as a whole, is ignoring the reality of the networked environment in which it operates. When AOL and Yahoo! struck aggressive deals with their dot-com partners in the boom years of the Internet bubble, they financially weakened their partners and set the stage for the collapse to come. It was not enough for the healthier financial domains to mask the inherent troubles of the weaker Internet firms. Although Yahoo!'s and AOL's actions may not have contributed to the individual performance of these financial firms as conventionally measured, the collective effect of their actions on the system as a whole was destabilizing—and ultimately catastrophic for the entire ecosystem, not just for the weaker domains. No one would argue that either of these firms was unaware of the fact that they were embedded in a network of interdependent firms: Both explicitly viewed themselves as hubs in these networks. Instead, what each lacked was a sense of the full impact of its actions as a hub. In essence, AOL and Yahoo! failed to appreciate the enormous power that hubs have on the collective dynamics of large networks. They thus proceeded to follow strategies that optimized short-term financial gains but potentially undermined the health of critical domains in their ecosystems. What they were missing was a framework for assessing network health that they could have employed to evaluate their actions.

What, then, makes a business ecosystem healthy? It is important to appreciate the novelty of this question. We are not assuming anything about given metrics of economic-theoretical health, such as number of firms or abstractions such as "competition" or "consumer choice," but instead are asking a different question: How can we assess the health of entire business communities of firms, products, and consumers? What we seek are measures of the extent to which an ecosystem as a whole is *durably creating opportunities for each of its domains*. It is not sufficient, for example, that an ecosystem have selective pockets of health that provide choice if the choices are not meaningfully different, nor is it acceptable that an ecosystem generates or supplies novelty if

FIGURE 3-1

Domains in the Microsoft Software Ecosystem

Data were provided by Microsoft Corporation, through a summary report of the aggregate number of Microsoft partner firms across thirty-two sectors. Only segments with 500 or more firms are depicted.

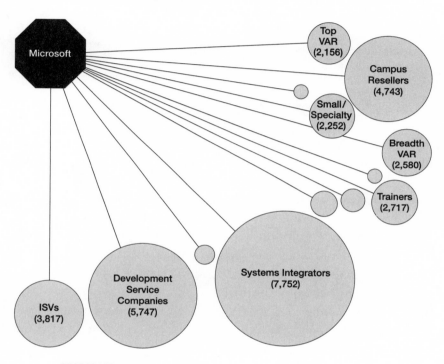

MICROSOFT

Total	38,338		
Partner Segment	**Firms**	**Partner Segment**	**Firms**
System Integrator	7,752	Mass Merchant	220
Development Srvc Co	5,747	Software Outbound	160
Campus Resellers	4,743	DMR	105
ISV	3,817	Computer Superstore	51
Trainer	2,717	ASP Aggregator	50
Breadth VAR	2,580	eTailers	46
Small/Specialty	2,252	Office Superstore	13
Top VAR	2,156	General/Aggregator	7
Hosting Srvc Prov	1,379	Warehouse/Club Store	7
Internet Srvc	1,253	Niche/Specialty	6
Business Consultants	938	Subdistributor	6
Support	675	Apps Integrator	5
Hardware Outbound	653	MS Direct (Rsir)	2
Consumer Electronics	467	MS Direct	1
Unsegmented Reseller	290	Network Equip Prov	1
Media Store	238	Network Srvc Prov	1

ISV = independent software vendor   VAR = value-added reseller the entire ecosystem vanishes or collapses at the first disruptive change in the environment.

To assess the health of business ecosystems in the sense we seek to capture, we propose examining three aspects of the ecosystem, inspired by our biological metaphor and expressed in terms of our ecosystem analogy: *productivity, robustness,* and *niche creation.* In what follows, we explain these measures and apply them to three different ecosystem communities: software application providers, biotechnology companies, and Internet service firms.

Productivity

Where are technologies reliably being transformed into new products? Where is capital and other investment being most effectively used? Where are these results achieved year after year? Different business networks show strikingly different performance along these dimensions. Over the same period that software firms averaged almost 10 percent return on invested capital, biotechnology firms' *losses* were over 5 percent; and whereas software firms were able to keep returns fairly stable over nearly a decade, those of Internet firms were highly unstable. At the same time, numerous technology transformations and upheavals, both large and small, have hit each of these industries—from online retailing to instant messaging, from the sequencing of the human genome to digital photography. Yet only software firms have consistently and effectively transformed these inputs into new products. These differences among these networks reflect differences in a critical aspect of ecosystem health: their productivity.

In the literature on the conservation of biological ecosystems, *productivity* is a widely used measure of ecosystem health and of its benefits to those who use the ecosystem: How effectively does the ecosystem convert raw materials into living organisms? This approach is a very good analogue to various forms of productivity analysis used routinely in economics, or to simpler measures such as return on invested capital, but is applied to different ecosystems or ecosystem areas. However, in biological ecosystems the set of inputs does not change significantly over time. The business ecosystems we are interested in are strikingly different: They are constantly subject to new conditions in the form of new technologies, new processes, and new demands.

By analogy, then, measures of productivity should also capture the effectiveness of an ecosystem in converting innovation into lowered costs and new products and functions. This suggests at least three types of productivity-related metrics:

1. **Factor productivity.** Leveraging techniques used in traditional economic productivity analysis, ecosystems may be compared according to the productivity of their participants in converting factors of production into useful work. The most widespread measure of this kind is focused on returns on invested capital, or ROIC. Figure 3-2 illustrates the kinds of comparisons between

FIGURE 3-2

Productivity Differences Among Ecosystems

To measure the ROIC in three ecosystems (software, biotechnology, and "Internet"), we assembled a systematic list of all public firms in those areas and calculated the average aggregate ROIC.[1] This list includes all public companies that fall under Standard Industrial Classification (SIC) 737, 3570, 3571, and 3575 for the software ecosystem, and SIC 2836 for biotechnology. The list of Internet firms was assembled from lists of all firms with IPOs from 1995 to 2002, from which we then manually identified Internet firms.[2] There were approximately 800 software firms, 231 biotechnology firms, and 130 Internet firms on the list.

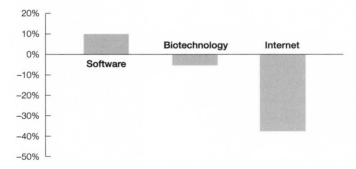

[1] The average aggregate ROIC is calculated by dividing the total net income in the ecosystem by the total invested capital in the ecosystem for each year (each calculated by adding the values for the individual firms identified as composing that ecosystem), and then averaging across 1990–2002.

[2] Currently, there is no SIC classification for Internet firms. The Internet firms we used were taken from www.bullsector.com/internet.html, www.wsrn.com/apps/internetstocklist, and www.internetstockreview.com.

ecosystems that are possible using this measure and demon-
strates that striking differences in ecosystem health exist
between software, biotechnology, and Internet firms.

2. **Change in productivity over time.** Do the members of the
   ecosystem and those who use its products show increases or
   decreases in productivity measures over time? Are they able to
   produce the same products or complete the same tasks at progressively lower cost?

   Figure 3-3 depicts data on ROIC for software, biotechnology,
   and Internet firms over time. The Internet plot is particularly
   interesting. It shows plummeting productivity numbers between
   1996 and 1997, which incidentally is when tough traffic-sharing
   agreements began to become entrenched in the sector. What is
   fascinating about the picture is that the plummeting ROIC
   numbers precede *by more than three years* the actual collapse
   of the Internet sector. Clearly, an awareness of network health

FIGURE 3-3

Productivity Differences Among Ecosystems over Time

This figure shows the same data as Figure 3-2, broken down by year.

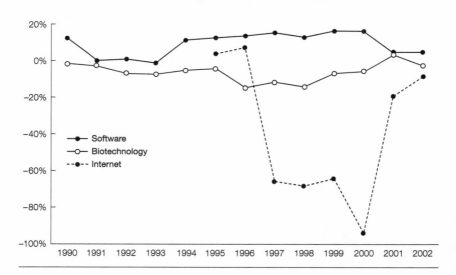

considerations might have helped firms like Cisco reduce their dependencies on such a precarious domain.

Comparing the data for the biotechnology and software ecosystems is also interesting. Why is the ROIC pattern so different for the two communities? Why is the software community consistently higher? And why, given these data, does the biotech community keep attracting so much capital? The data highlight what appear to be systematic differences among ecosystem communities. In the following chapters we will relate some of these systematic differences to the behavior of organizations that form ecosystem hubs, and explain the collective impact of keystone and dominator strategies.

3. **Delivery of innovations.** Other measures of productivity can also be applied to the analysis of ecosystems. One interesting point of view, somewhat less common in traditional economics, is to examine an ecosystem's propensity to share and promote innovation. Does the ecosystem effectively deliver new technologies, processes, or ideas to its members? Does it lower the costs of employing these novelties, as compared with adopting them directly, and propagate access to them widely throughout the ecosystem in ways that improve the classic productivity of ecosystem members?

The software industry provides some interesting examples. One measure of this aspect of ecosystem health is the time lag between the appearance of a technology and its wide dissemination—for example, the surprisingly short lag between the first beta version of the Mosaic browser in 1993 and the inclusion of Internet Explorer (IE) in every copy of Windows (along with all of the technologies, such as TCP/IP, HTML, HTTP, URL, and SSL, required for built-in Internet connectivity) in 1995.

Another measure is the decline in the difficulty of using an innovation—for example, the differences between the situation in the late 1980s, when establishing a network connection within the same building (let alone over phone lines to remote sites) required considerable expertise and time, and the situation today. Another measure is the degree to which the potential offered by an innovation is harnessed—for example, something that is used in many different ways by many different existing components of the ecosystem, such as the ubiquity of HTML as a generic standard for marking up text for presentation in applications ranging from accounting packages to system help.

The last measure, delivery of innovations, is an important one because it encourages us to follow specific novelties as they are developed and delivered through the ecosystem and then to assess the costs and benefits of employing them, but the first measure, productivity, can serve as a convenient proxy. It allows us to at least demonstrate that innovations are having a real collective effect on ecosystem members in cases where we are unable to examine individual innovations. Note also that we require that productivity improvements be sustained: It is not sufficient that an ecosystem provide one-time improvements to those who join it.

Robustness

Existing frameworks for the analysis of the impact of technological innovation are generally shaped by a view that sees technological change advancing in discontinuous waves through industries as organizational response is impaired by inertia.[1] But networks governed by these idealized dynamics are not healthy in the sense we seek here. To provide durable benefits to those who depend on it, a biological ecosystem must persist in the face of environmental changes. Similarly, a business ecosystem should be capable of facing and surviving perturbations and disruptions. If a business ecosystem dies or is radically altered by each new technological transformation or external perturbation, those who depend on it are less likely to be in a position to continue to benefit from the opportunities it provides.

The generic benefits to a firm from being a part of a robust ecosystem are obvious: The firm operates in a relatively predictable environment that absorbs shocks and buffers it against changes that could threaten it. This benefit has several dimensions that contribute to firm health, each of which can be used to assess this aspect of ecosystem health.

Measures of robustness should first of all examine survival rates in a given ecosystem. In its most basic form, a healthy ecosystem will promote the survival of a diverse set of firms that populate a variety of niches and undergo the variety of inevitable disruptions. Survival rates are only the most basic indicators, however, and more sophisticated analyses should focus on a variety of metrics:

1. **Survival rates.** Ecosystem participants should enjoy high survival rates, either over time or relative to other, comparable ecosystems. Figures 3-4 and 3-5 show numbers of firms over time in the software, biotechnology, and Internet ecosystem communities. In the software community, we see a strong growth rate over a decade, with some contraction around the technology recession of 2001. The biotech community is relatively flat in growth, which masks a lot of industry churn. What we see is significant turnover in firms as start-ups replace firms that go out of business. As expected, the Internet ecosystem shows a dramatic collapse in 2002. Again, it is interesting to note by how many years the ROIC collapse shown in Figure 3-3 precedes the collapse in the number of firms shown in Figure 3-5.

FIGURE 3-4

Numbers of Firms in the Software and Biotechnology Communities

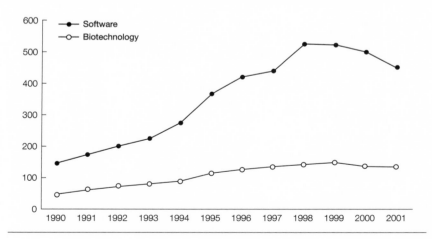

FIGURE 3-5

Numbers of Firms in the Internet Ecosystem

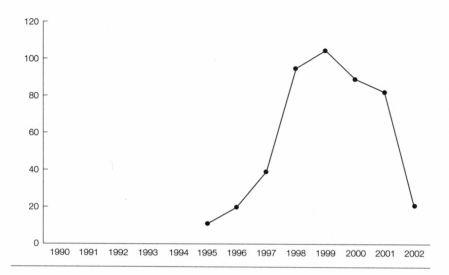

2. **Persistence of ecosystem structure.** In a robust ecosystem, changes in the relationships among ecosystem members are contained; overall, the structure of the ecosystem is unaffected by external shocks. Most connections between firms or between technologies remain. Notably, those who depend on the ecosystem (including many members of the ecosystem itself) can rely on certain structural features of the ecosystem—its details may change, but changes in the "way it works" are gradual and largely predictable. We will discuss some applications of this measure in later chapters.

3. **Predictability.** Change in a robust ecosystem structure is not only contained, it is predictably localized. The locus of change to ecosystem structure will differ for different shocks, but a predictable "core" will generally remain unaffected. Conceptually, a good example of this is the evolution of the PC desktop environment: Although it has gone from being a document creation and management environment to a much richer one, coping with

everything from shopping to communication to movie viewing and game playing, it has done this without major upheaval.[2]

4. **Limited obsolescence.** In a healthy ecosystem, there is no dramatic abandonment of "obsolete" capacity in response to a perturbation. Most of the installed base or investment in technology or components finds continued use after dramatic changes in the ecosystem's environment. Again, the adaptability of the PC is a good illustration: Through the adoption of tools for high-end digital image editing to digital photography, the incorporation of technology for fast transfer of data to external drives, and the extension of the file browsing user interface to support common photography-related functions (thumbnails, previewing, and even ordering prints online), the PC has adapted itself to a completely novel domain of application. Rather than being displaced by special-purpose tools (e.g., the digital camera), it has become an essential component of their use.

5. **Continuity of use experience and use cases.** The experience of consumers of a robust ecosystem's products will gradually evolve in response to the introduction of new technologies rather than being radically transformed. Existing capabilities and tools will be leveraged to perform new operations enabled by new technologies.[3] An example is the kind of consistent "user model" that has evolved on the PC desktop—for example, viewing Web content is largely indistinguishable from viewing other kinds of documents and is becoming increasingly seamless. This is partly enabled by the kinds of stable APIs that lead to predictability. One of the reasons that, for example, users can apply the same conceptual model to files on a hard disk and to files on digital camera is that they use the same underlying API.

Not all of these measures will apply or be available in every circumstance, but as a collection they should provide an effective set of tools for assessing robustness. As highlighted in our earlier discussion of what we call "domains," such an analysis should not necessarily be centered on whole industries characterized by firms competing in similar markets, but more generally on networks of firms that share common nodes. As highlighted in our discussion of the literature on networks, there is strong general evidence that networks with certain structural features—notably the presence of hubs—are more likely to exhibit the persistence of structure and predictability in the sense defined here. In a networked structure, the hubs will effectively leverage the network to mount responses to new, uncertain conditions. New product components or new service characteristics can be provided to a customer by leveraging the capabilities of other network participants as long as enough diversity is present. As a result, the presence of a stable hub and a diverse community of interconnected entities is a strong indicator of ecosystem robustness.

Niche Creation

The PCs on our desktops have the same outward appearance and general architecture as those of more than a decade ago. Like the cars in our garages, they would seem at first glance to have undergone few meaningful changes since their basic plan was stabilized. The difference could not be more striking, however. Whereas automobiles have added almost no major functionality in a generation (indeed, the "bells and whistles" that they slowly add seem almost forced at times), PCs have continuously increased the variety of functions they perform (from financial record keeping to digital photography, from game playing to telephony), as have the opportunities for a growing diversity of firms that specialize in these new capabilities.

The automobile and computing industries clearly exhibit very different dynamics. Indeed, whereas the computing industry has actively embraced new technologies with an enthusiasm that has led to the sustained creation of opportunities for entirely new classes of firms, the automobile industry has historically sought to prevent the emergence of such new niches. This difference suggests another dimension for assessing ecosystem health. Robustness and productivity do not completely capture the character of a healthy biological ecosystem; both in the ecological literature and in popular conception, it is also important that these systems exhibit variety or diversity—that they support many different species. Although diversity is often considered a positive attribute of these ecosystems, it is by no means an absolute good; some highly productive and valuable ecosystems, for example, are not diverse.[4] Moreover, as has already been mentioned, many business ecosystems are characterized by considerable diversity, but are stagnant or in decline. Furthermore, like evolved complex systems such as social insect colonies, business ecosystems have the capacity to create entirely novel capabilities through integration and innovation.

For all of these reasons, diversity alone should not map directly to a positive health measure for business ecosystems. What matters in these systems is the capacity to increase meaningful diversity over time through the creation of new valuable functions. In terms of the ecosystem metaphor, this is the capacity to create new valuable niches. We can thus begin to assess this dimension of ecosystem health with two related measures:

1. **Growth in firm variety:** The number of new firms created within the ecosystem community in a given period of time.

2. **Growth in product and technical variety:** The number of new product options, technological building blocks, categories, products, or businesses being created within the ecosystem in a given period of time.

For example, a crude measure of the variety of functionality supported by Microsoft operating systems is provided by the count of APIs that software developers can use in building applications (see Figure 3-6). As is the case with DOS and Windows, healthy ecosystems should rest on foundations in which such measures are large and growing.

Note that these metrics are connected to our productivity measures, particularly to the delivery of innovations: One way of delivering innovations is through the creation of new businesses. Thus, a fairly direct way of measuring niche creation is to determine the extent to which new technologies are appearing in the form of a variety of new businesses and products.

Because it is not just any diversity that matters, but rather diversity that creates value, it is essential that the new categories of business be *meaningfully* new: that they provide new functionality, enable new scenarios, or expose new technology or ideas.[5] One way of exploring this important aspect of ecosystem health is to examine the relationship

FIGURE 3-6

Growth in the Functionality of Microsoft Operating Systems, Measured by Counts of Application Programming Interfaces (APIs)

API numbers for Windows were derived by adding the counts of the "function" and "interface" entries in the Win32.API.Csv list of APIs supplied in Microsoft's Software Development Kit for each full-release version of its operating systems.

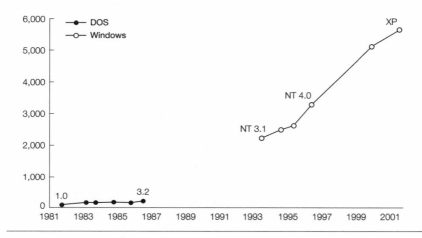

between diversity and consumer experience: Does the variety of firms and their products map to a variety of consumer experiences and to convenience and effectiveness in achieving those experiences or building downstream products?

Although healthy ecosystems should exhibit net creation of niches over time, it does not follow that old niches need persist: Diversity of niches may actually decrease in some areas. In fact, as we shall explore in some detail when we examine the process of integration in the computing ecosystem, it may be the case that decreases in diversity in some areas enable the creation of niches in others. This is consistent with the process through which new system-level capabilities arise in biological evolution: Diversity at one level is reduced to create a platform that enables greater and more meaningful diversity at higher levels.

Taken together, all the measures discussed in this chapter define what we mean by a healthy business ecosystem that is durably growing opportunities for its members and for those who depend on it.

They represent relatively clear, measurable metrics that can be applied to the direct comparison of different ecosystems and ecosystem areas.[6]

Collective Improvements

In the months after the collapse of the B2C community almost put them out of business (and virtually destroyed many of their lesser competitors), Yahoo! and Cisco both put in place substantial changes in their business practices. They both now actively examine the health of their business ecosystem and assess how to move their business toward healthier customer communities. Both have systematically lessened their dependencies on unhealthy supplier/partner communities and have increased their focus on products and services that are attractive to more traditional, "safer," blue-chip customers. Additionally, both have moved away from internal practices that might decrease the health of ecosystem communities.

The days of flaky, cash-loaded customers or superaggressive business development may yet return, but at least the businesses that lived through the worst of the Internet bubble seem to have learned a valuable lesson: The critical effects that a hub firm can have on the collective health of the networks of which it is a part cannot be ignored.

II

Ecosystem Strategies

CHAPTER FOUR

Operating Strategies

Why eBay Isn't Enron

Enron and eBay approached similarly daunting challenges in the late 1990s. Each attempted to be the hub of a massive business network of trading partners, and each attempted to use the potential of Internet technology to build hundreds of individual markets. The first started by leveraging its established, unique position in the energy sector, its extensive existing assets, and its aggressive blue-chip managerial talent and focused on improving vast, high-value, traditionally fragmented, and inefficient markets. The second started with very little and focused initially on the narrow collectors market.

In the years that followed, both Enron and eBay moved to start and scale hundreds of different markets. In doing so, eBay worked hard to share the wealth generated and managed to create an enormous, healthy ecosystem of trading partners. Enron, in sharp contrast, took away as much of the value as it could by exploiting any imperfection in information and market structure to its own advantage. The results are fascinating. eBay was cash-flow positive from the start and ended up generating huge profits, whereas Enron hid massive market losses in illegal partnerships. Why did the company that shared the wealth end up making so much more money?

What emerges from a variety of examples like this one is that a pattern of operating decisions based on creating, shaping, and leveraging a healthy ecosystem can make for strong, sustainable business performance. eBay and Enron followed fundamentally different operating strategies and achieved fundamentally different results. Clearly, many factors contributed to eBay's success and Enron's demise, but their approach to managing a business ecosystem was among the most important and has been the least discussed.

The previous chapter argued that the concepts of shared fate and collective behavior should motivate firms to take a close look at the health of their ecosystem communities. But this is only the first part of the solution to the puzzle of effective, sustainable performance in a networked environment. The second and more challenging part is to identify the strategies through which firms—whatever their role in the environment—can (and should) act to operate effectively within it. This chapter identifies key behaviors of network participants that can actively influence the collective properties of their business networks as well as their own individual performance. In the process of exploring this topic, the chapter identifies specific operating strategies that firms can employ to leverage the vast potential of a networked business environment.

Strategies

How does this networked view of the world help explain the difference between eBay and Enron? Critically, eBay and Enron played very different roles in their ecosystems, and these roles had an enormous impact on overall ecosystem health and sustainability. To capture the implications of these ideas, it is useful to view these different roles as contrasting operating strategies.

Whether explicit or implicit, a firm's strategy is revealed by the pattern of operating decisions made by an organization. For best overall performance, this pattern should match the organization's environment.[1] In a networked setting, these decisions should also be influenced by the structure and dynamics of the business ecosystem in which the firm finds itself and be consistent with the role that it decides to play, as well as the capabilities that it decides to develop.

Over the last decade, research in a number of industries has documented wide variation between competitors in critical dimensions of performance such as productivity, quality, time to market, customer satisfaction, and profitability.[2] This empirical evidence underscores the success of some firms in creating and sustaining significant advantage over their competitors. Although strategic moves (such as capacity additions, investments in R&D and advertising, and alliances) and structural considerations (such as strategic groups and barriers to mobility) may partly explain observed differences in performance, research on the sources of those differences points to critical capacities for action that are far more effective in practice at some firms than at others. Some firms are simply more able than others in ways that matter in competition, and these differences may be ascribed to operating strategies and their foundations in capabilities.

This connection between capability and competition has also been an important theme in recent work in economic history and business strategy.[3] The notion of a firm's "distinctive competence" has a venerable history in the study of business policy, but more recent work on the resource-based view of the firm, the notion of core competence, and the learning organization has emphasized the dynamic nature of the operational capabilities that are critical for sustainable firm performance.[4] Recognizing the dynamic nature of the interactions among the market, technical environment, and competence base of the firm, work by a variety of authors has also focused attention on the importance of innovation in building and renewing capabilities over time.[5]

However, most of the work performed so far has focused on the *internal* nature of these operational and innovative capabilities. This emphasis pervades the management of both operations and innovation and has several common themes: capability building, commonly linked to the management of improvement and learning; the internal implementation of information technology; the management of focused product development teams; and the management of resource allocation. Even when authors have focused on the operational challenges of managing the relationships between firms, the typical focus has been on bilateral relations or at most on relations among small groups of organizations. Examples are relationships between manufacturer and supplier, user and manufacturer, or designer and manufacturer.[6] A common thread runs through most of this work: The tighter the coupling between parties (manufacturer and supplier, co-design team members, etc.), the better the performance. The same is also true for many theories of quick response in supply chains, in which the better the relationship between firms, and the tighter the exchange of information, the better the performance of the supply chain system.[7] Relatively little attention has been focused on the study of extended supply networks, which are characterized by vast, loosely coupled networks of organizations and are fraught with a variety of problems, ranging from deep information and incentive asymmetries to the imperfect quality of information.[8]

The innovation management literature has generally followed this same focus. Much of the work so far has focused on the fragile nature of competitive advantage in situations of significant technological and market upheaval. Authors have applied punctuated equilibrium models to understand the impact of technological change on organizations, but the nature of the change has generally been treated as an exogenous variable.[9] Authors have analyzed changes that are competence destroying, attacking the firm's "core"; architectural, fundamentally changing its organization; or disruptive to the firm's business model. But in virtually all cases, the changes were analyzed as an exogenous shock or trend that influenced a single firm (or even a single organization within the firm). The critical interaction between that firm and its network of business partners was left largely untouched. Although the interaction of the firm with its "value network" is analyzed in Christensen's work, this interaction is generally perceived as a problem that increases the challenges faced by an organization. In all of these frameworks, the network is seen largely as a source of inertia, not as a dynamic factor that can enhance productivity and innovation.

However, a stream of literature in the finance and strategy domains has recently underlined the importance of industry fragmentation and industry networks.[10] This literature highlights the general impact of modularity, product standards, and network externalities. Most notably, Baldwin and Clark introduced the concept of an "industry cluster," made up of the many organizations that are linked to each other via modular interfaces in the design of a product, and set the stage for the significant operational implications of this phenomenon. As Carl Shapiro and Hal Varian point out, "There is a central difference between the old and new economies: the old industrial economy was driven by economies of scale; the new information economy is driven by the economics of networks."[11] Gawer and Cusumano extend this perspective by highlighting the critical role played by industry "plat-forms" such as Intel, Microsoft, and Cisco, and argue for the impor-tance of standards and distributed innovation.

These writings clearly highlight that distributed industries behave differently, but the implications of this difference for the formulation of strategy and for the management of innovation and operations are still underdeveloped. This leaves unexplored the challenges of manag-ing innovation or operations in the kinds of very large, loosely con-nected networks that characterize eBay's and Enron's environments as well as an increasing number of key industries. In this book we attempt to fill some of this gap by formulating a framework for under-standing and analyzing operating strategy in a networked environ-ment. We develop the framework by drawing analogies between *roles* in biological ecosystems and *strategies* in business networks. Our dis-cussion begins by linking the structure of a network to its effectiveness in performing tasks.

Network Structure and Performance

There is a growing appreciation that many phenomena in both the nat-ural and the man-made worlds can be viewed as networks of individ-ual agents.[12] From the understanding of the spread of forest fires to the accurate portrayal of the effects of crowd panic in a burning building, network approaches are yielding insights that conventional approaches have failed to produce.[13] Similarly, there is a growing awareness that by structuring problems so that they can be viewed as networks of smaller problems, difficult tasks can be completed more efficiently. This basic insight is the inspiration for a wide variety of applications, from the design of routing algorithms in communications networks to traffic flow management on highways, and has even inspired military thinkers to take a serious look at radical approaches. These military theories range from "fire ant warfare" employing "swarms" of small, lightweight networked vehicles and munitions as a replacement for the costly and vulnerable monolithic components in use today, to the use of fruit flies as a model for battlefield communications. A general conclusion of this literature is that by connecting even simple components *in the right way,* complex and difficult problems beyond the abilities of the individual components can be solved, and new capabilities acquired. The network becomes much more than the sum of its parts. Indeed, in almost every field, from geopolitics to medicine, there are advocates of "network approaches" and "swarm intelligence" who argue that breaking things up into large numbers of small interconnected components will solve almost any problem and make the system as a whole almost magically better.[14]

But what is the right way to connect components? Are some network structures more effective than others? The answers to these questions lie at the heart of understanding how complex systems work, and are essential if we are to begin to understand how firms can operate effectively to influence network health. The literature on complex systems suggests that networks of many kinds naturally possess "key players" or "hubs" that enhance efficiency and certain kinds of network stability. Many networked structures, ranging from relationships among friends to the pattern of links in the World Wide Web, exhibit a characteristic property: They have a pattern of connections in which a small number of nodes in the network are much more richly connected than the vast majority of the other members of the system. It turns out this structure will always emerge if networks evolve their connections over time and if these connections are "costly" to traverse or establish—for example, if they are constrained by physical location (participants need to be near one another to interact), require specialization (a plant requires special adaptations to live near the roots of another), or simply take time (as in navigating the Internet).[15] Critically, these hubs form regardless of the nature of the system, the internal details of the participants within the system, or the specific nature of the connections between members of the system.[16]

One important property of networks with hubs is that degrees of separation between nodes—the number of network nodes that, on average, need to be visited to get from any one node to an arbitrary other node—are small. Indeed, hubs are part of the reason behind the whimsical "six degrees of separation" theory.[17] Perhaps the most dramatic illustration of this rule of network structure is the pattern of links among sites on the World Wide Web.[18] Here a system with a huge number of diverse participants and no initial macro-scale structure evolved rapidly to have a structure in which a vast number of sites can be reached through a surprisingly small number of "jumps."

Both positive and negative consequences arise from the existence of a hub structure. For example, Web hubs make hundreds of millions of pages accessible through about nineteen degrees of separation, but the "bow tie" structure of the Web has left many sites stranded in fragmented "tendrils."[19] If the system is subject to growth or change, especially rapid or discontinuous change, hubs can be displaced over time as new hubs emerge to take over their function: Hubs will always exist, but specific hubs will rise and fall. Often, early movers in such "scale-free" networks are more likely to become hubs than those who join the network later. Moreover, the sudden removal of a hub results in the loss of a disproportionate number of network connections, resulting in the effective collapse and fragmentation of the network. Networks with hubs are vulnerable to malicious or targeted attacks.

Despite the danger from targeted attacks, network hubs exhibit an important and unambiguous aspect of network health: They are robust in the face of random disruptions. It is hubs that account for the robustness of nature's webs. Removal of arbitrary nodes from networks with hubs leaves most of the network intact.[20] Robustness of this kind has been documented both theoretically and experimentally for a wide variety of networks with hub-governed structures.[21] Conversely, it has been clearly shown that "the tolerance of networks to different types of perturbation depends critically on the network structure"; specifically, that networks lacking hubs are far more vulnerable to random disruptions.[22] In such networks, local disruptions can have far-reaching effects that damage or destroy the entire network.

Roles

Hubs can play an enormously important role in the collective performance of a network. They have the potential to increase the ease with which different network nodes connect to each other and thereby decrease the complexity involved in the coordination and integration efforts necessary for improving productivity and achieving growth.

Additionally, they have the potential to increase the robustness of the network to many kinds of environmental shocks. However, not all hubs will serve in such a beneficial role. In a business network, this potential can only be translated into reality by the decisions that managers in these organizations actually make, by the capabilities they develop, and by the business models they define. The impact of business network hubs such as Enron and eBay is therefore critically shaped by the roles that these organizations decide to play.

In nature, networks are rarely homogeneous, and different members play distinct and unequal roles. Critically, the ecosystem analogy suggests that by pursuing specific roles that foster (or hinder) ecosystem health, hubs can affect their own performance and survival. This provides a useful and vivid way to extend our perspective on networks and make it concrete. We pursue this by identifying specific roles for ecosystem members and relating these roles to the collective properties of their ecosystems. Three roles are of particular significance: keystone, dominator, and niche player. Each of these affords different opportunities to shape network health, and distinct opportunities to benefit from it.

Keystones

The biological literature suggests that a species that serves as a hub in a food web or other network of ecosystem interactions can improve its overall chances of survival in the face of change by providing benefits to the ecosystem as a whole. This literature identifies *keystone species* as having specific characteristics that produce such benefits for the ecosystem and its members.[23] Removal of biological keystones can have dramatic cascading effects through the entire ecosystem, whereas removal of other species, even species involved in many interactions, can have little effect beyond the loss of those connections.[24] The former type of effects include decline in important measures of health, such as loss of diversity, loss of productivity, and extinctions.[25]

Biological ecosystems are characterized by a large number of interactions among their members. Although often essential to survival, many of these interactions are indirect and have effects that are remote from their sources. The pathways of interaction often pass through the keystone species, whose influence on the survival and health of the entire ecosystem thus extends far beyond its obvious sphere of influence.[26] As a result, these species serve as keystones in the most literal sense of the word: Their removal results in a collapse of the ecosystem as a whole. This fact sets up a self-reinforcing dynamic in which the ecosystem and the keystone depend on each other for their survival. Because of this dependency, keystones naturally exert a variety of effects on their ecosystem that contribute to its health. These effects can be broadly placed in three overlapping categories: stability, diversity, and productivity.

Keystones can enhance the productivity of their ecosystems in a variety of ways. Some do so by directly removing or limiting the numbers of species that would otherwise disproportionately reduce productivity. An example of such a "keystone predator" is the sea otter. The reduction in sea otter populations in coastal ecosystems in the Pacific Northwest in the previous century resulted in the reduction in near-shore productivity of a wide variety of species of fish and other organisms. This collapse of coastal ecosystems occurred because sea otters are apparently the only (nonhuman) predator capable of effectively controlling populations of sea urchins, which, left unchecked, overgraze a variety of invertebrates and plants, including kelp, which in turn supports a food web that is the engine of near-shore productivity.[27] Recent reintroduction of sea otters has in fact resulted in the reestablishment of kelp in the areas affected and has led to a parallel increase in productivity in a variety of fish and invertebrate species and has even reduced coastal erosion.[28]

Keystones can also enhance productivity from the bottom up by providing a foundation on which other species rely. To some extent, this is the role played by kelp in the near-shore ecosystems influenced by sea otters: It provides not only shelter and habitat for a variety of fish and invertebrate species, but also serves as the basis for a detritus-based food web. These two keystones also provide contrasting examples of the conspicuousness of keystones in their ecosystems. Kelp functions as a keystone partly because of its conspicuous presence: It is significant in providing both nutrients and shelter precisely because it is conspicuous and abundant. Otters are another matter: Although they are only a small part of the biomass of their communities, they exert tremendous influence, largely through their ravenous appetites.[29]

Diversity in ecosystems often directly enhances stability by ensuring that the ecosystem has the capacity (in terms of genetic and behavioral variation) to respond to environmental changes. As a result it is not surprising to find that keystones often exhibit diversity-enhancing features. Again, selective keystone predation often plays a role. Sea otters enhance not only productivity but diversity as well; other predators, from coyotes to sea stars, have much the same effect.[30] However, diversity is also often maintained by seemingly passive behaviors. Through the simple act of grazing, bison prevent any one fast-growing plant species from dominating the grassland ecosystem in which they live, thus maintaining its biodiversity.[31]

Naturally, the most direct way for a keystone to ensure its continued survival is to directly maintain the stability of its ecosystem. Therefore it is to be expected that keystones act to encourage stability directly in addition to encouraging it indirectly through their effect on diversity. The most dramatic demonstrations that keystones in fact serve this function come from "removal" studies in which a keystone is either deliberately or accidentally removed or impaired. Among the many examples of this kind of experiment, the best documented demonstrate a "wholesale reorganization" of ecosystems when environmental stresses become so great that they exceed the tolerances of a keystone species.[32]

Close examination of the role played by such keystones reveals that they in effect provide a platform on which much of the rest of the ecosystem is built. Prairie dogs, for example, serve as an essential food source for mountain plovers, ferruginous hawks, black-footed ferrets, swift foxes, and a variety of other animals. Many animals preferentially graze where prairie dog burrows are present, and a large number of birds (including burrowing owls, upland sandpipers, and McCown's longspur) and other animals (including the prairie rattlesnake and the Great Plains toad) use prairie dog burrows for shelter.

All these contributions to ecosystem health are of course overlapping and often reinforce one another. Thus, for example, as discussed in chapter 2, figs contribute not only to stability indirectly through their contribution to diversity, but also enhance it directly by providing a stable ecosystem platform. Less obvious but more important, there are often trade-offs among these contributions—notably between diversity and stability. The case of figs is again instructive: One might argue that a greater diversity of fruit sources in place of figs might enhance the stability of the ecosystem. But diversity alone is not sufficient. Unless these sources also provided all of the platform benefits on which the ecosystem relies—complex fruiting patterns and specific sets of nutrients—increasing diversity at this level could actually destabilize the ecosystem by undermining the predictability of its foundations and leading to a loss of diversity at all other levels.

Keystones and keystonelike behavior are not restricted to biological ecosystems. Keystones are, in fact, a general phenomenon of networks with members that have the capacity to act in ways that influence other network members. Consequently, we should expect to find keystone roles as a phenomenon in many networked systems. We believe that keystones play a crucial role in business ecosystems.

First of all, firms that follow keystonelike behavior are important in business domains that are characterized by frequent or significant external disruptions. The diversity they support serves as a buffer, preserving the overall structure, productivity, and diversity of the system in the face of change that may eliminate other, nonkeystone species. Such firms have the potential to preside over significant turnover in ecosystems over time. The individual members of the ecosystem may change, but the system as a whole, along with its keystones, persists. For example, the successive waves of transformation that have spread through the software industry (starting with the rise of the PC, and followed notably by the rise of the graphical user interface and of the Internet) resulted in significant changes in the software ecosystem, but its overall structure, productivity, and diversity have been unhurt, and its keystones— among them Microsoft, IBM, and Sun—have persisted.

Similarly, keystone species often displace or hold in check other species that would otherwise dominate the system (i.e., not just take over the keystone's role, but also the roles of many other species). Moreover, because keystones can preside over significant turnover within an ecosystem, and because diversity and responsiveness to change preserve the ecosystem against encroachment, keystones improve the chances of their survival by either directly or indirectly *encouraging* change. This is what the IBM-Microsoft-Intel ecosystem achieved with respect to Apple: For many years, Apple refused to license its operating system and produced a highly integrated product (including hardware, a software platform, and many applications) that performed the functions of many potential other "species"—acting in effect as a dominator. But it failed in the face of Microsoft, IBM, and Intel, which acted as effective keystones. Microsoft focused its business model on software platforms, licensed its platform and tools broadly, and distributed innovation to a wide variety of ISVs and other technology and business partners. The sheer diversity of approaches, the productivity, and the pace of innovation that Microsoft's keystone approach unleashed could not be matched by Apple's approach.

Fundamentally, a keystone acts to improve the overall health of the ecosystem and, in doing so, benefits the sustained performance of the firm. It does this by creating and sharing value with its network by leveraging its central hub position in that network, while generally occupying only a small part of that network (see figure 4-1). Chapter 5 explores in detail examples of keystones in business networks, applying the concept of a biological keystone to analyze the critical and active role firms can play in their business ecosystem by following a keystone strategy.

Dominators

The literature on keystones also suggests a contrasting *dominator* role.[33] Dominators are easily recognized, and easily distinguished from keystones by two characteristics. The first is metrics of physical size or abundance—in contrast with dominators, keystones are often a small part of their ecosystems, by many measures. The second is that to the extent that they fail to encourage diversity, dominators must either take over the functions of the species they eliminate or eliminate those functions altogether. Ecosystems that are in the grip of an invasive weedy species provide a good example of the effects of a dominator: Not only is much of the biomass of such ecosystems made up of the dominant invader, but also these ecosystems simply "do" less. This is essentially the situation that has played out as a consequence of the introduction of the zebra mussel (discussed in chapter 2), and is the fate of many North American wetlands, which have become dominated by the invasive purple loosestrife.[34] These wetlands have become increasingly uniform swaths of a single plant species and have

FIGURE 4-1

An Idealized Keystone in a Business Network

In this schematic representation of a business network, a keystone (thick lines and large nodes) is shown occupying only a small proportion of the total nodes in the network; the remaining nodes (thin lines and small circles) are available for occupation by other firms. The nodes that a keystone occupies are those that serve collectively or individually as hubs in the network: They are the most richly connected and thus lie at the network's "core."

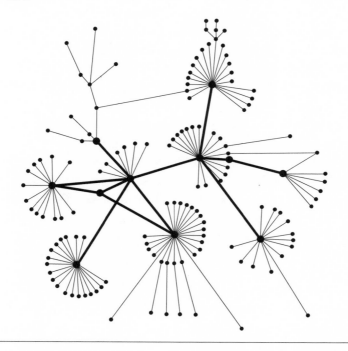

lost many native species of plants and animals—in effect, they *become* the single dominating species.

Of course, conspicuousness alone is not sufficient to make a species a dominator or to disqualify it from being a keystone. Some species, such as kelp in the near-shore ecosystems in the Pacific Northwest, are keystones partly *because* of their conspicuous presence. But such species leave many thriving niches unoccupied, and their removal damages the health of the entire system.[35] The distinction we wish to highlight here is that keystones do not occupy a large number of the nodes in the ecosystem network, whereas dominators do. Dominated ecosystems often suffer the same fate as systems with poor keystones: They can become unstable or vulnerable to disruptions. This most commonly occurs when they become subject to some external shock or stress, and is largely because dominated ecosystems simply do not have the diversity to respond to these changes.

As in nature, dominators in the man-made world can come in many forms and can seek to exercise their control along a variety of dimensions. In business networks, two are of particular importance. A *classic dominator* acts to integrate vertically or horizontally to directly control and own a large proportion of a network. In so doing, dominators become directly and solely responsible for the majority of both value capture and value creation in their networks, leaving little opportunity for the emergence of a meaningful ecosystem. A value dominator, or *hub landlord,* in contrast, eschews control of the network and instead pursues control of value extraction alone. In so doing it provides little new value to its network, while at the same time taking what value there is for itself, leaving a starved and unstable ecosystem around it. Chapter 6 explores these two kinds of dominator operating strategies and highlights the potentially adverse impact a single influential firm in a hub position can have on the health of its business ecosystem.

As mentioned previously, Apple is an example of a classic dominator. Many other examples of failed attempts to dominate a business ecosystem exist in both the computer and other industries—from the disappearance of all the computer technology vendors that did not open up their vertical stacks in the 1960s and 1970s (Wang is a classic example) to the rise of the open VHS standard over Beta, which was controlled by Sony. The examples just cited fall into the first category: These classic dominators sought to directly control large parts of what could have been a thriving ecosystem of numerous firms by providing a single integrated product. In effect, they occupied a significant number of the nodes in the network of technologies and products produced by their ecosystem, leaving little room for others. Such dominators provide a striking contrast with keystones, which often occupy relatively few nodes.

We explore this taxonomy (summarized in Table 4-1) in considerable detail in subsequent chapters, but for now it is worth noting that it helps

TABLE 4-1

Taxonomy of Network Strategies

Strategy	Definition	Presence	Value Creation	Value Capture	Focus and Challenges
Keystone	Actively improves the overall health of the ecosystem and, in doing so, benefits the sustained performance of the firm	Generally low physical presence for its impact; occupies relatively few nodes	Leaves vast majority of value creation to network; what value it creates internally it shares widely	Shares value widely throughout network; balances this with capture in selective areas	Focused on creating platforms and sharing solutions to problems throughout the network. A significant challenge is to sustain value creation while balancing value extraction and sharing. Deciding which areas to selectively dominate is another challenge.
Dominator	Integrates vertically or horizontally to manage and control a large part of its network	High physical presence; occupies most nodes	Responsible for most value creation itself	Captures most value for itself	Primary focus is on control and ownership—defining, owning, and directing most of what the network does.
Hub landlord	Extracts as much value as possible from its network without directly controlling it	Low physical presence; occupies very few nodes	Creates little if any value; relies on the rest of the network for value creation	Captures most value for itself	A fundamentally inconsistent strategy. Though landlords refuse to control their networks while relying on them as their only source of value, they simultaneously extract so much value from those networks that they put their existence at risk.
Niche player	Develops specialized capabilities that differentiate it from other firms in the network	Very low physical presence individually, but constitute the bulk of ecosystems where they are allowed to thrive	Collectively create much of the value in a healthy ecosystem	Capture much of the value they create	Focused on specializing in areas where they have or can develop capabilities, while leveraging the services provided by the keystones in their ecosystem.

to identify some of the crucial differences between the firms we introduced at the start of this chapter: eBay and Enron. eBay serves as a keystone for a vast and diverse ecosystem of traders—buyers and sellers ranging from individuals to established firms—by providing an array of tools that create a platform on which the members of the eBay ecosystem can rely. Through this platform, eBay creates and shares value with this community in ways that make it an essential hub in the network of traders that has grown to depend on it. Like eBay, Enron focused on occupying a small part of its network, actively seeking central hub positions in a variety of markets. Unlike eBay, however, Enron completely failed to share value with these networks in ways that could sustain them. Enron pursued an aggressive hub landlord strategy that ultimately drained its network of all hope of growing into a thriving ecosystem.

There are important subtleties in the distinctions among these strategies. Effective execution of a keystone strategy, for example, requires a careful balancing of value creation and value extraction: By taking too much value out of its network, a hub can turn itself from a keystone to a landlord. Similarly, it is important to note that despite their beneficial effects on the ecosystem as a whole, keystones will not be viewed by all members of an ecosystem as being directly beneficial specifically to *them*. In biological ecosystems, this is particularly true in cases where keystone predators improve the productivity of their ecosystems by directly removing or limiting the numbers of species that would otherwise reduce productivity. Controversial examples of this behavior by business keystones are all too familiar. The point here, which we elaborate in chapter 5, is that such "aggressive" and "predatory" behaviors, in which keystones act as dominators of selective domains, can in fact be beneficial to the ecosystem as a whole.

Niche Players

In addition to keystones and dominators, a third kind of species is implicit in the literature's discussion of ecosystem structure: *niche species*. Niche species individually do not have broad-reaching impacts on other species in the ecosystem, but collectively they constitute the bulk of the ecosystem both in terms of total mass as well as variety. They are thus critical to shaping what the ecosystem is. In a sense, keystones shape what an ecosystem does, whereas niche species *are* what it does.

In business ecosystems, most firms follow (or should follow) niche strategies. A *niche player* acts to develop or enhance specialized capabilities that differentiate it from other firms in the network, leveraging resources from the network while occupying only a narrow part of the network itself. Examples are NVIDIA and Broadcom in the chip industry, or Siebel Systems and AutoDesk in the software applications industry. These firms focus their businesses on areas of relatively narrow expertise by leveraging powerful platforms provided by others. For instance, NVIDIA leverages the process technology and manufacturing capabilities provided by TSMC, but it focuses on the design of high-performance integrated circuits for graphics. In this way, the company benefits greatly by being able to focus on the development of critical competencies in a narrowly defined arena, and it shares its destiny (along with many other fabless semiconductor design companies) with that of its keystone firm—TSMC.

Effective leveraging by niche players also serves to enhance the health of the entire ecosystem. By avoiding duplication of effort, niche players implement a more efficient division of labor within the ecosystem. As we shall see in later chapters, the choice of what to leverage and what to duplicate can be a complex one, but in natural systems the trend is clear. Repeatedly in evolving natural communities, members have increased the tightness of their integration and the efficiency of their collaboration by losing the chemical apparatus or anatomic features required to perform functions that their partners perform for them. This process is one of the engines driving complexity building through integration and produces efficiencies that lead to competitive advantages between competing biological systems. This aspect of niche players has important implications for keystones as well: They must encourage niche players to leverage whenever they can and dissuade them from duplicating effort in areas of functionality already supported by the keystone.

A further critical function served by niche players is the role they play in inducing central players to pursue effective keystone strategies. Even in a world where there is only one ecosystem and only one hub in that ecosystem, the incentives for the hub to preserve the ecosystem and keep growing it are strong, but they are held in check by forces that push the hub to extract as much value as possible from the ecosystem and keep it for itself. In such systems we would expect to see powerful hubs driving all members of the ecosystem to the edge of survival. It would still make sense for these niche players to participate in the ecosystem, but just barely. The choice in such cases is between being in the ecosystem and doing nothing.

When there are multiple ecosystems for niche players to choose from, or multiple hubs in the same or overlapping ecosystems, niche players can not only protect themselves by hedging their bets and relying on several keystones (a strategy that, as we shall see in chapter 7, has "cross-platform" costs associated with it in business ecosystems), but can also increase their leverage with keystones by doing so. Because the keystone relies on the presence of the niche players to populate its ecosystem, it must, in effect, leave more on the table for them. The end result is that more value is distributed through the ecosystem than would have been the case if the niche players did not pursue this strategy. We will have much more to say about niche players in business ecosystems and the strategies they pursue in chapter 7.

Fallacies

The view we are developing here helps to dispel three common fallacies about the role of key firms in industries. The first is what one may call the "all peers" fallacy. It is sometimes argued that an industry with many small equivalent players, or *peers,* fiercely competing in all domains would be more productive, stable, or innovative because that is the natural way. However, the reality is that there is very little evidence for this kind of system in nature. Almost all evolved networks of interacting elements (from biochemical pathways to social networks) have their stability and function governed by keystones, hubs, or some form of centralized or shared control. Even "neutral" hubs (such as often occur in social networks or as is the case in the Web) help reduce important measures of complexity, while active keystones (such as keystone herbivores) additionally encourage diversity where it can do the most good in increasing stability and productivity. This fallacy is more often disseminated by the popular press than by economists, who are well aware of the limited capacity for innovation and productivity improvements in low-barrier and low-differentiation industries. Such industries, like lobster fishing or clothing manufacture, generally end up being characterized by vast numbers of equivalent players. This fallacy is quite widespread, however, among advocates of "distributed approaches" to problems, although even here there is often an acknowledgment that the "hard part" is in devising globally applied (and therefore centrally disseminated) rules for coordinating the activities of individual components.[36]

A second fallacy is the "dominator" fallacy. The fact that keystones persist over time in the face of what is often significant turnover within the ecosystem, and the fact that they influence, directly or indirectly, the behavior of a majority of the participants in an industry, leads to the mistaken view that they must somehow dominate that industry. However, biological keystones are often small players by most obvious measures, and have no presence at all in most niches in their ecosystem. Their influence is exerted not by size, but by the relationships that make them essential for the overall health of the system. One way of differentiating dominators from keystones is to focus on the ratio of biomass to impact. In contrast to dominators, keystones can often exert an impact on the ecosystem that is many times greater than what would be expected from their relative share in biomass. Similarly, business keystones often have an impact that extends far beyond the number of nodes they occupy in their business networks.

The third fallacy is the "inhibitor" fallacy. Because keystones sit astride critical pathways in the network of interactions that make up an industry, it is often suggested that they occupy "choke points" that inhibit both innovation and the free flow of information and value through an industry. But a keystone that followed this strategy would quickly be displaced. To survive and prosper, a keystone needs to increase the resilience and diversity of the ecosystem. Thus, firms in an industry and that industry's keystones together seek to increase the pace of innovation throughout the industry; the obstruction of important flows (of information, value, or intellectual property) through any of the critical pathways would be against the keystone's own interests.

Different Roles and Different Outcomes

By 2003, the ecosystem that formed around eBay's market platform was thriving. A vibrant and diverse community of 62 million users was actively trading on its site, with 195 million listings in more than 18,000 market categories. During the previous two years (and during a recession), eBay's revenue increased from $224 million to $748 million, and its net income grew from $10 million to $91 million. During the same time period, now-bankrupt Enron closed down virtually all of its online markets. The electricity industry as a whole has shut down so many trading operations that it is experiencing a serious liquidity crunch, and the viability of a large number of companies in this industry has been tentative at best. The reasons for this difference are obviously complex and reach beyond the frameworks presented here. However, as we will argue in the next two chapters, our perspective is a useful starting point in understanding how the drastically different roles played by these firms in their respective business networks may have been instrumental in shaping the outcomes.

This chapter set the stage for this discussion by identifying three roles that can be played by species in biological ecosystems as they influence ecosystem health and evolution: niche player, dominator, and keystone. These terms provide metaphors that will serve as a framework for analyzing the behavior of firms in business networks. The next three chapters develop this framework in some detail and focus on the many differences among keystone, dominator, and niche player roles in business networks. We do this by framing them as different operating strategies, each defining a deeply contrasting pattern of operating decisions followed by some businesses operating in a networked environment. In doing so, we shift our emphasis to a more pragmatic discussion of these ideas' implications for business leaders and policy makers.

CHAPTER FIVE

Keystones

When he was seventeen years old, Bill Gates worked with Paul Allen to develop a BASIC compiler for the newly introduced MITS Altair microcomputer. After Gates had the compiler working (it used less than four kilobytes of memory and was carried around on a paper tape), he went to all the microcomputer manufacturers of the time and somehow managed to convince them to make his compiler the standard on each of their machines. Few people remember that back in 1980, when you booted an Apple I or a TRS-80 computer, what you got was Microsoft BASIC. Gates thus introduced one of the first real standards in the microcomputer industry—a programming tool that would enable the emergent community of microcomputer programmers to write a broad variety of applications.

It is essential to understand that since its earliest days, Microsoft has been focused on creating a powerful developer platform, from BASIC all the way to .NET. What Gates realized was that Microsoft would have the greatest influence, reach, and impact not as an applications company, but as the platform that would enable applications to be written. The success of this strategy is renowned. Within a few years, Gates's small project became the tail that wagged the dog of the computer industry, shaping the destinies of huge entrenched firms like IBM. Before long that "tail" became the foundation of a thriving network of firms. In doing so, Gates and Microsoft pursued what may have been the most successful keystone strategy of all time.

Keystone Strategies

Biological keystones maintain the health of their ecosystems through specific behaviors that have effects that propagate through the entire system. In a surprisingly similar fashion, companies such as Microsoft, eBay, Wal-Mart, and Li & Fung all act as regulators of the health of their business ecosystems. They perform similar roles, whether the organizations in their communities write software applications, trade used cars, sell shampoo, or manufacture apparel. In each case, the keystones occupy richly connected hubs that provide the foundation for creating many niches, regulate connections among ecosystem members, and work to increase diversity and productivity. They provide a stable and predictable platform on which other ecosystem members can depend, and their removal would lead to the catastrophic collapse of the entire system. Moreover, they ensure their own survival and health by directly acting to improve the health of the ecosystem as a whole. It's important to understand that these firms don't act this way because of altruistic reasons—they do so because it is a great strategy.

In each case, these companies have successfully deployed what we call a keystone strategy. A *keystone strategy* is an operating strategy that improves the overall health of the ecosystem and, in so doing, benefits the sustained performance of the firm. The central feature of this strategy is its focus on managing external resources, shaping the structure of the external network, and maintaining and harnessing external health.

Keystones achieve these goals by creating and leveraging important resources and capabilities across the network. They effectively improve the productivity and efficiency of their ecosystems in a variety of ways by sharing information, intellectual property, and physical assets—from tools to interfaces, and from customer contacts to manufacturing capacity. They achieve powerful and successful positions not by dominating large parts of their industries, but by recognizing the potential that arises from being a hub in a business network and by actively managing the natural possibilities for efficiencies and innovation that arise from occupying that position.

Keystone strategies focus on making sure that these efficiencies actually happen and then on sharing their impact, efficiently, with the rest of the ecosystem. Keystones thus provide a critical service to an ecosystem, promoting its health, increasing the ecosystem's productivity, robustness, and niche creation capabilities. They enhance productivity by simplifying the complex task of connecting network participants to each other, and by making the creation of new products by third parties more efficient. Furthermore, they increase network robustness by consistently investing in and integrating new technological innovations and by providing a reliable reference point and interface structure for other ecosystem participants. Finally, they encourage niche creation by offering the innovative technologies to a variety of third-party organizations and investing in new fundamental infrastructure.

Ultimately, these widely different firms are pursuing a similar and consistent set of actions that achieve these results by actively focusing on the way that their behavior influences the health of the network of which they are a part: Each has recognized the significance of its position as a hub in its network and has adopted an operational strategy that explicitly takes into account the implications of shared fate. Let's look in some detail at how Microsoft does this.

Microsoft

Microsoft serves as a crucial hub in the computing ecosystem, forming a nexus in the network of thousands of hardware manufacturers, software developers, consultants, and IT departments. There is no question that Microsoft's reach and impact on its ecosystem is enormous: By almost every obvious measure of influence, Microsoft is *the* significant player in the computing ecosystem. Because of Microsoft's business model and evangelization methods, Microsoft has had decisive influence on the way businesses and independent software vendors (ISVs) develop software. Indeed, Microsoft's sway extends well beyond what can be measured by the number of software products that Microsoft licenses or the number of developers that it employs. Much of the impact of Microsoft on the computing industry is better measured by looking at what goes on *outside* the company.

One obvious way to measure the importance of Microsoft to software developers is to examine the number of firms and developers that create software for Windows platforms. CorpTech, the most comprehensive source of data on technology companies, indicates that, as of 2000, approximately 84 percent of software firms developed at least some software for a Microsoft platform.[1] Surveys published by the Evans Data Corporation (EDC) provide further support for the assertion that a majority of developers and IT managers (upward of 70 percent) use Microsoft platforms to write most of their applications.[2] Many additional studies report consistent results: Despite its public image as a giant software company, Microsoft's influence is not achieved by being physically large or by occupying significant parts of the networks of which it is a part.[3]

A similar pattern exists in the ecosystem of business partners that provide components for extending Microsoft products and platforms and of firms that leverage those same products and platforms, a definition that encompasses a large number of organizations—ranging from component providers such as Intel and AMD to system providers such as Dell and Hewlett-Packard, and from ISVs such as AutoDesk and Intuit to enterprises such as American Express and Merrill Lynch. In the context of this web of interdependent firms, Microsoft is quite small (see figure 5-1). Currently, the company has around 40,000 employees, mostly located in its Redmond, Washington, campus. Although this is a sizable number, it pales in comparison with the number of developers not at Microsoft who currently program on Microsoft's platform, which currently totals more than 5 million.[4] The story is essentially the same if one looks at Microsoft's revenues over time. Microsoft's revenues were $20 billion for the year 2000, which corresponded to slightly over 11 percent of total packaged software revenues, and less than 1 percent of the total revenues if we include hardware and component vendors (and naturally much less if we include the entire ecosystem).[5]

Another interesting point of analysis focuses on Microsoft's market capitalization. Although very large, Microsoft's market capitalization is a fraction of the market capitalization of the software provider domain in the ecosystem, ranging between 20 and 40 percent over the last few years. In contrast, during the 1960s IBM enjoyed more than 80 percent of the total market capitalization of the much larger ecosystem of software, component, system, and services providers, as well as most of that ecosystem's revenues.

FIGURE 5-1

Measures of Firm Presence for Microsoft

Microsoft, despite its pervasive impact on the computing ecosystem (all software firms), remains a small part of that ecosystem by any physical measure (here using revenue, number of employees, and market capitalization). As expected for a keystone, its revenue presence is somewhat (though not much) greater than its employee presence. Its market capitalization is much greater—again, as one would expect given its influence as a keystone.

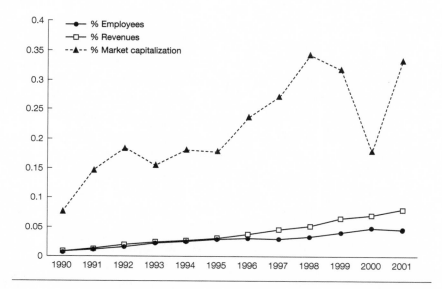

It is interesting to compare the percentage of employees to the percentage of revenues or the percentage of market capitalization. In strict measures of size (e.g., employees), Microsoft takes up a much smaller fraction of the industry than in measures of value (revenues and, even more so, capitalization), which is exactly what one would expect from an effectively implemented keystone strategy. In biological ecosystems, keystones typically have their pervasive systemwide effects despite being a small part of their ecosystems by most measures. The same holds true for Microsoft. Unlike a dominator species, it is not "taking over" the ecosystem, and the fraction of "industry mass" that it contains is relatively small, while the impact and value it has are very large—all characteristics of a firm pursuing a keystone strategy.

Microsoft's Keystone Strategy

Although limited physical presence in an ecosystem is one hallmark of a keystone strategy, it is ultimately a firm's impact on ecosystem health that determines how effectively a firm serves as a keystone. In what follows we provide an analysis of Microsoft's impact on the health of its ecosystem factored according to the basic aspects of ecosystem health defined in chapter 3. This analysis highlights the usefulness of our framework as a lens through which to examine the behavior of influential firms in their ecosystems.

Productivity. It is natural to begin our analysis with direct improvements in productivity, since Microsoft's very first product was a tool for creating other products: a BASIC compiler for the MITS Altair computer, a product that was quickly licensed to every major microcomputer manufacturer of the time and had an enormous impact on its industry.

Improving developer productivity has been central to Microsoft's strategy from the start and has led to a variety of innovations and improved product features, ranging from the p-code incremental compiler to the introduction of Visual Forms and programming components. Microsoft has also actively focused on ways to enable developers to leverage and reuse solutions created by other developers, through technologies such as Visual Basic Controls and ActiveX and through the integration of these technologies into developer tools. Indeed, Microsoft has inspired the growth of thriving industry segments devoted to the construction and exchange of such components, and has consistently focused on delivering powerful development tools that ease and automate the process of code development as much as possible (see figure 5-2). Recently, Microsoft expanded these efforts by making subsets of these tools available for free download.[6] This combination of freely available tools and automatic generation of code is a particularly important one because it not only improves productivity directly, but also expands the population of developers who have access to the Windows platform.

There are many anecdotal accounts that illustrate the effectiveness of Microsoft's tools in improving productivity in a broad variety of software companies and information technology departments over a wide

FIGURE 5-2

Impact of Tools on Software Development Productivity

The figure shows estimates of the proportion of code generated and maintained automatically by Microsoft's Visual Studio .NET integrated development environment (IDE), as measured by percentage of actual lines of code.[1] These are all small programs, but they represent the basis of the core functionality of typical simple applications built with .NET (Windows UI, Web UI, database access and manipulation, Web services, Web services clients) and thus are fairly representative of the assistance that Visual Studio provides in common Web development scenarios.

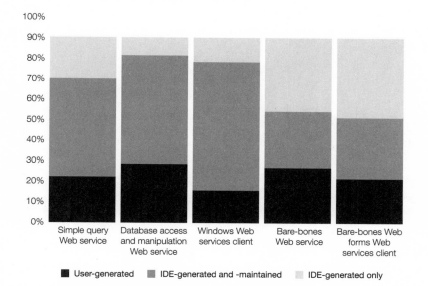

[1] Lines of code are a subjective measure, so we simply counted each noncomment line (including attributes). In some cases lines were omitted where there was obvious redundancy simply to support the IDE's automation of code maintenance. The net effect is to *underestimate* the proportion of code generated and maintained by the IDE. Furthermore, no attempt was made to count the significant amount of IDE-generated and -maintained "code" in the form of XML (Web Form definitions, database schema definitions, Web service WSDL specifications). Again, this results in an underestimate of the functionality automatically supported by the IDE.

range of applications.[7] In rare direct productivity comparisons using lines of code required as a measure of programmer effort, Microsoft's Visual Studio.NET was shown to exhibit significant advantages over competing platforms.[8] Although the exact numbers involved in any such comparison are clearly open to dispute, and the nature of their interpretation subject to discussion, even fierce competitors often praise the quality and effectiveness of Microsoft's efforts in this domain.

We can also gauge the impact of Microsoft's platforms on third-party developers by looking at the revenues generated in this fashion. According to data from IDC, in 2000 approximately 38 percent of worldwide packaged software revenue ($64 billion) was derived from software written for 32-bit Windows platforms.[9] Additionally, approximately 34 percent of systems infrastructure software revenue was derived from software written for Windows platforms, and this share is increasing. IDC forecasts that shares of packaged applications software and systems infrastructure software will increase to 54 percent and 42 percent, respectively, by 2005.[10] These ecosystem niches indeed appear to be enjoying a healthy growth rate.

Microsoft's latest development tools further increase productivity by offering interoperability among programming languages, a set of powerful class libraries, and a unified model of programming with Web Forms, Windows Forms, and Mobile Controls. These features are combined with a blurring of the boundaries between Web servers and clients that makes it far easier for developers to move software from one target environment—Web server, local machine, or mobile device—to another, or to have it span environments.

Robustness. Microsoft has provided a crucial degree of stability in the software industry by ensuring that its application programming interfaces (APIs) remained consistent across different generations of technology. Application developers write programs that call on various APIs to perform routine functions, which greatly reduces the cost of writing software programs. It is important to developers that an operating system have a consistent set of APIs because it ensures that programs that work on one version of an operating system will also work on other versions. Software developers can also be confident that their software applications will not break when new versions of the operating system are released. This, in turn, ensures a familiar experience for developers (and ultimately for end users) and reduces learning costs. Although Microsoft has aggressively evolved the scope of its APIs, it has also worked to avoid sudden or arbitrary changes to those APIs, often adapting old APIs to perform new functions so that old applications do not suddenly break as the platform evolves.

The fact that Microsoft offers a reliable, consistent, and widely distributed operating system benefits ISVs, original equipment manufacturers (OEMs), businesses, and individual consumers alike. ISVs benefit from consistent and well-documented APIs, standards, and tools, and from access to a broad base of users. OEMs benefit because a standardized Windows interface reduces consumer confusion and thus the volume of support calls, for which OEMs are largely responsible. Businesses benefit in at least two ways. First, as with ISVs, businesses benefit from well-documented and consistent tools and standards when they develop proprietary software applications for the Windows platform. Second, because the Windows user interface is widely used and basically remains consistent across different software features, training costs for workers are reduced. Consumers benefit from having a stable and consistent platform and from having a broad range of applications to run on the platform.

In addition to Windows, Microsoft has supported, developed, or contributed to some fifty different standards, ranging from Bluetooth to Universal Plug and Play (UPnP). In some cases, Microsoft has developed proprietary technologies (for example, the programming language C#) and has subsequently obtained certification by a standard-setting body. Microsoft often cooperates with other firms to jointly develop standards such as Universal Description, Discovery, and Integration (UDDI; developed with Ariba, IBM, Intel, and SAP) or Advanced Configuration and Power Interface (ACPI; developed with Intel and Toshiba). In other cases, Microsoft simply supports existing standards (for example, HTML) and includes them in products such as Windows and Office.

Taken together, these efforts provide the kind of predictability and continuity of experience we stipulate as measures of robustness. Moreover, the general outlines of the network structure of the ecosystem parallel that of the hub-governed networks that exhibit inherent stability with respect to random changes.

Niche creation. As mentioned previously, stability is also about providing a buffer against external shocks so that they do not disrupt the system. In fact, an effective keystone should seek to find ways of harnessing the energy of such shocks to further enhance diversity by creating new niches. Here Microsoft's .NET strategy provides an interesting example by exploiting what otherwise might have been a disruptive new technology for the advantage of the ecosystem as a whole. The Internet represented a dramatic threat to many existing software architectures, as well as significant challenges to many businesses that rely on software. The .NET architecture, via its language neutrality, through-the-firewall exposure of business logic (through standards such as HTTP and SOAP), and facilitation of data exchange (through XML), allows existing firms and their products to evolve and participate in the Internet rather than being threatened by it. At the same time, it effectively recruits new participants to the ecosystem by, for example, enabling COBOL or Python programmers (and the business logic they maintain) to more easily participate in the ecosystem.

In contrast with most other software companies, from the very first days of its existence Microsoft's strategy has been to license its programming tools to an increasingly large community of independent software vendors. These tools have included compilers, integrated programming environments, programming components, and, most recently, Web services. Microsoft tools are currently being used by more than 20,000 software companies and information technology departments. They have been used to develop an incredible variety of applications, ranging from wireless platforms to channel management systems. In all, more than 70,000 applications have been written for Windows, far more than for other operating systems.[11]

The number of applications written for Windows is due at least in part to Microsoft's business model, which places a premium on developer support and evangelization of the Microsoft platform. Microsoft dedicates many resources to encouraging developers to write applications for the Windows platform and to take advantage of new features in its operating systems. The Microsoft Developer Network (MSDN) is key to Microsoft's relationship with developers. Through MSDN, Microsoft communicates with its community of developers and provides them with technical information and support. MSDN currently has approximately 5 million members around the world.[12] Microsoft employs at least 2,000 full-time personnel who are dedicated to supporting developers, and it invests more than $600 million per year for this purpose.[13] In contrast with many other companies in the software industry, Microsoft has thus targeted the creation of a wide diversity of applications for its platform by directly nurturing its developer community. According to IDC, "Microsoft is viewed as a pioneer in the developer market and is considered by some vendors to be the benchmark in the industry."[14] The *New York Times* recently noted that "[m]uch of Microsoft's success over the years can be traced to its understanding of and catering to rank-and-file developers."[15]

A fundamental part of encouraging niche creation in the computing ecosystem is increasing functionality by expanding the range of things that computers can do, increasing the variety of ways in which those things can be accomplished, and increasing the scenarios in which they can appear. Microsoft's .NET architecture is designed to directly enhance this aspect of diversity: The combination of language independence and the potential for a unified framework of functionality that is available on a wide range of devices means that a greatly expanded community of developers can now reach a huge audience of potential users.

Core Components of a Keystone Strategy

Broadly speaking, there are two foundational components of an effective keystone strategy. The first is to create value within the ecosystem. Unless a keystone finds a way of efficiently creating value, it will fail to attract or retain members. Unless the other members of an ecosystem are trapped in that ecosystem and unable to escape (a point to which we will return in chapter 7), the ecosystem will wither. The second is for the keystone to then share the value within the ecosystem. It is not sufficient to create value: In order to sustain an entire network of firms, that value must be effectively shared with other participants in the ecosystem. A firm that creates value but fails to deliver it to the ecosystem as a whole will find itself perhaps temporarily enriched, but ultimately abandoned. One way of exploring the structure of a keystone strategy is along the lines of these two components.

Value Creation

A keystone strategy systematizes value creation in a large network by creating what we call *operating leverage*. By this we mean a series of assets that can be easily scaled and shared by a broad network of business partners. These assets may be physical, as in the case of a large and highly efficient manufacturing network; intellectual, as in the case of a broadly available software platform; or financial, as in the case of a venture capitalist's portfolio of investments. The key to creating leverage is to make sure that the value of these assets divided by the cost of creating, maintaining, and sharing them increases rapidly with the number of ecosystem members that share them.[16] This enables the keystone player to effectively generate more value than it "needs," and thus to effectively create the potential for sharing this surplus with its community.

It is critical in the calculation of operating leverage to subtract the true system costs of administering the hub and sharing its assets. In the days of the network boom, many business models failed because although the theoretical benefit was increasing with the number of customers (what some economists have defined as "the network effect"), the operating cost was increasing also. Many business-to-business (B2B) marketplaces, for example, continued to increase revenues at the expense of decreasing margins (which became highly negative), which led to the collapse of their business models.

Operating leverage can be obtained by the development of physical, intellectual, or financial assets. Examples of physical assets that create leverage are high-scale, general-purpose manufacturing or retail assets (e.g., a contract manufacturer like TSMC or a large retail chain like Wal-Mart), direct customer links (e.g., Dell), and network integration hubs (e.g., Li & Fung). Examples of intellectual assets are uniform standards (e.g., Linux), state-of-the-art tools (e.g., Visual Studio), shared Internet components (e.g., .NET or Java Beans), and information hubs (e.g., Yahoo!, eBay). Examples of financial assets are equity investments in start-ups (such as Benchmark's $5 million investment in eBay) and in the acquisition of complementary firms (e.g., Microsoft's $1.3 billion acquisition of Navision). A few examples will illustrate how each of these classes of assets can be employed in distinct ways to create an effective keystone strategy.

Create high-value, sharable assets. TSMC is the world's largest foundry for semiconductor components. Its business model is founded on the premise that it can manufacture a broad range of integrated circuits more efficiently than a vertically integrated manufacturer, particularly one with lower volume. The efficiency of its process increases sharply with its participants, thus creating a concave value curve, all the way up to reaching full capacity. This naturally makes capacity planning crucial and links TSMC's strategy to additional intellectual assets, such as component libraries and design tools.

Leverage direct customer connections. Dell's keystone strategy begins with its ability to leverage direct connections to its customer network. These connections effectively create a customer hub that has enormous value not just for Dell, but also for its community of suppliers. The productivity and robustness improvements created by improved forecasting abilities are thus shared with its operating network.

Create and manage physical and information hubs. Just by virtue of its position, a hub is the ultimate shareable resource. The essence of Li & Fung's strategy is to leverage its vast network of business connections. These are composed of both physical assets (such as EDI- and XML-based integration links) and intellectual assets (such as decades-old relationships).

Support uniform information standards. One can obtain significant network leverage by fostering uniform information standards. Information such as APIs, orders, purchase histories, and demographics stored within the keystone's or any other member of the ecosystem's databases or directories can be made readily available to network participants. If the information is not stored in a uniform manner, then it falls upon the keystone to drive creation of this standard.

Create, package, and share state-of-the-art tools and building blocks for innovation. These shared elements increase the productivity of network members, quickly propagate new innovations through the network, and encourage potential members to join the keystone's ecosystem. For example, eBay and TSMC both provide valuable tools and modules for their ecosystems. eBay provides a "seller's assistant" to help new sellers save time in preparing professional-looking listings with HTML templates, clip-art pictures, and other online formatting assistance. eBay also provides the free Turbo Lister service to list, track, and manage thousands of bulk listings on home computers. TSMC's wide-ranging manufacturing platform and comprehensive Web-based component library are offered at no charge to fabless chip design firms. The components are optimized to run on TSMC's manufacturing platform and to integrate with their semiconductor design tools.

Establish and maintain performance standards. Keystones can enforce performance standards via customer evaluations and partner incentives. eBay's sellers and buyers rate each others' conduct over the course of any given transaction by three criteria: disclosure, honesty, and fulfillment. The ratings themselves follow a rather simple three-point scale: 1 for positive, 0 for neutral, and −1 for negative. If a seller obtains at least 100 unique feedback results, 98 percent of which are positive over three months, the seller will attain eBay's PowerSeller status. However, a cumulative score of −4 will result in the suspension of the offender's eBay membership and exclusion from future transactions.

Charles Schwab provides another example. Schwab's online system refers customers to over 6,000 independent financial advisors and provides transaction services to those advisors. Schwab monitors the performance of this ecosystem of advisors and reserves the right to intervene if a member's performance or integrity falters.

Build or acquire financial assets for operating leverage. Venture capital is the classic example of using financial assets for operating leverage. Benchmark's initial investment of $6.7 million in eBay is now worth more than $4.48 billion, possibly making it the most lucrative venture investment of all time. In corporate venture capital, financial assets can be combined with other aspects of a keystone strategy to create and share operating leverage, promoting the health and growth of an ecosystem. A variety of firms, ranging from IBM to Dell, have leveraged this model effectively.

Reduce uncertainty by centralizing and coordinating communication. A keystone can have tremendous impact on the organization's ecosystem simply by centralizing and simplifying communication about key trends and opportunities. For example, IBM is one of the very few players in its industry that can proactively reduce uncertainty by decreasing information gaps and providing crucial context for niche players in its ecosystem. IBM can (and does) communicate its architecture vision and development decisions to reduce both technology and market uncertainty for a large variety of companies. Its activities range from widely publishing documents clarifying standards and frameworks to holding more private sessions to promote open dialogue with top venture capitalists, and from sharing IT strategies and road maps to participating in standards bodies. IBM can thus add tremendous value simply by sharing information and decreasing uncertainty for niche players. In recent years, the company has leveraged this capacity by endorsing the Linux operating system.

Reduce complexity by providing powerful platforms. Microsoft's platforms dramatically reduce the complexity to which ecosystem members are exposed. By crafting programming interfaces that hide and structure access to the underlying technology, Microsoft effectively provides a centralized and predictable—and above all simplified—technology foundation for its ecosystem. In effect, such APIs embody a statement about how and where niche players can contribute to their ecosystem. Apple made a similar, almost revolutionary contribution to its ecosystem in the early days of the Macintosh with its "phonebook" API guide, which not only provided a carefully crafted API but also included some of the most effective and clear communication about how to employ it and what to expect from it. This facilitation of the participation of developers, along with clear communication about the form that participation should take, helped to produce the rapid and enthusiastic growth of the Macintosh developer community, which was at least as important a factor in the Macintosh's spectacular initial success as its clean design and ease of use.

Value Sharing

Ecosystem health will suffer if a network hub does not share some of the value it creates. Ecosystem participants will start failing and attempt to switch to other hubs. If other hubs do not exist, or if no hubs share value, the whole ecosystem may collapse. The dot-com and telecommunications crashes are striking examples of how suddenly and dramatically an unhealthy ecosystem can fail.

Value sharing is important in differentiating a dominator from a keystone, and a business ecosystem will be more robust if a hub shares value with its partners. Take eBay, for example. Its incentives reinforce performance standards and member behavior, both of which serve the larger interests of the ecosystem. This distributes control and diminishes the need for centralized monitoring and feedback systems. Although eBay may take up to 7 percent of a given transaction, that is well below the typical 30 percent to 70 percent margins that most retailers would charge. For example, Ambient Devices manufactures a wireless gadget (the Orb) in China for around $35 apiece. Brookstone, which sells the device for $149, pays Ambient Devices $55 apiece, which just covers product design, tooling, offshore manufacturing, and operating costs. However, when Ambient Devices listed the Orb on eBay, it sold for a little over $100. After subtracting 10 percent for eBay's fee and other various transaction costs, Ambient Devices receives a 30 to 40 percent profit. It is important to stress that eBay does this because it is good business. By sharing the value, it can continue to expand its own healthy ecosystem and thrive in a sustainable way.

Effective keystones often couple value creation with value sharing. The software examples mentioned earlier are paradigmatic of this pairing: Carefully crafted platform architectures, especially APIs, not only embody the value created by firms like Microsoft or Apple, but also package, distribute, and provide access to it so that it can be shared by others. This linkage, the ability to share created value in a way that easily scales, is an important enabling feature for keystones. Firms that can find a way of doing this—notably through software, intellectual property, or information licensing—have a particularly powerful tool in their hands for the execution of a keystone strategy. This is especially true because it allows the keystone to set a balance between value sharing and value capture for itself through relatively simple licensing agreements, even for very complex products or underlying technologies.

Value sharing is not simply a matter of deciding to share value; it is also a significant operating challenge. What we are talking about here is the ability to share value with what is likely to be a massive network of business partners. The cost of sharing value with each individual partner must therefore be very low and must decrease with the size of the network. In other words, estimations of operating leverage should include the cost of creating the assets as well as sharing them. This is why certain types of assets with clear, simple, and easy-to-use interfaces (such as APIs or tools, for example) can be more effective in providing foundations for a keystone strategy than more traditional assets, such as customer relationships.

Let's focus on Wal-Mart again as an example, to examine in some detail how the value creation and sharing components of a keystone strategy can be deployed.

Wal-Mart

One of the most important roles played by keystones is their creation of a stable platform that simplifies the complexity of the world in which the members of their ecosystem operate. Perhaps the most dramatic success in this regard is the retail giant Wal-Mart, the number one company on the *Fortune* 500 and the world's largest retailer. Wal-Mart's ecosystem embraces a vast web of firms that constitute its supply chain, stretching from manufacturer to consumer. Seen in this way, Wal-Mart's role takes on a different character from that often portrayed in media reports about its aggressive business practices. Although these practices certainly contribute to the firm's success, the foundation of Wal-Mart's success is its pursuit of a strategy that creates and shares value with its network.

Value Creation

Over several decades Wal-Mart has established a centralized supply chain infrastructure that has significantly improved the efficiency of its retail ecosystem and thereby lowered prices for consumers. In developing this ecosystem, Wal-Mart has created new value by introducing a massive new channel for vendors large and small to reach consumers worldwide.

The creation of the immense and robust Wal-Mart retail ecosystem has been enabled largely through the relentless implementation of business processes and technologies that improve the efficiency of the retail supply chain, streamlining information flow and interaction between Wal-Mart and the firm's thousands of vendors. Wal-Mart's successful efforts to continuously improve the efficiency of the entire supply chain, from factory to shopping cart, has allowed it to create a thriving ecosystem of partners, suppliers, and vendors, displacing the competition in the process. (See figure 5-3 for an analysis of the cost differences between Wal-Mart and its competitors.)

FIGURE 5-3

Wal-Mart's Cost Advantage

The data are from the grocery sector, compared with industry averages. The 22 percent overall advantage is broken down by source. CPFR stands for collaborative planning, forecasting, and replenishment.

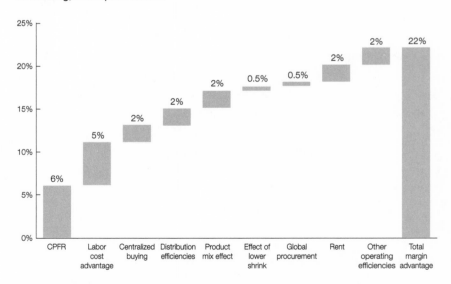

Source: Authors' estimate.

Wal-Mart's system captures detailed customer information, analyzes it in real time, and shares it with its supply chain (see figure 5-4). A striking example of Wal-Mart's information management skills was provided on September 11, 2001, and in the days following the terrorist attacks on the United States:

FIGURE 5-4

Expansion of Wal-Mart's Retail Information System (in terabytes of data)

After implementing the use of data terminals in 1974, followed by point-of-sale (POS) scanners in 1983 and satellite communications in 1986, Wal-Mart began the accumulation of retail data, which ultimately grew to a vast 175-terabyte database (each terabyte is equal to approximately 200 million pages of text). This database is second in size only to that of the U.S. government, and dwarfs those of competitors Kmart (70 terabytes) and Target (3 terabytes).

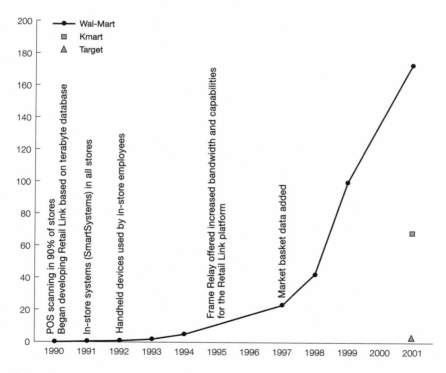

Source: Company data; MVI Research.

Sales from every scanner in Wal-Mart's stores are instantly tabulated, sorted and analyzed by a giant computer system at the corporation's Bentonville, Arkansas[,] headquarters. The proprietary system, called Retail Link, a technological behemoth whose database capacity is second only to the U.S. government's, offers a look into the psyche of the American consumer during a week of widespread uncertainty. . . . [L]ast week was hardly average. Wal-Mart says sales nationwide on Tuesday, the day of the attack, were 10 percent below the same day a year earlier. At Wal-Mart stores around New York and northern Virginia, where the terrorists struck, sales plummeted as much as 30 percent to 40 percent for the day, the retailer says. . . . [B]y evening, however, customers began flooding back, stocking up on staples and emergency supplies. Sales of gas cans spiked 895 percent. Gun sales jumped 70 percent, and ammunition sales surged 140 percent. Sales of TV sets jumped 70 percent and antenna sales leapt 400 percent. On Tuesday, Wal-Mart sold 116,000 American flags, compared with 6,400 the same day a year earlier. . . . [T]he chain sold 200,500 flags on Wednesday, compared with 10,000 a year earlier. . . . Wal-Mart says by Friday its overall customer count had returned to within normal ranges, and comparable-store sales gains returned to around 5 percent. Still, the size of the average purchase lagged, the company said.[17]

Building on this information management platform, Wal-Mart has created an extraordinarily efficient system for managing inventory and vendor relations that benefits all members of Wal-Mart's ecosystem. In an effort to effectively manage hundreds of thousands of stock-keeping units (SKUs) from thousands of vendors, Wal-Mart instituted a formal vendor-compliance program, which governs the preparation of store-ready merchandise as well as transportation and logistics issues. When Wal-Mart Stores introduced these rules for suppliers in the early 1990s, vendors were concerned with the impact on their business. Wal-Mart suddenly was dictating how the goods they received would be labeled, how they would be packaged—anything that made it easier for them to receive and handle goods and clear them through the store with minimum inventory. One key element of this strategy was the push for prepackaged vendor displays, which cost more to ship but required less labor and time to handle once they got to the store.[18]

Value Sharing

Wal-Mart's retail system works because its value is shared with its massive supply chain. We can think of Wal-Mart's retail assets as a massive platform for the generation of supply chain information. This information is packaged and shared with its business partners through a variety of interfaces, which connect with different types of supplier information systems. At a high level, Wal-Mart's retail platform's interfaces perform a function that is similar to Microsoft's Windows APIs. They reduce the uncertainty and complexity faced by the company's supply chain partners and provide new opportunities for innovation.

The company's efforts in these areas date back decades, but gained prominence in 1987 when a partnership was forged with Procter & Gamble to improve supply chain efficiency. The work focused on connecting Wal-Mart's budding information systems to P&G's forecasting organization through the deployment of EDI links. This had an enormous impact, reducing inventory and improving the accuracy of plans and stocked products. It also affected the relationship between the two companies: "[I]t really changed things from an adversarial price negotiation to a win-win situation."[19] Today, Procter & Gamble's $6 billion per year relationship with Wal-Mart is so important to both firms that P&G maintains a 150-person office in Bentonville, near Wal-Mart headquarters.[20] Vendors such as Procter & Gamble are given full access to real-time data on how their products are selling, store by store. By sharing information that other retailers guard, Wal-Mart allows suppliers to plan production runs earlier and offer better prices.

Wal-Mart's integration of business processes with its suppliers is enabled through the use of technology and promoted through a corporate philosophy of sharing inventory, logistics, and even detailed financial information with suppliers. As Wal-Mart's CIO Randy Mott puts it:

> We share everything with our vendors that they need to know
> to have a profit-and-loss statement with Wal-Mart. . . . We share

markdown information, return information, claims, sales, shipments and inventory levels. We actually put that information out on the applications that we supply to the vendors so they know what their profitability is. We give them a comparison on how they do within their category, a sort of benchmark. When they come in to sit down with a buyer, there's not a lot of wondering whether they have inventory bulges or markdown or return opportunities. . . . Both parties know the same information, so the discussion centers around actions. We think that's a very constructive relationship.[21]

Competing retailers will often admit that their systems and processes are not as detailed or as advanced. In the words of Office Depot CIO Bill Seltzer, "We don't do as much knowledge sharing as Wal-Mart. . . . I think Wal-Mart has really led the way in teaching us that."[22]

The impact of Wal-Mart's keystone interactions with its own partners and suppliers has had a ripple effect throughout the industry, forcing competitors to improve their own productivity through improvements in systems and processes for supply chain management. Thus, Wal-Mart continues its drive to increase the productivity of the retail ecosystem and provide even more consumers worldwide with the "everyday low prices" that are the company's ultimate goal. Significantly, these contributions have had a ripple effect extending far beyond Wal-Mart's own ecosystem and out into the wider economy. As noted by Bradford C. Johnson, "More than half of the productivity acceleration in the retailing of general merchandise can be explained by only two syllables: Wal-Mart."[23]

Understanding Keystones

The idea of a keystone is virtually absent from existing theories of management. Just as existing theories of operations do not effectively account for keystone strategies, so too the idea that a firm might do more than just leverage switching costs for maximum profit is absent in much of the work based on network economics. The idea of a keystone is also missing in most prevailing policy and legal frameworks, which are actively hostile to firms that follow them. As demonstrated in the Microsoft antitrust trial, existing frameworks had to be stretched to account for the complex dynamics of networked industries. Although we will not directly focus on such topics in this book, it is worth keeping in mind that many of the strategies we discuss in what follows run the risk of being misunderstood or resented if they are not clearly articulated and explained.

The most frequent misunderstanding is that, as with keystone species in nature, firms do not pursue keystone strategies for altruistic reasons: They have positive effects on network health for the simple reason that it is good for the keystone's own effectiveness and sustainable performance. To work well, a keystone strategy relies on competitiveness, and often attacks individual competitors. The ecosystem cannot benefit from a keystone that does not aggressively defend its competitiveness and continually develop new products and capabilities. For Microsoft to continue to enhance the capabilities of its platform in ways that realize the benefits of new technologies for its ecosystem, it must continually evaluate the threats and opportunities that emerge. If, for example, Microsoft were to eschew development of its own media technologies or of Web-based computing technologies like .NET, it would compromise its ability to provide an effective foundation for new and important activities in its network. A critical component of a keystone strategy is thus keeping an eye on important emerging domains and striking a balance between attacking and absorbing threats there in ways that ultimately add to the keystone's capabilities as the provider of a comprehensive platform for the ecosystem.

Just as it is possible to ignore the positive impact of keystone strategies, it is also possible to overemphasize the "goodness" of firms that have employed keystone strategies in the past. Although we may have thus far occasionally referred to "keystone firms" as if the firm as a whole is a keystone, what really makes a firm a keystone is the extent to which it pursues actions that serve keystone functions. Although we will sometimes use the shorthand of "keystone" to refer to firms, it is essential to keep in mind that what we are focusing on are the actual *practices* of such firms that are consistent with a keystone role. Microsoft, Wal-Mart, and eBay are not keystonelike in everything they do, although we believe that much of their success is explainable by their implementation of keystone strategies. Microsoft, for example, is hardly a pure keystone in everything it does, nor is it always the best-behaved company. In many cases, such as financial software or console gaming, one could argue that Microsoft has only been prevented from acting like a dominator by the restraining influences of effective competitors. Moreover, Microsoft, like all mature keystones, must struggle against the pressure exerted by its growth imperative to cannibalize niches in the ecosystem for short-term gain at the expense of long-term ecosystem growth and health. The point is simply that, on balance, Microsoft, far from being the dominating monopolist that is axiomatically a burden on its industry, has pursued a keystone strategy. Moreover, Microsoft must, perhaps now more than ever, focus on that strategy and look for ways to grow its ecosystem.

It is also important to understand that a given firm may act as a keystone in one domain while acting as a dominator or a niche player in others; in fact, as we shall see, firms may adopt contradictory stances, with one business unit pursuing a keystone strategy while another pursues a niche or dominator strategy. The firm may even serve as a keystone in several domains. Again, Microsoft serves as an example. By measures of market share and extracted value, Microsoft's Office suite clearly dominates the office productivity application domain, but Office also serves as a platform for a huge ecosystem of add-ons and business infrastructure, while the features and integration of Office with Windows help to enhance the value of the Windows platform. Moreover, these different strategies may either conflict or work in synergy. Indeed, as we shall see in subsequent chapters, in healthy ecosystems we should expect to find niche players that eventually grow their niches into ecosystems in their own right, for which they serve as a keystone. Similarly, we should not be surprised to find examples of firms that use a keystone role in one domain to dominate another.

Did Bill Gates or eBay's Pierre Omidyar fully understand what they were doing when they embarked on what turned out to be phenomenally successful and influential keystone strategies? Although it would have been impossible for either of these entrepreneurs to fully understand the impact of what he was starting, they did share one common belief—that the key to success was appealing to a community of people that was much larger than their own organizations. What Gates and Omidyar engineered from the earliest days of their efforts were platforms that connected an increasingly vast network of people and organizations and provided real, meaningful value to them. Whether it was writing applications for the cool new microcomputer medium or trading unusual collector's items, Gates and Omidyar fueled the enthusiasm of passionate communities that catapulted Microsoft and eBay to the forefront of modern business as keystones of their domains.

CHAPTER SIX

Landlords and Dominators

"The market loves Enron because president Jeffrey Skilling and CEO Kenneth Lay seem to have come up with a business model that works for just about anything."[1] In August 2000, when these words appeared in *Time* magazine, there were many investors who would have enthusiastically agreed. Enron's stock traded at a P/E of over 60, and banks enthusiastically loaned the company billions to expand into new markets. In November 2001, however, Enron filed a letter with the Securities and Exchange Commission declaring that $690 million in debt had to be paid almost immediately. Within a few months it filed Chapter 11.

Value Thief

The misconceptions about Enron's approach and performance form one of the most intriguing puzzles of recent business history. How could so many people have held the company in such high regard? Certainly, Enron's widespread and now well-known deceptions and ethical violations hold much of the answer. But it is all too easy in hindsight to believe that Enron's shady dealings *caused* its spectacular failure. It is interesting and important to inquire whether in fact Enron's business model and strategic approach should take at least some of the blame, or whether the losses incurred as a result of poor operations might have sparked some of the unethical behavior in the first place.

Many industry experts have argued that Enron's business model deserved significant praise. David Campbell and Ron Hulme, two principals at McKinsey & Company, wrote as recently as 2001:

> Enron has built a reputation as one of the world's most innovative companies by attacking and atomizing traditional industry structures—first in natural gas and later in diverse businesses such as electric power, Internet bandwidth and pulp and paper. In each case Enron focuses on the business sliver of intermediation while avoiding the incumbency problems of a large asset base and vertical integration. Enron no longer produces gas in the United States, no longer owns an electric utility and has never held a large investment in telecom networks. Yet it is a leading value creator in each of these industries.[2]

Understanding the failure of Enron's strategy and operating model sharpens many of the arguments made in this book. Like many of the keystones in this book, Enron pursued strategies that gained control of important hubs in its business ecosystem. Unlike those keystones, however, Enron believed that it could extract almost unlimited value from the networks it dominated. Enron pursued a deliberate strategy of establishing itself as the extreme case of what we call a *hub landlord,* following an unsustainable strategy of value extraction that eventually choked off the health of the ecosystem on which it depended.

One of the reasons that Enron's collapse was so devastating and had such widespread effects was that, ironically, the company and its many advisors understood the importance of occupying critical hubs in business networks. Enron envisioned itself as "carrying out . . . transactions rather than . . . owning the infrastructure and commodities themselves"—and not just any infrastructure, but the crucial minimum of assets necessary to establish a hub position.[3] "For each industry it serve[d], Enron figure[ed] it need[ed] about 2 percent of the physical product *in the right locations.*"[4] Enron thus implemented an approach that eschewed physical assets unless they were absolutely necessary for occupying a nexus in the web of trading interactions in the industries it sought to enter. This "asset light" approach is indeed an essential component of an effective keystone strategy: Good keystones ought to avoid taking over the activities of their ecosystems, leaving room for a wide variety of other participants to grow and thrive. This is the feature of Enron's approach that rightly drew much praise. But in establishing itself as a hub in so many different networks, Enron also acquired a responsibility for the health of those networks, which it failed to fulfill. This is where the company went wrong.

Early in its history, Enron seemed to have been on the right path to combine its occupation of network hubs with innovative businesses and technologies in the way that keystones should. As one of the first firms to take advantage of the Federal Energy Regulation Commission (FERC) order that set natural gas deregulation in motion, Enron took a leading role in redefining energy markets and quickly acquired a reputation as an innovator.[5] Enron was the first to create futures markets for natural gas and later for electric power, and EnronOnline transformed the way business was done in these industries.[6] Overseas, Enron was the "battering ram" that broke down regulatory barriers and opened the way for complex new trading structures for natural gas and electricity.[7]

However, although these innovations may have reduced inefficiencies in the markets Enron served, they did so entirely for Enron's own benefit. The "innovation" for which Enron was for a time renowned was not about creating new platforms on which other ecosystem members could build, or about packaging intellectual property for reuse and leveraging by ecosystem members, or about sharing information, lowering costs, reducing complexity, or creating stability. It was about inventing ways to capture new value for Enron, often by plainly avoiding the kinds of information sharing and complexity simplifying that effective keystones make a part of their strategy. Enron's EnronOnline operations, for example, did not employ clear price transparency, although the corporation told energy companies using the service that it did. Enron traders have frequently claimed that Enron greatly benefited from the general lack of price transparency. Senator Lieberman noted in a FERC report that "only Enron would know valuable information about the actual volumes and prices transacted on its trading platform—and, of course, how the prices charged in any particular transaction were set or how they compared to those charged in other, similar transactions."[8]

Enron prided itself on what its managers believed was a highly entrepreneurial approach to creating new businesses and products. As Lay himself would describe his commitment to innovation in 1996, "We expect that five years from now 40 percent of our earnings will come from businesses that did not exist five years ago. It's a matter of re-creating the company and the business we're in."[9] Many new businesses and business models—from EnronOnline to weather derivatives—grew out of this culture of "not getting corporate approval" in which "you just do it."[10] Enron created an environment in which profit-motivated "stars did what ever they wanted" and in which "the needs of the customers and the shareholders were secondary to the needs of its stars"—an environment where it was thus almost impossible to pursue a strategy that focused on broader issues of ecosystem health.[11] Although this created the "innovative" record for which Enron was admired, it meant that almost all of the company's creativity was focused not on improving ecosystem health through value creation or value sharing, but squarely on *value extraction*.

This was Enron's crowning failure: What little value Enron might have brought to its networks by improving their efficiency, it quickly captured for itself by creating a variety of novel tools for enriching itself at the expense of those networks. Many of these were nothing more than new ways to game the market. Such schemes included "Megawatt Laundering," "Daisy Chain Swap," and "Death Star."

Death Star

In 1998, California gave responsibility for matching supply and demand to an independent system operator (ISO). The ISO would buy from providers (e.g., Enron) and sell to middlemen (e.g., Pacific Gas & Electric) as necessary. The ISO would even pay providers to take excess electricity out of the state.

Enron was one of the firms that entered this market. Using power trading strategies in California devised to game the market, Enron took advantage of the fact that the ISO would pay congestion fees to traders "to either reduce the power they were selling into the state's system or to transmit power away from California" if "the amount of power scheduled for delivery into California exceed[ed] the capacity of some of the transmission lines." These congestion fees could run as high as $750 per megawatt hour. To exploit this, "Enron would schedule power deliveries it never intended to make just so the state grid would seem like it would get congested in certain areas; the ISO would then ask it to reverse those deliveries," and Enron would receive the congestion fees. "A similar technique Enron called 'Death Star' routed power around the ISO to send power away from a transmission jam, also to collect congestion fees."[12] Enron was being paid to remove excess energy that it never actually put in. In doing so, it extracted value that was never created in the first place.

Enron also "took advantage of the fact that the California ISO sometimes paid firms not to use power that they had scheduled for use in the real-time market." Enron would schedule excess power purchases in the day-ahead market. The next day Enron would decide not to buy the power, thus getting paid for giving up electricity it never really needed. Thus, Enron "was buying and selling commitments it had never made."[13] Another Enron tactic, "Ricochet," played on price differences between California's day-ahead and real-time power markets. "Enron would buy energy on the day-ahead and sell it to an out-of-state trader. The next day, Enron would buy that electricity back and sell it into the real-time market, which was often dominated by power-hungry utilities willing to pay higher prices. This helped artificially boost electricity prices without helping supply and demand."[14]

These strategies are almost the opposite of what we would expect of a keystone. Enron's trading strategies certainly did not benefit its ecosystem. Instead, they were designed to maximally exploit its hub position in the domains of which it was a part to extract the maximum profit for itself, regardless of its effect on the ecosystem. The impact was significant. In 2002, California saw electric bills that were as much as 67 percent higher than in 2000. "[T]he price of a megawatt hour, which was $43.80 at the beginning of 2000, skyrocketed to $292.10 by the end of it. Death Star had struck."[15] Many California residents, including Governor Gray Davis, now believe that Enron traders manipulated the rules of the system to make "maximum profit regardless of the effect on consumers."[16]

Failed Network Strategies

Enron is a tragic and dramatic illustration of an important aspect of network strategies. The dynamics of ecosystems set up forces that can not only benefit firms but also seriously hurt them. The previous chapter explored one of the defining opportunities for firms in the special position to leverage a hub position in the network structure: the pursuit of a keystone strategy. As we have seen, effective keystones can create successful business opportunities both for themselves and for large numbers of other firms by actively harnessing and channeling the dynamics of their business ecosystem. But the forces at work in networks, particularly if they are not recognized or appreciated, present many challenges to firms that seek to chart a course as a keystone. Enron's failure can be seen as that of a *faux* keystone—a firm that appreciated the crucial position that could be achieved by seeking out and occupying a nexus in a web of business interactions, but which ignored (or even actively damaged) the health of the networks it served.

As we have seen throughout this book, opportunities for creating network strategies have existed for a wide variety of organizations. These opportunities have met with varying degrees of success, and some with spectacular failure. In particular, it is clear that there are different ways that firms in a hub in their ecosystem can leverage the potential efficiencies that their position enables. One way to fail is to not create these efficiencies in the first place, instead using the power of a hub position as a beachhead for extracting as much value as possible from the ecosystem. This is the hub landlord strategy followed by Enron in a variety of its businesses. Another way to fail is to create efficiencies, but to burden the core efficiencies with additional costs that eventually overwhelm them as the network grows (many failed B2B exchanges are examples of this).

This brief tour through the potential dangers facing a firm at the hub of a business ecosystem should serve as a cautionary—perhaps frightening—counterpoint to the hopeful summary of the positive potential for keystones presented in the previous chapter. It highlights an especially important point: Any firm occupying a hub in a business network faces powerful temptations to exploit that position for short-term gain to the great detriment of the entire network of firms that are connected to that hub. Firms like Yahoo!, Enron, AOL, and Microsoft all have the opportunity to drain all the value out of their ecosystems, and although they may temporarily enrich themselves in doing so, in the end they sow the seeds of their own demise because they undermine the health of the ecosystems to which their fates are bound.

What distinguishes an Enron from a Microsoft is not just the dramatic difference in value creation by these two firms, but also the relative emphasis placed on value creation and value extraction. We believe that Enron went way too far in pulling value from its ecosystem, to the point that the viability of its own position was threatened. Moreover, Enron almost certainly did this deliberately: It was no mere failure as a keystone, but in fact actively squandered its keystone potential in draining value from its network. Such behavior need not always be deliberate, however. Perhaps the most interesting thing about hub landlords is that they can trigger Enronlike collapses without fully understanding the extent of the damage that they are doing, or the way in which that damage may come back to hurt their own companies in the end. That is why it is worth spending a little more time on this strategy.

Landlords

A landlord strategy is problematic because it renders the ecosystem fundamentally unstable. A *hub landlord strategy* is an operating strategy that extracts as much value as possible from an ecosystem or ecosystem domain without integrating forward to control it.

Landlords follow a fundamentally inconsistent strategy. They refuse to integrate forward to control assets that are crucial to their operation. However, they extract so much value from the ecosystem that they make the business models of the needed niche firms unsustainable. These landlord firms recognize that networks have exceptional potential to create value indirectly, but they capture too much of it for themselves.

We have seen, in our discussion of Enron, what can happen in extreme cases of this strategy when a firm loses all focus on ecosystem health and develops an aggressive culture focused entirely on inventing new ways of profiting directly from its hub position. But a landlord strategy can take more subtle forms and need not be the result of reckless disregard for ecosystem health. Often this can be a simple mistake of timing or of overestimation—a miscalculation of how much value it is safe to extract from the ecosystem, or even simply a misunderstanding of how much power a hub truly has on overall network health. Yahoo! and AOL, in their earlier incarnations, were susceptible to these problems. In effect, they often acted like landlords, extracting high rents from their hub real estate. What they did not necessarily understand was that their role was so fundamental to the ecosystem that extracting a little too much value, if done in a large number of cases, could help bring down the whole thing.

Internet portals such as Yahoo! and AOL are worth looking at more closely. Between 1995 and 2000, their strategy hinged on the development of two different communities: users and business partners. Their pricing and value capture model, however, was overly generous to consumers and overly onerous to business partners. They felt that as long as they had the traffic, the business development partners would flock to them. They therefore attracted large numbers of consumers by providing high value-added services for free (e.g., My Yahoo!, e-mail) and extracted enormous rents from business partners in terms of slotting fees, traffic-sharing agreements, and so forth.

The fascinating thing is that Yahoo! and AOL did this in large part because they simply did not realize how damaging their impact on the Internet economy would be. In each individual business development deal, leveraging their business power appeared to make enormous sense. Start-ups viewed an announced "partnership" with AOL as the ticket for a successful IPO in the boom years.[17]

However, it was difficult to recognize that portals in fact wielded so much power that they could materially influence the likelihood of one of those domains collapsing. These firms thought they understood the value capture piece of network strategy, and even the potential of value creation by other members of the ecosystem leveraging their platform, but they ignored the implications of shared fate and collective behavior. By driving their partners to the wall, they left them unable to cope with even the slightest downturn in their markets. In the second half of 2000, the dot-com partner community completely collapsed. The following quarter, the portals themselves experienced severe declines, as the revenues that AOL was extracting from the ecosystem dried up.

The contrasting case of eBay makes clear the effect that these failed network strategies had on the health of their ecosystems. As illustrated in previous chapters, eBay uses its powerful hub position to extract value, but balances its value capture with actions that enhance the health of its ecosystem. As a result, eBay has managed to support a healthy and thriving ecosystem through the same downturn that crushed the weakened networks of many other firms.

In the aftermath of this collapse, Yahoo! has completely restructured its approach and balanced the different sides of its market. It is now charging both sides, consumers and partners, in a much more equitable way. Yahoo!'s current sales and profit growth is in pay services, such as advanced e-mail, job searches, and personals. Additionally, the company has completely restructured its business development practices, decentralizing the function and having targeted business development support for each deal. This has been enormously successful and has created true win-win situations with key business partners such as SBC, which co-markets broadband access services with Yahoo!

Dominators

Although the landlord strategy has problems, there are effective alternatives to pursuing a keystone strategy in an ecosystem. In its purest sense, a dominator strategy is aimed at maximizing both internal value creation and capture. Whereas being a hub landlord is always dangerous, selective domination of certain niches can be effective and successful.

A *dominator strategy* is an operating strategy that integrates vertically or horizontally to manage and control an ecosystem or ecosystem domain. Dominators are firms that control both value capture and value creation in an ecosystem domain. These firms are vertically integrated and in many ways follow the example of the classic (prenetwork) diverse firm in an industry delivering a complex product. Such firms take upon themselves the entire task of delivering these products, often producing closed architectures that eliminate the possibility of other firms leveraging, building on, or extending their products.

As with keystones, these firms occupy critical hubs in their ecosystem. However, unlike keystones, dominators progressively take over their ecosystem. In biological ecosystems, dominators start by eliminating all other species in their closest niche and gradually move on to other niches. The analogue in business ecosystems is clear: firms that seek to eliminate other firms in their market, often expanding into new markets that they subsequently dominate or even eliminate.

Business history is filled with dominator strategies. Examples range from the early days of AT&T and IBM to the more recent history of Digital Equipment Corporation (DEC) in the minicomputer market. In each of these cases, the firms provided the comprehensive set of products and services that was necessary for an end customer to perform its tasks, and left essentially no space for other organizations to leverage their services and enhance them by providing additional functions. In the 1960s, IBM produced every technological component that went into its mainframes and provided virtually every service that the customer needed to get the most from the products it bought, from the creation of memory components to custom software applications, and from installation services to financing. Similarly, DEC leveraged internal components and services for its line of minicomputers.

To preserve their futures, dominators must invest in internal R&D to make sure that substitutes cannot be created that offer their customers better price/functionality characteristics. To a dominator, technological innovation is an internal necessity, a hedge against potential competitors. Thus, Bell Laboratories and IBM's Thomas J. Watson Research Center were created for the explicit task of making sure that their parent companies could never be blindsided by a competitor that offered superior technologies.

Over time, a dominator reduces the diversity of organizations that populate its ecosystem, and reduces the ecosystem's robustness to external shocks. It is therefore quite likely that over time the entire ecosystem occupied by the dominator will be threatened by neighboring ecosystems that offer substitute functionality. If these competitive ecosystems are characterized by a healthier structure, including one or more effective keystones, the dominated ecosystem will likely be replaced. Such was the fate of both the mainframe and minicomputer ecosystems when the PC ecosystem started to provide comparable performance. The dominated ecosystems, each largely driven by the efforts of a single firm, simply could not compete with the combined efforts of the thousands of organizations linked by the PC platform.

Our approach in this work suggests that in situations of significant technological or market change, keystone strategies may be preferable to dominator strategies because they encourage long-term innovation and niche creation for the ecosystem and appear to be a more effective and sustainable way for leading organizations to do business. In areas susceptible to turbulence, dominator firms may produce extraordinary returns in the short and medium term, but may eventually lead to ecosystem collapse, massive dislocation, and the creation of a substitute keystone structure. Even in cases where dominators do not take their ecosystems to the point of collapse, they can leave them weakened or at least keep them from developing their full potential.

In this context it is interesting to consider the case of Apple versus the "Wintel" platform. If Apple was always truly innovative, as many have argued, why did it lose out? There are many explanations, but the view espoused here would suggest that in creating an integrated "appliance computer," Apple courted a dominator role: It controlled everything from operating system to hardware, from applications to peripherals. Indeed, one could view the evolution of Apple as a constant struggle in striking a balance between its original conception of the Macintosh as an integrated "appliance" and a more open conception of it as a platform.

Interestingly, many of the classic examples of incumbent failure captured by leading authors (minicomputers, mainframes, glass making, automobiles, disk drives, etc.) can be related to the ineffective behavior of dominant firms.[18] In the case of both minicomputers and mainframes, for example, we see ecosystems that were dominated by players (IBM and DEC) that did not open up their platforms to third-party organizations. They leveraged proprietary hardware (such as IBM's SLT technology in the 1960s, or DEC's Alpha chip in the early 1990s) and proprietary software (such as IBM's MVS and DEC's VMS operating systems). Despite many predictions to the contrary, neither ecosystem threatened the other (because their rate of innovation was comparable). However, when a different type of ecosystem structure began to encroach into their territory (the personal computer, with its vastly more productive and innovative structure), both minicomputer and mainframe ecosystems collapsed virtually simultaneously.

The model pursued by such firms is to dominate in both the value creation and value capture side of the opportunities available to a network hub. The leverage that is created internally—through operating efficiencies and broad programs of costly and fundamental R&D—is exploited by classic dominators to give them an unassailable advantage against potential niche players, with which they directly compete. It is precisely these ecosystems that are threatened by changes in technology or business environment. The strategy may work well in mature businesses or as long as things stay fixed, but when conditions change the whole system may crash or be overwhelmed by a more innovative ecosystem.

Landlords, Dominators, and Ecosystem Health

Clearly, both landlords and dominators have the potential to do considerable damage to their ecosystems, either directly (as in the case of those, like Enron, that drain value from their ecosystems) or indirectly (by taking over nearly all value creation and thus "becoming" the ecosystem in the way that the vertically integrated minicomputer firms of the 1970s and 1980s did).

Situations in which dominators can play a constructive role in their ecosystems do exist. In terms of the balance between value creation and value capture, the negative effects of landlords are clear. The case of classic dominators is not as clear, however. These firms not only take control of the vast majority of value capture in their ecosystems, but also take responsibility for creating the majority of the value in those systems. Thus, whereas landlords can kill their ecosystems outright—or eliminate the potential for creating ecosystems in the first place—dominators can have more subtle effects on ecosystem health. In comparing the effects of these two different kinds of strategies, it is helpful to look closely at their differing effects on our measures of ecosystem health.

Productivity

The two strategies differ significantly in their impact on ecosystem productivity. Landlords cripple the ability of their ecosystems to deliver the necessary variety of functions because they not only drain incentives for creating and delivering innovations but also fail to create any themselves. What innovative activity there is, as we have seen in the case of Enron, is often focused on improving the landlord's ability to extract value. The impact on productivity is thus clearly negative.

Dominators differ. These organizations integrate forward and take it upon themselves to deliver innovations. The health of the ecosystem with respect to delivering value is, in effect, determined by the productivity of the dominator's internal efforts at R&D and operations. This difference suggests that physical dominators may have their place—namely, where the pace of innovation is slow; where innovations require large, focused, highly coordinated efforts; where transaction costs between firms are high; or where innovation has risks that simply cannot be absorbed by a more diffuse or decentralized market structure. In these cases, although the productive part of the ecosystem is constrained to a small number of competing dominating firms, overall productivity may nonetheless exceed that which could be achieved by a true networked ecosystem of many firms. This may be the case, for example, in the pharmaceutical industry, which has partly resisted the pressures for fragmentation experienced in other environments.

Niche Creation

Landlords stifle niche creation in their ecosystems. They extract so much capital from their networks that there is nothing left on the table for other firms to use in building new businesses or establishing new niches. Dominators may also prevent niche creation and diversity by occupying niches themselves or by otherwise preventing niches from forming outside the firm. But when more than one dominator is present, competition in the environment will usually encourage dominators to create and expand into new ecosystem niches themselves. For example, during the late 1950s and early 1960s, IBM and its competitors (the "seven dwarfs") introduced a number of crucial innovations and created a variety of new businesses in the computer industry, ranging from semiconductor components to leasing services.

The differences in the impact of landlords and dominators on their industries are therefore significant. Because landlords do not take responsibility for vertically integrating and creating their own internal niches, they preside over industries that perform few functions. Such industries are always unambiguously worse off for the presence of such strategies: What little such networks do is limited to what happens in the few firms that survive the landlord's value stranglehold.

The effects of dominators are quite different: They inhibit diversity, but to the extent that they vertically integrate and take on and dominate other ecosystem niches themselves, they do not eliminate these roles completely. The effect is not so much a loss of functions as potentially less diversity in the way those functions are provided. As with productivity, there are cases in which this can be beneficial or appropriate. Where too much variety threatens stability or leads to incompatibilities or redundancies among products or technologies, a firm that eliminates unnecessary diversity can play an important role. Just how much diversity is good for an ecosystem is difficult to determine and is an issue beyond the scope of this book.[19] The point here is simply that diversity—especially arbitrary diversity—can come at a cost (in terms of complexity, redundancy, confusion, etc.) and that some degree of reduction in niche creation may be beneficial so long as at least one instance of the function provided by the niche is supported by the dominating firm.

Robustness

As we have argued in several places, one of the ways in which effective keystones enhance stability is by supplying a stable and predictable core around which the rest of the ecosystem can organize itself. A point we have finessed, however, is that this core is itself, in effect, often "dominated" by the keystone. This highlights another important distinction between landlords and dominators. Landlords, in their most extreme definition, are focused simply on extraction and not creation of value, and do not control a meaningful stabilizing core of their ecosystem. Dominators are instead focused on precisely that: the construction of a stable system for which they take responsibility. Although there are other ways of constructing such cores—by formulating open standards or by building open shared components, for example—one obvious way is to own them: to ensure stability by guaranteeing that there is only one such core and that it is owned and maintained by a single firm.

Over time, however, the lack of diversity in any dominated ecosystem is likely to backfire. Dominated ecosystems are bound to be less resilient to shocks, such as architectural, radical, or disruptive innovation. This implies that over long stretches of time, one would expect dominators that leverage different technologies, architectures, or business models to displace each other or to be displaced by ecosystems organized around keystones.

Mixed Strategies

As the foregoing points should make clear, the impact of landlords and dominators on their ecosystems is complex. Whereas landlords like Enron are inherently destructive, dominators can have beneficial effects. In very mature industries, for example, where little innovation is taking place and where what change there is occurs at a slow pace, a small number of highly integrated firms that perfect well-established products may be more effective than a more open ecosystem structure.

More important for our present purposes, however, is to note that firms often pursue mixed strategies, acting as keystones in one domain while dominating a different domain. Usually, there exist domains within any industry wherein pursuing some degree of domination is effective. Clearly this is often the case with some core aspects of any platform for which a keystone is responsible. A keystone will usually want to control (or at least strongly influence) those aspects of the platform to ensure the health of its ecosystem. Microsoft needs to control the many crucial facets of the Windows platform, just as TSMC seeks to control its manufacturing assets. IBM is no exception: While leveraging the largely external Linux operating system, it also owns and controls the WebSphere platform and a comprehensive set of programming tools (which motivated the acquisition of Rational Software).

A keystone might also want to extend by dominating a domain because it perceives it to be mature. Microsoft Office, for example, is not in itself a platform to the same degree that Windows is; however, it represents a mature and fairly stable constellation of functionality. In this view, Microsoft's "domination" of office productivity software stabilizes this segment of the software industry, shifting diversity and ecosystem effort to other areas where it may be more appropriately applied. Moreover, the presence of a reliable, stable, and predictable tool for one of the most important and well-established uses of personal computers enhances the value of Windows as a platform, which brings benefits to the ecosystem as a whole.

Enron Backlash

In the months following Enron's collapse, the world witnessed a pushback against networked, "asset light" models of business operation. In the electricity industry, this has had an enormous impact, essentially causing the shutdown of most trading operations. This backlash appears to have gone much too far and is causing a major liquidity crisis in the sector. This suggests why it is so critical for operating managers to reflect on the real operational dynamics of business ecosystems and to understand, at a deep level, why Enron failed, why Yahoo!'s business development strategy may have been flawed, and why Enron and eBay are so fundamentally different.

This kind of understanding is important not only for managers in firms that make up important ecosystem hubs, but also for managers in niche firms. Niche players should understand how ecosystem structure and dynamics influence them, and should develop appropriate strategies. This is the subject of the next chapter.

CHAPTER SEVEN

Niche Players

Close to 24,000 people lived in and around the city of Prato, Italy, at the end of the fourteenth century. The bulk of the population worked as textile craftsmen and merchants, mostly organized in tiny independent operations. These typically included a handful of people and focused on highly specialized "niche" crafts such as weaving, carding, spinning, fulling, and dyeing.

This mass of niche players formed a business ecosystem much like the ones discussed in the previous chapters and was coordinated by two tiers of intermediaries. The first tier was made up of the *lanivendoli* (wool sellers), who bought in small lots from the craftsmen and sold the materials in larger amounts to the powerful *lanaiuoli* (wool merchants). These wool merchants made up the second tier of intermediaries and acted as the most powerful trading hubs in the ecosystem. The lanaiuoli were typically structured as significant formal companies, with clear accounts and specialized managerial expertise (such as production, selling, or bookkeeping), and provided critical functions of production coordination, quality control, and even financing. The lanaiuoli were among the first keystone players in Western business.

During the fourteenth and fifteenth centuries, the mass of specialized niche players in the wool and related trades functioned as a highly interrelated collective system, in which organizations connected with each other in a variety of ways. In some cases, relationships were defined by family ties. In other cases, formal partnerships were signed, including joint ownership of assets, effectively creating networks of holding companies. Niche players in Prato and in other European cities involved in wool and textile trading had many of the same challenges faced by niche players today: how to trade off the benefits of integration and tight affiliation with one wool merchant against the risk of hold-up and the advantages provided by keeping relationships flexible.

It is difficult for us, focused as we are on modern information and communications technologies, to appreciate that these "primitive" trading ecosystems were easily as vast and as highly distributed as the most fragmented of today's industries. One of the most fascinating examples is provided by Francesco di Marco Datini, who acted as a keystone in a vast ecosystem of hundreds of specialized organizations, reaching out to close to a hundred cities across Europe. The fact that Datini managed to hold this ecosystem together despite the drawbacks of fourteenth-century information technology and communications is an amazing testament to the resilience and robustness of healthy business ecosystems. Key to Datini's operations were meticulously kept accounts and a vast amount of written correspondence, part of which was preserved over time and provides insight into how Datini's ecosystem worked.

The companies in Datini's ecosystem were largely independent and ran as almost autonomous operations. However, like current effective niche players, these organizations deployed strategies that leveraged each other's strengths, assets, and capabilities in order to pursue opportunities that would never have been open to any individual operation acting in isolation. This naturally led to a complex set of connections and interrelationships among ecosystem players, which built relationships among trades as different as jewelry, insurance, and textiles, as the following example describes:

> Each . . . was an independent enterprise, and each in dealing with the others would charge commission and interest. The only common link was Francesco. The various branches . . . promoted each other's business as much as possible. When, for instance, the wool dyeing company of Francesco di Marco and Niccolo' di Piero in Prato sent some cloth to the company of Francesco di Marco and Stoldo di Lorenzo in Florence, to be sold in Venice, the cloth was consigned to Bindo di Gherardo Piaciti, the company's Florentine correspondent in Venice, who, instead of sell-

ing it, exchanged it for pearls belonging to Messer Andrea Contarini (108 strings of 74 pearls each) and these were then insured and forwarded to the company of Francesco di Marco and Luca del Sera in Valencia, to be sold in Catalonia. When the transaction was completed, the Florentine branch credited the amount due to the company in Prato.[1]

As was the case in Datini's Renaissance ecosystem, the majority of business ecosystems are composed of small, focused players who individually seem to have little influence on their surroundings. However, the performance and effectiveness of these niche players is essential to an ecosystem because they typically provide the majority of its actual functionality in terms of activities and available products and services. As seen in Datini's ecosystem, the ability of the majority of niche players to leverage a broad set of capabilities and opportunities provided by their ecosystem is one of the quintessential characteristics of a functioning keystone strategy.

This chapter explores the role of these niche players in business ecosystems and focuses on how they can take the most advantage of the opportunities available while avoiding some of the pitfalls that confront them.

Niche Players

One way of identifying a niche player is as a business that exhibits a "typical" (or less than typical) number of relationships with other ecosystem participants.[2] By definition, such businesses are the most numerous members of the ecosystem and usually greatly exceed other types of businesses. In the software industry, the ratio between niche players and others is greater than a factor of ten, even if we only include public firms in the analysis. The ratio becomes much larger if we include all businesses. Niche players are thus critical because they make up the bulk of their ecosystems.

Because many niche players locate at the "fringes" of the ecosystem, where new innovations are actively being pursued and where new products and services are being developed and new markets explored, they are critical drivers of innovation. These "edge firms" are vital to the health of the ecosystem because they are the locus of precisely the kind of meaningful diversity that we believe is essential to its robustness.

Examples of effective niche players are obviously quite numerous and range across a variety of settings. They include companies such as NVIDIA in the fabless integrated circuit domain and Intuit in software applications. NVIDIA and Intuit are well-established players and occupy well-defined segments in their respective industries of graphics accelerators and personal accounting software. Examples of "edge" firms (niche players that are currently opening up new ecosystem niches) might be Groove Networks and MobilianAvnera—the first in peer-to-peer applications, the second in cross-platform wireless connectivity solutions.

As was the case in Datini's time, the key to success for a niche player is specialization. By leveraging symbiotic relationships with other ecosystem players with complementary assets, niche players can achieve deep specialization while at the same time assembling the complex, system-level solutions that are so often demanded by customers.

Symbiotic Relationships: IBM and deNovis

The 2002 agreement among Empire Blue Cross Blue Shield, IBM, and deNovis provides a good example of a symbiotic relationship between a keystone and a niche player. IBM complemented the niche capabilities of deNovis by leveraging its software and service assets, combining its technologies, technological expertise, sales force, and industry reputation.

DeNovis, Inc., is a Lexington, Massachusetts–based company focused on the needs of health care payers. The deNovis software has the ability to electronically read policy statements, rules, and regulations and make appropriate payments automatically. This ability enables carriers to offer customized health plans for each family member and offer customer service online. This complements a variety of IBM hardware, software, and services, including the operation of the computer network for the new service and the systems for charging insurers based on each claim submitted.

The first end result was a ten-year, $930 million Solution Engagement Agreement with Empire Blue Cross, which encompassed the deployment of the deNovis solution on IBM's platforms, including hardware and database and infrastructure software. IBM also transferred the functions of 22 million lines of old software from Empire to the deNovis program. What's more, IBM lent deNovis its marketing and sales muscle to push the technology to other health care companies.

DeNovis would never have closed the Empire deal without IBM. "DeNovis is the gold standard for ventures benefiting from an ecosystem strategy," noted one prominent West Coast venture capitalist. "DeNovis, a young startup, was seeking the credibility and assurance of a large company while IBM was on the lookout for an application that would provide value and access to the health care market. At the same time, Empire/Blue Cross Insurance needed to modernize their claims processing; which was costly because of complex contracts with diverse health care providers. Ecosystems are not about technology. They are about solutions for would-be Empire customers."[3]

IBM thus acted as an effective keystone for deNovis, providing needed complements to its technology and integrating an effective solution based on deNovis's focused technological components. Faced with a competitive proposal from their competitor, EDS, IBM and deNovis proposed to integrate their next-generation claims processing engine with Empire's health care system. DeNovis's claims processing application is able to adjudicate automatically more than 95 percent of health care claims with 100 percent accuracy.[4] This is double the automatic adjudication percentage possible using most existing systems, which depend on the manual review of at least half of all claims. With these systems, the average cost per claim is as much as $12 and ultimately costs the industry an estimated $250 billion or more. DeNovis's ability to automatically adjudicate has the potential to decrease claims administration costs by 50 percent.

Recalling the prominent characteristics of successful keystone strategies, we observe that in terms of robustness, deNovis is garnering enormous business and technological stability by combining its focused solution with the IBM platform. IBM is providing de facto insurance for both deNovis and the end customer. IBM is also dramatically increasing deNovis's sales and operational productivity by leveraging

IBM's assets and capabilities, ranging from its sales force to its technology. Finally, IBM is driving niche creation by leveraging its platforms to open a novel area of innovation by third parties. The deNovis deal will not be the last one.

IBM, having shed the landlord features that characterized it during the 1960s, is also improving the productivity and robustness of its customer's ecosystem. IBM and deNovis helped Empire dramatically reduce the time-consuming manual labor and drudgery of processing claims, saving billions of dollars. This product line could significantly affect the entire health care industry. By acting as the integrator (and using its assets to solidify emergent applications), IBM added robustness and helped find the correct solution to Empire's cost problem. In the process, it expanded its ecosystem by fostering the emergence of a new niche company.

Niche Strategies

A *niche strategy* is an operating strategy that specializes capabilities to differentiate a business within an ecosystem domain. The fundamental advantage of a niche player such as deNovis is specialization. Niche players specialize by leveraging the services provided by the keystones in their ecosystem and by concentrating on the acquisition of business and technical capabilities that directly support their niche strategy. It would be madness for Intuit to squander its resources on the technical details of disk compression or hardware driver implementations (which are Microsoft's concern), or for Mobilian to invest its precious cash in the creation of manufacturing facilities (as TSMC does). Their advantage instead resides in their ability to build and nurture specialized capabilities that are unique to their domain.

Niche players are naturally dependent on other businesses. The essential step in defining a good niche strategy is therefore to analyze the firm's ecosystem and map out the characteristics of its keystone and dominator players. Do strong keystones exist? Are there multiple keystones that compete to play the same role? How far removed are the dominators? How many keystones should the firm tie into?

A classic niche firm in the software industry is Integrated Development Enterprise (IDe), which leverages Microsoft's platform (relying greatly on technologies such as Active Server Pages, ActiveX, COM, and ADO) to build its products. Because IDe can rely on Microsoft to provide stable and evolving tools and components, IDe is able to stay completely focused on building Internet-based development chain management (DCM) solutions. Moreover, by integrating its products into Microsoft Project and Microsoft Excel, IDe in effect allows users to leverage these applications in their own deployments of IDe's products.

IDe is also typical of a firm pursuing a niche strategy in that it effectively takes the platform provided by a keystone for granted as a kind of foundation upon which all else relies. Not only do Microsoft's technologies free IDe from worrying about all kinds of details that have little or nothing to do with its focus on DCM, but because tools like Visual Studio "hide a lot of things that it intimately integrates," developers are able to focus on the correct "level of abstraction" in their work, which, among other things, greatly facilitates IDe's ability to rapidly "throw things in front of customers and ask for feedback," which is "critical for IDe's business effectiveness."[5] One indicator of the extent to which niche players rely on the efficiencies they achieve through effective leveraging of keystone platforms is CTO Ralf Brown's response to a hypothetical scenario in which his firm is forced to stop using Microsoft's platform (even if it only meant switching to another one): "It would be the end of the world."

To the extent that niche players focus their own activities narrowly on a specific domain while using existing solutions for everything else, they improve their own productivity and efficiency. This has important implications for product architecture: Niche firms should view their products not as standalone entities designed from the ground up, but as important, specialized complementary components in an interconnected ecosystem of elements in which conventional product boundaries may not always be distinct or clear to the end customer.

This presents considerable challenges because firms must balance the need to distinguish and brand their products with the need to support and complement other ecosystem offerings. Ultimately, this tends to have positive implications for overall ecosystem health: Niche firms are driven to distinguish themselves not through artificial or superficial attributes but through the core contribution of their products in complement with other members of their community.

Despite the best, highly specialized strategies, niche players will find that over time they will come into conflict with other complements, other niche players, keystones, and especially dominators. Typically, innovation will be critical to their success in these battles, emphasizing continued specialization and differentiation. Niche players that do not or cannot actively advance and evolve their products toward the edges of the ecosystem may find that the frontier of constantly advancing platforms will approach the niche they occupy.[6] Such firms face a crucial decision between dealing with keystones and dominators in ways that promote the incorporation of the niche player's products into the platform or resisting this process. Recognizing when this decision needs to be made and choosing the correct path are important elements of a niche firm's strategy that have important implications for ecosystem health.[7]

In certain ecosystems, firms following keystone strategies will avoid confrontation with niche players by making clear and very public decisions not to compete in certain areas. That is the case with regard to IBM and software applications, for example—IBM offers an effective platform through its WebSphere product line and will explicitly not compete with any of the application companies that are potential WebSphere customers and users. TSMC made the same kind of decision with regard to designing specific integrated circuits. TSMC will thus not compete with its customers in chip design and will focus only on providing a manufacturing platform.[8]

NVIDIA's Niche Strategy

NVIDIA is a textbook case of a highly successful niche player in the business ecosystem of semiconductors and integrated circuits. By leveraging physical assets (such as TSMC's awe-inspiring manufacturing facilities) as well as intellectual assets (such as third-party design tools, libraries, and standards), NVIDIA is able to stay highly specialized and focused on its core domain: the design, development, and marketing of graphics and media communication processors and related software for PCs, workstations, and digital entertainment platforms.

Leveraging Physical Assets: TSMC's Manufacturing Platform

As a fabless chip company, NVIDIA has outsourced fabrication of its graphics processing units to TSMC, which has served as one of its keystones. NVIDIA's fabless manufacturing strategy thus leverages the manufacturing assets provided by TSMC as well as other assets in such areas as assembly, quality control and assurance, and even reliability and testing. NVIDIA graphics processors are primarily fabricated by TSMC and assembled and tested by Advanced Semiconductor Engineering, ChipPAC Incorporated, and Siliconware Precision Industries Company Ltd. NVIDIA receives semiconductor products from subcontractors, performs incoming quality assurance, and then ships them to computer equipment manufacturers, stocking representatives, motherboard manufacturers, and others. Generally, these manufacturers assemble and test the boards based on NVIDIA's design kit and test specifications, then ship the products to the retail, systems integrator, or OEM markets as motherboard and add-in board solutions.[9]

This complex web of relationships enables NVIDIA to avoid the significant costs (many billions of dollars) and risks associated with owning and operating manufacturing, assembly, and test operations. These suppliers are also responsible for procurement of most of the raw materials used in the production of NVIDIA chips. As a result, the company can focus resources on product design, additional quality assurance, marketing, and customer support. In the words of NVIDIA's founder and engineering vice president Chris Malachowsky, "This has tremendous value for us. It would be a nightmare for us to have to develop the capability to do all that. It clearly allows us to focus on what we do best, and it's critical to our strategy."[10]

Because of NVIDIA's niche/keystone relationship with TSMC, NVIDIA CEO Huang Jen-Hsun can log on to a TSMC Web site and track the production status of his company's chips in Taiwan. "We get daily feeds on where every single wafer is in the process," raves Huang. He claims he can make late engineering changes and even cancel an order at the last minute without incurring a heavy penalty. "A lot of people would like to have our business,'" says Huang. But the "chemistry" he says his engineers have with those of TSMC is a major reason NVIDIA gives the foundry some $500 million in orders every year.[11]

Leveraging Intellectual Assets:
Optimized Design Libraries and Standards

Through its relationships with TSMC and TSMC's library partners (Artisan and Virage), NVIDIA is able to improve the efficiency of its graphics processor design and fabrication by using third-party design tools and building blocks. As part of its growing emphasis on customized service, TSMC uses the Internet to make information on designs and products available to customers twenty-four hours a day. "Access to our fabs is very important, so we are turning to e-commerce," says TSMC chairman and founder Morris Chang. "The emphasis is for the customer to access the information they need without any human intervention. We have a library of technologies available for them and they should be able to find out 90 percent of our technologies without any human assistance."[12]

The concept of an optimized technology library is at the center of TSMC's business model. Chang sees the company as not just a manufacturer but a design and technology broker. For example, if NVIDIA had designed a new graphics chip and needed a standard circuit to link the chip with other computer operations, a search of TSMC's database would provide such a circuit. Moreover, the library circuit would already be optimized to have high yield in TSMC's manufacturing fabs. TSMC could then pull the designs together to make a single, integrated, optimized product. Chang calls this "acting as the honest broker on intellectual property," adding: "The fact that we don't do any design and don't compete with any of our customers is a big advantage."[13]

TSMC launched its design library in August 1998 when it signed an agreement with Artisan Components, a Silicon Valley design house. Artisan doesn't charge TSMC any fee up front, but receives royalties when TSMC produces chips using Artisan designs. In effect, TSMC customers such as NVIDIA get free initial access to the designs, making their cash flow easier—an important consideration for companies both small and large.[14]

Another example of leveraged intellectual property is the use of testing standards. As with most three-dimensional chip companies, quality and performance are NVIDIA's prime concerns when testing prototype integrated circuits. Once in production, millions of these devices are shipped. The complexity of these devices makes it a challenge to bring them into production quickly with a high level of quality. For instance, NVIDIA's latest integrated circuit includes 15 million transistors in a 0.25-micron CMOS (complementary metal-oxide semiconductor) with a complexity on par with today's leading microprocessors, including a high level of logic function, internal caches, and speeds of 200 MHz and beyond.[15] Fabless semiconductor companies do not have internal resources for testing prototype integrated circuits. Instead, many fabless companies rely on outside services such as DTS in San Jose, California, which has the type of sophisticated testing equipment needed.[16] NVIDIA hardware and software development teams work closely with these external testing services, certification agencies, Microsoft Windows Hardware Quality Labs, and OEM customers to ensure that both boards and software drivers are certified for inclusion in the OEMs' products.[17] Quality standards for chip production are maintained by TSMC and by Microsoft and Silicon Graphics, Inc.[18]

Core Components of a Niche Strategy

The essence of a niche strategy is to achieve specialization by taking explicit advantage of the opportunities provided by the ecosystem while avoiding the kinds of traps that challenge firms in such environments. Our observation of a variety of niche strategies in action highlights a few critical components.

Value Creation

The first driver of an effective niche strategy is value creation.

Specialize in unique capabilities. An effective niche strategy creates value by selecting a specialization that is truly different and whose differences are sustainable over time. A classic mistake made by a variety of new ventures during the venture capital boom of the late 1990s was selecting areas that had no staying power, such as Web calendars or Web-dispatched limousine services. Over time, it was inevitable that these new niches would merge with existing ones. The services are now broadly offered, but the firms that started developing them have ceased to exist as independent entities. In those cases in which the skills and capabilities that characterized new ecosystem domains were distinct enough to justify a truly focused strategy (for example, personal financial accounting or customer relationship management software), these strategies have endured for many years and enabled the growth of large and successful firms (such as Intuit and Siebel Systems).

A well-executed niche strategy, because of its focus, will exhibit strong defenses against a keystone and dominator trying to expand. Intuit is again a strong example here, with the continued success of its Quicken application against Microsoft Money. The key is finding a large enough market that requires specialized capabilities.

Leverage other capabilities from keystones. Effective niche players recognize that they are no longer bound by the constraints of vertical integration. As with IDe or deNovis, they create system solutions by combining their specialized assets with complementary products and platforms provided by other niche players and keystones. They embrace the opportunity to be lightweight and focused and leverage the tools, technologies, services, and products available through the ecosystem.

In doing this, niche strategies trade off risk with productivity. Strong economies can often be found by niche players by leveraging a single platform—for example, NVIDIA can optimize its designs for yields on TSMC's production lines. If a strong, trustworthy keystone is present in the niche player's ecosystem, there may be no apparent reason for the niche player to connect to multiple platforms. However, because of the risk of keystone collapse and keystone hold-up, niche players may want to diversify and invest in connecting with multiple hubs. As we discuss in some detail later, the crucial factor in figuring out which of these strategies to pursue is developing an understanding of the necessary "coupling strength," which defines the switching costs between keystones.

Sustain innovation. Whether dealing with one or multiple keystones, the heart of technology strategy for a niche player is to continually innovate by integrating technology available from the ecosystem to sharpen the niche offering that it is crafting. It is important to examine technological threats coming from the edge, and to leverage the ecosystem in crafting response strategies. This lets focused players develop specific solutions and concentrate on integrating these with key specific assets inside the firm. Intuit enabled its application, Quicken, for the Web by integrating technology components provided by Microsoft.

This implies a fundamental change in technology strategy models. In a vertically integrated setting, a company needs to develop into a massive organization and cover a broad variety of business areas in order to scale and survive. This makes scaling the company very challenging and requires a massive amount of capital. Additionally, it makes the company highly vulnerable to technological changes and other types of shocks. In a distributed business ecosystem, a firm can scale more easily and respond to shocks by leveraging capabilities provided by others.

Healthy business ecosystems will support a large number of niche firms for long, sustained periods of time. In the software industry, a large number of niche players have endured for many years, constantly generating a variety of product innovations (see figure 7-1). Despite the contraction caused by the crash of 2000 and the recession that followed, the ecosystem is still enabling *thousands* of different firms to survive.

Value Sharing and Risk Management

How can a niche player influence the way that value is shared in an ecosystem? How can it protect itself against the risks of hold-up or keystone obsolescence? One of the most critical factors is the *coupling strength* of the implied interactions. Tight coupling (or high coupling strength) implies that a given niche player needs to develop highly specific internal assets to leverage the assets provided by a third party. NVIDIA needs to spend a significant amount of time optimizing its designs to TSMC's manufacturing process. This in turn implies that

FIGURE 7-1

Niche Creation in the Computing Ecosystems

The figure represents numbers of firms that target a given platform along with at least one other platform (e.g., the UNIX line represents the number of firms that target any version of UNIX in addition to at least one other platform). Note that not only do large populations of firms continue to exist around each platform, but also that several platforms coexist and show a general trend of growing their ecosystems over time.

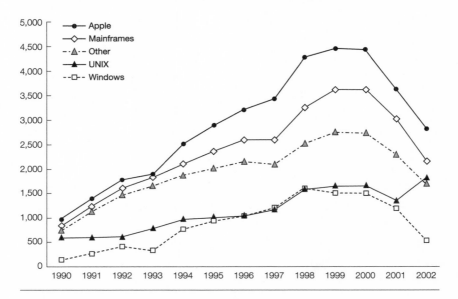

once committed to a given partner, the cost of switching is very high. Loosely coupled interactions instead imply minimal asset specificity and enable a niche player to easily switch from one relationship to another.

Tight coupling: Manage risk and dependencies. Tradition holds that tightly coupled relationships are by nature more efficient; for example, close collaboration between customers and suppliers is usually favored in existing management theories. However, tightly coupled models also have many disadvantages.

First, the tighter the coupling between organizations, the higher the risk of hold-up and the more power that platforms have over niche players. Thus, niche firms are much more at risk if a keystone decides to dominate its environment. Additionally, if the coupling strength is high, niche firms are more vulnerable to significant changes in technology and business models, which explains the many challenges and incumbent failures highlighted in a variety of research.[19]

A common failure of niche players is to bind too tightly to a keystone, which increases the power of the keystone over the niche player and can ultimately compromise the health of the entire ecosystem. Figure 7-2 shows that multiplatform firms in the software industry enjoyed higher net survival rates than single-platform firms throughout the 1990s.

Loose coupling: Embrace mobility and flexibility. The heart of operating strategy for a niche player is to leverage the broad-based efficiencies offered by connecting up with several players in an ecosystem, while

FIGURE 7-2

Growth Rates for Multiplatform and Single-Platform Firms in the Software Ecosystem

Each group is treated as a distinct population, and the year-to-year change in the number of firms in that population is used to calculate a growth rate. After 1992, the multiplatform population grows consistently faster (and contracts more slowly) than the single-platform population.

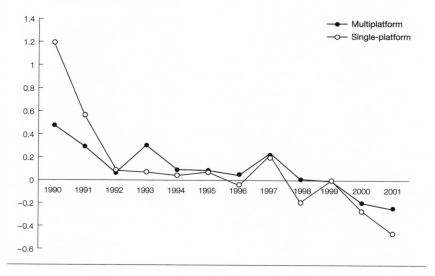

managing the dependencies that are created. This kind of behavior is made much easier by the emergence of loose coupling, as described in chapter 2 for the computing ecosystem. The essence of the argument is that less invasive, "minimalist" interfaces between organizations and technologies have the great advantage of minimizing technological risk and hold-up.

The emergence of loose coupling has enormous implications for niche firms because it means that an organization is no longer as threatened by the replacement of one technology with another. Because interfaces in loosely coupled systems are lightweight and noninvasive, firms can change much more easily in response to massive shifts in the technological environment. In essence, this means that they can much more easily "plug in" to a different way of doing business. Examples are provided by NVIDIA easily cutting across generations of semiconductor technology, or by enterprise IT departments easily embracing the Web.

In the software industry, for example, we have witnessed how the emergence of loosely coupled interfaces has enabled the majority of application companies to leverage multiple platforms (see figure 7-3). The same is true in the semiconductor and retail industries. The reality is that loosely coupled interfaces such as XML are quite powerful, so that reasonably strong efficiencies can be achieved with little commitment of platform-specific assets. Niche players can connect to both TSMC and UMC, or to Wal-Mart and Target, or to Microsoft and Apple. They can exchange design rules and purchase orders, and can optimize supply chains across different systems.

Niche leverage: Power over keystones. Finally, the emergence of loosely coupled technology interfaces has another critical implication for niche firms. Because loose coupling enables mobility, niche firms acquire enormous collective negotiating power with respect to keystones. The same mobility that allows them to escape devastating technological transitions allows them to potentially "leave" a keystone that is trying to extract too much value from the system for itself or that is not creating a platform that enhances opportunities for value creation.

Niche players, in effect, can use this leverage to keep keystones honest and to prevent them from straying into becoming dominators.

FIGURE 7-3

Growth in the Proportion of Multiplatform Firms in the Computing Ecosystem

The figure depicts the fraction of the total number of firms in the software industry that target more than one platform.

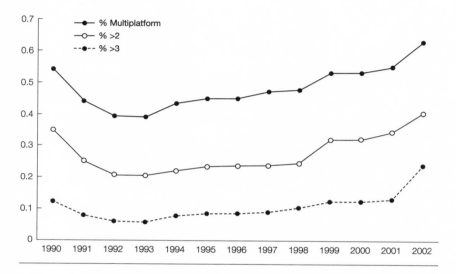

It is in fact in this sense that ecosystems compete: They compete with each other for mobile niche players. And it is precisely this competition that keeps ecosystems healthy: Without niche players who understand and exercise this leverage, ecosystems will be less healthy than they could be and may fall into sickness if their keystone loses sight of its role.

Innovation and Niche Evolution

Firms that pursue a focused niche strategy have an ultimate advantage in the creation of novelty. This is partly because a focused new idea can more closely correspond to a new firm than is possible in vertical or modular industry structures: Everything beyond the scope of the firm can be integrated from external sources, or, conversely, a new product or technology offered by the firm can be easily integrated into the existing ecosystem as an extension or addition to its capabilities.

Firms that actively seek out new terrain in this way have the further advantage that as they distinguish themselves in new domains they may create platforms and become keystones themselves. NVIDIA is a great example of this kind of pattern.

NVIDIA's Emergent Keystone Strategy

NVIDIA has grown rapidly to become not only a vibrant niche player in the integrated circuit ecosystem, but also to serve in some ways as a keystone itself, supporting the development of firms in the adjacent hardware and software communities. By following a successful and focused niche strategy, NVIDIA built a firm foundation for the next step: the transformation of its niche into an ecosystem in its own right, with NVIDIA as its keystone.

NVIDIA's Select Builder program, for example, supports system builders for PCs, laptops, and workstations. NVIDIA also maintains reseller and distributor partnership programs for firms that promote the NVIDIA line of products.[20] In addition, the firm supports an active NVIDIA Registered Developer program to provide software developers in sectors ranging from video games to engineering simulation with training, tools, and support for application development tailored to exploit the unique capabilities of NVIDIA graphics processors.[21] NVIDIA provides a significant set of tools, libraries, and standard interfaces that enable its own ecosystem to be more effective. This sharing of assets with channel partners and applications developers makes NVIDIA a keystone in its own right, with a role that is likely to increase in significance over time.

Building the Complexity of the Ecosystem

Firms like NVIDIA play a crucial role in structuring the complexity of an ecosystem in ways that make it accessible and manageable. In effect, they represent rungs in a ladder of ascending complexity that facilitate the power of platform leveraging: Hardware manufactures that build on the "NVIDIA platform" are not just leveraging NVIDIA's products; they are also leveraging those of TSMC. This "serial leveraging" enabled by firms such as NVIDIA that are both niche players (focused experts in a domain) and keystones (platform providers) is a critical source of the productivity and rapid advance in capabilities of their ecosystem. Such firms are woven into the fabric of the business ecosystem just as surely as the textile craftsmen and merchants and traders were woven into the textile business ecosystem in Datini's time.

III

Foundations for Competition

CHAPTER EIGHT

Architecture, Platforms, and Standards

Whether a firm has a central role in a business ecosystem or whether it focuses on a narrow niche, defining and executing strategy hinges on understanding three foundations for competition in a networked setting. The first foundation is *architecture,* which defines how companies draw boundaries between technologies, products, and organizations. The second foundation is *integration,* which effectively defines how organizations collaborate across these boundaries, sharing capabilities and technological components. The third foundation is *market management,* which shapes how organizations complete transactions across these boundaries, operating within the complex market dynamics that govern business networks. The next three chapters discuss these three foundations. We begin with architecture in this chapter, focusing on a discussion of platforms and standards, and follow with integration and market management in the next two chapters.

Designing a Payment Platform

The concept of architecture goes well beyond the technology sector. In 2002, Visa orchestrated more than half of the $1.5 trillion transactions executed through payment cards.[1] In what must certainly be one of the world's most leveraged organizations, Visa employs only 1,300 people to facilitate the trading activities of over 5 million merchants and 22,000 banks. The organization manages this enormous and dispersed community through the deployment of a well-designed platform—a collection of foundational technologies and simplifying standards that provide an incredibly efficient framework for value creation and sharing throughout the retail transaction ecosystem and that define Visa's role as a keystone.

Visa's platform has evolved over time. Payment cards were pioneered in 1950 by Diners Club, which gave away its cards to Manhattan customers and then persuaded restaurants of the benefits of accepting them. By 1960, Diners Club faced competition from American Express and Carte Blanche. A number of banks had also begun issuing cards to provide payment card services to retail stores in their geographic regions.[2] Bank of America's BankAmericard enjoyed an advantage over the rest of the bank-issued payment cards because of the size of the California market. Wanting to expand nationally, Bank of America franchised the BankAmericard system to seven banks outside California in 1966.[3] Within two months of the BankAmericard franchise announcement, American Express, Diners Club, and Carte Blanche offered similar franchise programs.[4]

These four franchised systems encountered a number of problems as they began to scale. First and foremost, the payment card systems were inconvenient. Merchants and customers experienced delays when they were required to call for authorization. Banks would often set a "floor limit," which allowed merchants to avoid calling for authorization if the transaction fell below the floor limit.[5] This helped with the delays but created significant risks. Furthermore, problems arose because processing transactions generated slips of paper that had to be moved physically from the merchant to its bank, to the cardholder's bank, and then to the cardholder for payment. Last, a complete lack of trust existed among the members of the franchise system. Some issuing banks would receive sales drafts, collect payments, and sit on the drafts for weeks to earn interest to which they were not entitled.[6]

In response to these challenges, different bank alliances combined to form the National BankAmericard system, which evolved into what we know today as Visa. In this system, banks agreed to design and leverage a common platform to solve their scale-up challenges (see figure 8-1). The platform was founded on a set of shared technologies, including merchant dial-in systems, magnetic stripe cards, and technology "oper-

FIGURE 8-1

Credit and Charge Transactions (millions) from 1971 to 2002, with Timeline of Key Events

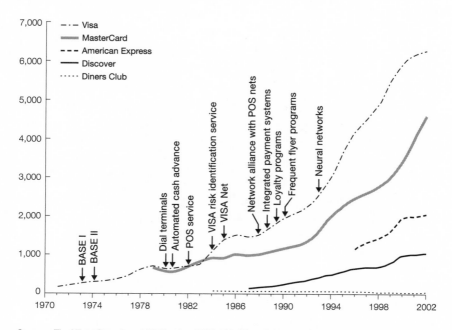

Sources: The Nilson Report, no. 780 (January 2003); The Nilson Report, no. 756 (January 2002); The Nilson Report, no. 759 (March 2002); The Nilson Report, no. 760 (March 2002); U.S. Census Bureau, <http://www.census.gov/hhes/income/histinc/h05.html> (accessed 12 December 2002); "The Trick Is Managing Money," BusinessWeek, 6 June 1970; and Irwin Ross, "The Credit Card's Painful Coming-of-Age," Fortune, October 1971.

ating systems" supporting automated authorization and bookkeeping, as well as systems to detect fraud and reduce risk. It started with the BASE I system (BankAmericard Authorization System, Experimental I), an international electronic network that carried messages authorizing merchants around the world to accept Visa payment cards for transactions twenty-four hours a day, seven days a week. Its introduction immediately cut authorization time from four minutes to only forty seconds.[7] The BASE II system, which became operational in November 1974, solved another major problem—the headaches of paper transactions. BASE I and II were gradually complemented by a variety of other technologies and services, ranging from integrated support for frequent flyer programs to neural network–based systems to detect fraud.

Visa network members accessed the platform through a set of standard "interfaces," including the agreement by different members to accept each other's transactions, clear rules for establishing membership, fees for membership and interchange, and formats for electronic exchange of data to ensure interoperability. This platform created a foundation through which the widely dispersed participants in the transactions ecosystem could interact efficiently, and enabled the system to scale to enormous proportions. In all other matters—fees, features, service, and marketing—the banks competed fiercely.

This common platform was the key to the ensuing strong growth in numbers of members, merchants, and cards, as well as the explosive growth in the volume of transactions. Today it continues to serve as the foundation of the successful keystone strategy pursued by the payment industry's leaders.

Architecture, Products, and Platforms

Whether we are talking about payment methods or about software, keystone strategies demand the efficient sharing of value with a dispersed ecosystem of organizations. The mechanism for this sharing is usually embodied in platforms such as Wal-Mart's Retail Link, TSMC's design tools and libraries, Li & Fung's supply chain system, or Microsoft's .NET. Understanding what platforms are and how they are designed is essential to understanding the dynamics of ecosystems and the tools that keystones have at their disposal to shape them.

Ecosystem Foundation

A *platform* is a set of solutions to problems that is made available to the members of the ecosystem through a set of access points or interfaces. In software these interfaces are called APIs (application programming interfaces). Although the API terminology is not usually used in other domains, the same basic approach is followed: Platforms serve as an embodiment of the functionality that forms the foundation of the ecosystem, packaged and presented to members of the ecosystem through a common set of interfaces. Ecosystem members then leverage these interfaces as a kind of toolkit for building their own products and think of them as the starting point for their own value creation (see figure 8-2). The platform is the "package" through which keystones share value with their ecosystems.

In computing, platforms such as Microsoft .NET or Apple OS X provide access to hardware capabilities while removing the need for developers to worry about how the hardware actually works. They link to basic functions such as access to disks and devices, security, support for basic user interface components, or drawing to printers or video screens. In semiconductors, manufacturing platforms such as TSMC and UMC offer manufacturing capabilities to a wide variety of design organizations. This dramatically lessens the latter firms' need to

FIGURE 8-2

Product Architecture as a Combination of Platform and Component Design

Platforms can be seen as embodiments of sharable solutions to common ecosystem problems. The areas of the rectangles schematically represent the proportion of effort (e.g., software code) needed to deliver a solution that bridges the gap between an underlying technology and the use for which it is adapted. As indicated, any product contains elements specific to a given use or solution and elements that are shared with many other products in an ecosystem. The latter represent an opportunity for the formation of a platform that can be leveraged by other members of the ecosystem to eliminate redundant effort.

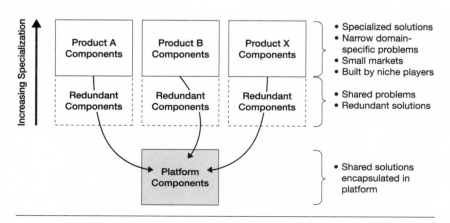

understand the details of the manufacturing process or to invest in manufacturing assets. The equivalent of APIs are formed by the design libraries that TSMC and UMC offer to their customers, which semiconductor designers can use to rapidly create circuits that are optimized to function with their processes. In the payment industry, platforms such as Visa and MasterCard lessen the need for individual banks to worry about the accuracy and risks of a transaction. Regardless of the details and complexity of the platform, or of the sophistication or formality with which its interfaces are packaged and presented, very different-looking platforms serve a similar foundational role and have a similar architectural structure.

Platform Architecture

Platforms can usefully be divided into two distinct types of components: the implementation and the interface. Platform *implementations* are proprietary approaches to solving problems and to bridging the gap between the underlying technologies on which an ecosystem is based and the set of solutions to problems that can be achieved using those technologies. Implementations are subject to invisible incremental improvement by their owners and to the incorporation of new technologies "underneath" the visible parts of the platform.

Platform *interfaces* are the visible embodiment of the solutions achieved in the implementation. They are the access points that ecosystem members use as the starting point for their own work. They are visible expressions of what the platform does and they establish the utility of underlying technologies. It is the design of these interfaces that ultimately determines what the underlying technology can do.

The notion of *coupling strength* describes the nature of the interface between components. A tightly coupled interface implies strong dependencies between components. A loosely coupled interface implies weak dependencies. If the interface between component A and B is weakly coupled, it is likely that we can change the internal properties of component A without influencing the behavior of component B.

Whether one is designing a broad-based platform or a focused service offering, it is crucial to have a crystal-clear idea of the "coupling" implications of one's decisions, from both a technological and organizational perspective. Most critically, a tightly coupled interface will engender higher switching costs than a loosely coupled interface. A loosely coupled interface will be more resilient to technological shocks and other environmental changes. This is true not only in the technical domain but also in the managerial domain, with implications ranging from organizational process design to the creation of strategic dependencies between firms.

The multipart structure of platforms means that what is seen and experienced by ecosystem members is the interface, so the details of the implementation can change as long as they don't "break" the interface. So long as interface components loosely couple ecosystem members to implementation components, the platform can endure major changes. This makes it easier for a keystone to manage technological change. Many technology improvements that do not radically transform the capabilities of the platform can be "hidden" from the ecosystem and will thus be unlikely to dislodge an established platform. Even discontinuous changes in underlying technologies will be unlikely to threaten an established platform as long as the platform can adapt and help its members to make the transition to using the new capabilities. Novel technology that has the potential to deliver meaningfully new functionality—that is, to result in the creation of new *interfaces*—represents the most significant threat to established platforms, because such technology may imply changes in the entire community that uses the platform. Considerations regarding these kinds of changes force keystones to constantly and aggressively incorporate new technologies into their platforms and to manage the impact of these changes on their ecosystem.

Dell's Operating Platform

Dell provides an interesting example of an operating platform that embodies loosely coupled interfaces. In its essence, Dell is a powerful hub in a business ecosystem that connects information technology suppliers and customers. Dell's business model is to retain the fewest internal assets necessary to build and operate the platform that makes up this hub, assuring a continuous, high-speed, two-way flow of information between its key customers and its supply base. Dell thus orchestrates the combined operations of its business ecosystem, connecting the assets of its supplier base to the needs of its customers. Despite having the least assets, Dell maintains the greatest supply chain velocity in its industry, responding to market demand much faster than its competitors.

The architecture of Dell's business network is key to its business model (see figure 8-3). It effectively divides the world into two parts: the tightly coupled core of Dell's operation platform, and the loosely coupled components that connect to Dell's customers. The interfaces connect to a variety of different systems, ranging from traditional enterprise resource planning (ERP) systems such as SAP to more recent Web-based solutions such as Ariba.

The architecture has been robust enough to endure a variety of technological transitions—from client/server systems to the Web, and from the Web to Web services. In essence, each technological transition was managed by the addition of new interfaces, which connected the stable operating core to a variety of novel technologies and interface types. The core of the platform has thus remained consistent over the last ten years, evolving through the incremental addition of new functionality.

Dell's architectural interfaces enable the organization to design its operations to integrate its assets with a diversity of new and old customers. They make it as simple as possible to exchange customized information with a variety of firms and form a critical foundation for its operating model.

Architecture and Ecosystem Dynamics

The architecture of products and services has a profound effect on the evolution of ecosystems. Well-managed platforms shape ecosystem dynamics as they grow to incorporate new functionality and create opportunities for keystones to expand their ecosystems; new platforms arise that threaten established ones, and entrenched and poorly maintained platforms age and become irrelevant.

How a platform evolves and responds over time shapes the ecosystem that depends on it: what firms survive, where diversity can

FIGURE 8-3

The Architecture of a Critical Part of Dell's Information Platform

The platform includes a tightly coupled core and an ability to interface with a variety of enterprise resource planning (ERP) systems.

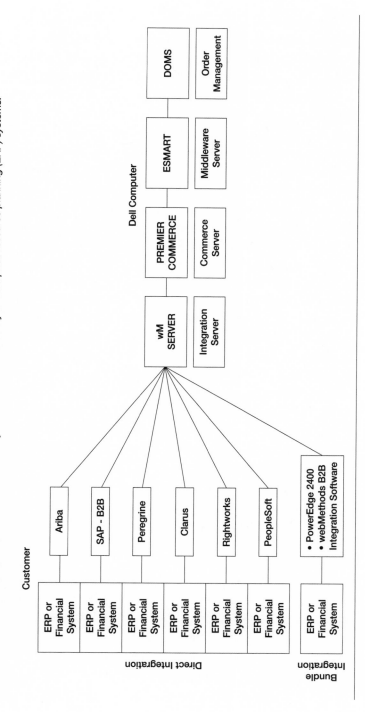

exist, what will be easy to do and what will be hard, which things in the ecosystem will do well with little effort, and which things will be challenging. This happens because platforms serve as an intermediary between the underlying technology and the ways in which it can be easily exploited. They define the "language" in which problems and opportunities are expressed and thus profoundly influence what problems are important and where those problems lie. Wal-Mart's platform, for example, set the stage for the impact of consumer information on performance in the retail sector. TSMC's and IBM's technology road maps have become central to the evolution of the semiconductor industry.

The powerful influence of platforms can lead to confusion and outright hostility when they produce the appearance of dominating behavior by the keystones that define and maintain them, or lead to harsh criticism when large and powerful platforms seem to stifle improvements and creativity. For example, an accusation often leveled against Microsoft is that it crushes companies that could be potential platform competitors, especially makers of so-called middleware.

To the extent that meaningful differences among products are inseparable from the rest of a product or technology, proliferation of multiple middleware competitors outside the scope of the platform can usefully continue; at some point, however, a significant portion of functionality has stabilized and can be incorporated into the platform—it *belongs* in the platform. The accretion of new functionality into platforms and the increasing integration of once-distinct functions is an inexorable trend. As we will see in chapter 9, this process of integration is a common component of both technological evolution and biological evolution. The process benefits almost all ecosystem members—but at the expense of firms (or specific implementations) that position themselves too close to the frontier of the platform without preparing for the consequences. As platforms grow in the range of functionality they support, and as once-new functionality becomes increasingly stable and tightly integrated into the platform, firms that staked out terrain at the frontier of the platform will be absorbed as the frontier shifts outward. This is the fundamental reason why, for example, so many software middleware firms have failed to scale as independent entities.

This argument is naturally of enormous consequence for niche players. Understanding the nature of the platform on which they depend and the likely evolution of its boundary is paramount. Effectively, the growth of the platform drives niche players away from the established core, which can be healthy for the ecosystem as a whole: It impels them to seek the frontier of innovation and look for where specialized expertise is required. Strong and expanding platforms will thus push innovation and exploration into areas that might otherwise not be served, partly by lowering barriers to entry into those areas (by providing foundations) but also simply because they are the only "safe" places to be.

The expansion of platforms also provides a way for different ecosystems to become connected to each other as they grow not only in terms of the functionality they support but also in terms of the markets they serve. Examples include the expansion of Windows and Linux into the telecommunications sector. Although threatening to many ecosystem members, platform expansion has significant benefits. These include not just opening up new markets, but also leveraging shared experience, transferring user models (e.g., similar user interfaces on PocketPC and PC devices), and using similar APIs on multiple targets (e.g., the ability to use the .NET frameworks to target both mobile devices and PCs using significant amounts of shared code).

The process of platform expansion is an important way for ecosystems to grow. However, it is important to understand that this growth can happen at the expense of other ecosystems or potential ecosystems. To the extent that Microsoft, for example, is able to make inroads into telephony, the established businesses of existing firms in that domain, from Nokia to Lucent, may be threatened. But consumers seeking consistent experience and integration—and firms in the Microsoft ecosystem seeking new opportunities—will benefit.

Managing Platforms

Platforms are only effective if they are widely used. The best platforms, those that become the foundation of a vast and varied ecosystem of products and activities, must create numerous opportunities for ecosystem members, must be understood and accepted by those who use them, and must evolve and expand in step with the capabilities of the underlying technologies (see figure 8-4).

Provide Solutions to General Problems

Platforms, to have any use at all, must unlock the potential of the underlying technology on which an ecosystem is organized or solve fundamental shared problems faced by members of the ecosystem. Microsoft's beginnings are telling: Its first product was not a complex operating system, but a relatively simple programming tool—a way of unlocking the potential of computers for a vastly wider audience than had previously been possible. Similarly, the beginnings of Wal-Mart's extensive multiterabyte Retail Link system were simple opportunities for sharing hard-to-get information. In both cases the focus was on making it easier for a community to solve problems.

Balance Implementation and Interface Design

The problem-solving focus should be the primary initial function of a platform that forms the basis of a keystone strategy, and should remain a guiding principle in platform design and evolution: What new features, tools, or concepts will be most effective in helping ecosystem members solve problems efficiently? What distinguishes one platform from another is the way it provides these solutions: the strength of the implementation and the expressive power of the interface. This is where the challenge for keystones lies. An effective keystone must strike a balance in its allocation of effort between perfecting the implementation and structuring the interface, while at the same time constantly evolving both the capabilities of the platform and the domains in which it applies.

Windows is typical of platforms that have been effective by advancing their technological frontiers, often at the expense of not improving the details of their technological plumbing. In a rapidly changing technological environment, it makes sense to neglect low-level optimizations to focus on expanding the platform's capabilities and improving its interfaces. As a consequence, platforms (like living systems) may accumulate inefficiencies, idiosyncrasies, and weaknesses that are the

FIGURE 8-4

Platform Architecture in Context

Although often portrayed as a simple "stack," platforms show considerable change in the diversity of solutions and approaches as one moves up or down the platform hierarchy.

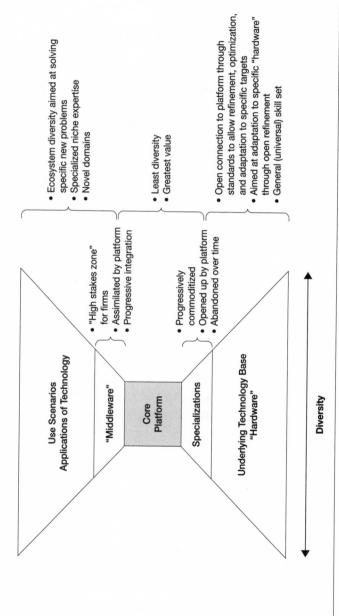

result of the historical evolution of the platform's functionality and that cannot be easily revisited or repaired. Moreover, if the platform has advanced significantly beyond these foundations, there may be little incentive to do so: All the perceived advantages and value of the platform are at higher levels.

Selectively Open the Platform to Balance
Distributed Innovation with Control Needs

One particularly thorny issue faced by keystones in this context is the extent to which they should retain control over the different levels of their platforms. As discussed earlier, these tend to become commodities over time, in the sense that the problems they solve are increasingly well understood by a wide audience at the same time that their age may begin to show as the platform faces new challenges or expands into new domains. The best way for a keystone to face these challenges may ironically be to "let go" of the lower levels of the platform: to open them up to adaptation and modification by a large segment of the ecosystem. For example, Microsoft has opened up Windows CE source code to enable better tuning to specific devices. This process represents an important opportunity for keystones, but one that may be difficult to see in light of the apparent loss of control it entails.

Identifying the right parts to open up or break off in this way is especially challenging because of the risks involved: The keystone exposes itself to losing control of its platform if it gives away the wrong parts. In this context it is important for keystones to recognize that different parts of the platform contribute unequally to its overall value. The parts that a keystone should seek to retain control of should sit on the locus of highest value; the rest can be outside the platform—"above" in niche players in the ecosystem, "below" in specialization, and "hard-coded" in commoditized components.

Shape Your Ecosystem

Finally, keystones need to be keenly aware that platforms provide them with a critical opportunity to shape and control their ecosystems. As participants in the Visa network or in the Li & Fung retail system invest in the systems and capabilities required to integrate and leverage the ecosystem's powerful shared assets, their fate will become increasingly shared with that of the platform. They will incur switching costs that provide an incentive to remain loyal to their keystone. This will in turn provide the keystones with a crucial level of predictability in the evolution of their business networks.

Keystones must not overestimate the power of the switching costs they engender. As technologies evolve toward increasingly open standards in environments ranging from computing to payment, the opportunities for niche players to leverage multiple platforms have expanded, which provides an enormous incentive for keystones to keep increasing the value created and shared by their platforms. Continuously creating value for ecosystem members is a much more sustainable strategy for keystones than relying on switching costs that, sooner or later, are bound to evaporate.

Niche players play a critical role in helping to shape platforms. Their participation in the design of interfaces is essential not only for improving the quality and relevance of the platform for real problems, which are the domain of niche players, but also for shaping the platform architecture so as to ward off potential threats to the niche players' mobility among platforms. Ultimately, niche players vote with their feet and switch away from established platforms if these do not provide the enduring value niche players need. This alone has an enormous influence in shaping platform evolution over time.

Implications for Managing Products

Product design is becoming to an increasing extent the art of leveraging platforms. The implications are many and have been discussed throughout this book, but it is worth highlighting a few key ideas.

Leverage Platforms Provided by Others but Manage Switching Costs

Above all, firms in an ecosystem should be aggressive about using platforms to the greatest possible advantage. Efficiency and productivity in an ecosystem are to a large extent determined by the effectiveness of niche players in taking advantage of the solutions that the platforms provide and in understanding the potential embodied in their interfaces. As they strive to leverage a platform, the best and most effective niche players must watch for two subtleties. First, despite what we have said about the invisibility of the implementation, niche players should keep a wary eye out for potential pitfalls and problems buried deep in the platform. Second, in pursuing the kind of platform-neutral niche strategy outlined in chapter 7, niche players need to avoid platform idiosyncrasies that make it harder for them to move between platforms or to support multiple platforms. Niche players should be aggressive about using the platform to save costs and to solve problems, but at the same time they should take care to avoid excessive reliance on *aspects* of the platform that surrender control over the fate of their application or product to the keystone.

Invest in Understanding the Architecture and Dynamics of the Platforms That You Use

Product design in a business ecosystem is a challenging task: Cost saving, efficiency, and smoother integration with the ecosystem drive toward a greater reliance on the platform, but the need to maintain a degree of independence and identity pushes in the other direction. Product design in a distributed environment is a *strategic* task—the dependencies built through everyday design decisions shape the future of firms. Niche players should thus invest in a deep understanding of platform design and dynamics, going beyond what is immediately necessary to design their specific product. This investment will pay off in spades by building critical expertise in the dependencies that are created and in strategies for managing switching costs.

Beware of the Platform Frontier

Ecosystem players that do not control a platform must understand platform design because they need to avoid its frontier unless they are prepared to be integrated into the platform. As the marketing director of one firm whose domain was assimilated by a platform (in this case,

Apple) puts it: "It's an unfortunate but natural part of the business. We know that if we do something that will make sense for them to add to the operating system, they probably will. Our goal is to stay ahead of them, to make our product better than whatever they're adding."[8]

Niche players that hope to survive and remain independent over the long term should stake out domains that lie as far as possible from the platform or that are highly specialized in terms of the market they serve or the technical expertise they require. Firms that find themselves close to a frontier may want to take steps that make them attractive acquisitions: playing along with the platform, becoming as compatible with both the implementation and the interface philosophy as possible, while simultaneously focusing on creating value in the domain in which they specialize. An alternative strategy for niche players is to become a keystone in their own domain, as NVIDIA has done for computer graphics. This is a challenging approach, but provides a bulwark against easy duplication by the keystone's platform and improves the chances of being in a strong position if assimilated—or provides a defense against irrelevance should the keystone attempt to duplicate the niche player's functionality.

Architecture and Standards

Standards play a crucial architectural role in a business ecosystem and deserve separate mention in this discussion. Hardly a day seems to go by without Microsoft or IBM announcing support for the latest standard, and tussles over who owns or controls a standard are almost as frequent. Standards are an elusive concept, however. Although they command considerable attention, they often seem surprisingly simple when examined closely. Money, perhaps the most important standard of all, is really nothing more than an accepted standard for bookkeeping—it has no content and no intrinsic value outside the context of its use.[9] XML, one of the latest promising families of standards in computing, is touted as a solution to just about everything—from separating data and its visualization on Web pages to transforming the entire World Wide Web into a huge distributed application—yet on close examination it is really nothing more than a simple set of rules for structuring information in text files.[10] Despite their simplicity, standards are a critical part of what makes ecosystems work: They are an essential tool for structuring ecosystems and an instrument used by influential players to exert power over others.

A *standard* is an interface that facilitates interoperability. This interoperability can be between organizations (as between the FBI and the CIA or between a firm's purchasing department and its human resources organization), between devices or technologies (as between a personal computer and a gaming console, or a digital camera and a television), or between data formats (such as different types of XML).[11] The usefulness of a standard is that it empowers participants in a network to interact with each other and to sustain those interactions over time even when their internal details change. Additionally, the best standards allow for growth in the nature of the exchanges that occur across interfaces, so that the same standard that is used on one setting or at one time can continue to be used when new demands are placed on it.

Perhaps surprisingly, this interoperability is often best achieved by simple designs. Often these appear as nothing more than a simple agreement about the language or currency of exchange among participants: the shape of a plug, the layout of a form, the format of a data file, or the order of values passed to a function call in a software program.

Standards are distinct from interfaces in general, and specifically from the kinds of interfaces used to package and provide access to platform capabilities. This distinction is important because it figures prominently in the subtleties of the role of standards for keystones. Interfaces that structure and provide access to platforms, such as APIs, are clearly a part of the value-sharing strategy of keystones and as such represent an obvious component of the way they shape their ecosystems. We will call these *access interfaces*. But standards, which can be thought of as *interoperability interfaces,* are quite different. In a sense they are orthogonal: Access interfaces shape the interactions between a platform and all others in the ecosystem built around that platform, whereas standards facilitate direct interactions among ecosystem members. This is the conundrum of standards: At first glance they would seem to undermine a keystone's ability to shape and control its ecosystem. In effect, they insert a publicly visible, open, and nonproprietary step in the connections among ecosystem members. Instead, for example, of requiring two software programs to use a proprietary Microsoft format for exchanges, which would demand an "all-Microsoft" connection between these programs, using XML means that even if both applications are running on Windows and both use Windows APIs to emit and consume XML, there is an intermediate step that anyone can potentially implement. Because the XML specification is public, it would seem to undermine Microsoft's "control." But this is not the whole story.

Standards are also a way of expanding the reach of the platform—increasing its functionality and enhancing its grip over those that depend on it. The act of identifying a place where standards can be "meaningful" is also the act of figuring out how to expand the platform's potential scope. The more general the standard, the greater its scope; the more specific vertical instances (under the umbrella of an encompassing standard) are explicitly supported, the more attractive the standard. One way of increasing scope is to provide standards that improve the opportunities for ecosystem participants to interact easily with others. The most powerful standards lower barriers for interoperability across the widest possible set of domains, even across different ecosystems. By enabling such wide-reaching interactions, the importance of the platform and its capacity to shape an increasingly large ecosystem are increased.

This is a critical point and one that is perhaps best appreciated through an example. Before XML, each application was essentially on its own with respect to deciding how to format structured data. Applications either supported one or more explicit proprietary formats (such as dBase, Access, Oracle, FileMaker, etc.) or de facto rudimentary standards (CSV, tab-delimited text, or even Windows "ini"), or they defined their own application-specific format. In almost all cases each application embodied the code for handling all of the critical semantics of the structured data from scratch. This had a critical consequence from the perspective of the software keystones: Their platforms were not being used to handle structured data. APIs for reading and writing data to files were being embedded in one proprietary application after another to solve a general problem. This was a lose-lose situation because application developers were writing more code than they should, and platforms were providing less value than they potentially could.[12]

The standardization of XML has the potential to create a dramatically different picture, but not for the immediately obvious reason. The "win" that is often cited for XML is that applications can now share data and interoperate more easily, but the critical win from the perspective of the relationship between keystones and those that rely on them is that the value of the platform has grown, as has its grip over those who use it. By providing extensive support for XML, Microsoft, for example, has not only made it easier for applications to handle structured data, but has also taken control of the details of managing that data. Huge chunks of proprietary code are now gone, replaced with a series of calls to Microsoft's XML APIs. These APIs *are* proprietary and moreover are embedded in a huge constellation of other APIs with which they interact and interoperate. The consequence is that to the extent that applications leverage Microsoft APIs and tools to adopt XML (a truly open standard), they contain much less platform-indifferent proprietary code and can thus be more tightly bound to the Windows platform (which is proprietary). This is the irony that leads to so much confusion about the role of standards in ecosystems: They have the potential to enhance the role of keystones. In fact, the more general and flexible the standard, the more potential it has to do so, because the more generic and broadly applicable the underlying standard, the more complex and widely employed the supporting APIs can be.[13]

This explains why the naive expectations that standards could lead to keystones "losing" ecosystem members are often unfounded. The platform's support for a standard, as long as it truly adds value to ecosystem participants, makes it more attractive to use that standard than a proprietary implementation. This can make it harder for ecosystem members to switch platforms. These considerations mean that ecosystem participants should be very savvy in how they manage standards.

Managing Standards

To be effective, standards should be as broadly applicable as possible and solve ubiquitous problems. In this context it is important to appreciate that the goals of keystones and other ecosystem players are aligned: Both want the most widely applicable, generally useful standards and both seek to establish them in precisely those domains where they will be most widely used. The motives of keystones and other players are distinct, however. Whereas most ecosystem members seek standards to simplify common tasks and interoperate with others, keystones endorse standards so that the value and importance of the platform is enhanced. This difference in motives has important and distinct implications for keystones and niche players that shape the kinds of standards they should endorse, and influence the way they implement and use standards.

Appeal to the Widest Audience

From the perspective of both keystones and other ecosystem members, an essential requirement of a meaningful standard is that it appeal to the widest possible audience. For a keystone, the desire is for the standard to lead to almost universal adoption of its platform. In this way, the standard serves as a broad-based method of solving a common problem—it impels other ecosystem members to adopt a (literally) standardized solution. Think of it this way: From Microsoft's perspective, the situation in which everybody was defining and writing their own code to handle structured data was a threat to the reach and longevity of its platform. What Microsoft in effect needed was a way to say "You should use this format and you should use our APIs." A standard lets Microsoft have the same effect by instead saying "Here's the best possible open format and we'll make it easy for you to use." From a keystone's perspective, good standards are decrees in disguise because they satisfy the first part of this goal: They specify a standard approach to solving a large class of problems.

Match Powerful Platforms with Powerful Standards

The second part of a keystone's goals in endorsing standards—ensuring that others use its platform to achieve compliance with the standard—is achieved though careful design of platform components that support the standard and through careful selection of standards that have the right level of richness. Overly simple standards, such as CSV or tab-delimited text for representing data, are often problematic for platforms. Not only do such standards have limited capabilities, but they also are simple to implement and thus create little incentive for reliance on the platform for ease of compliance. There aren't a lot of ways in which keystones can add value beyond the standard itself. Rich standards with many subtleties and a wide range of potential expressiveness and nuances are what a keystone typically seeks. Again, XML is an excellent example. While it famously represents a lightweight solution to a wide range of complex problems, which allows its specification to be relatively simple, it also creates the potential for a complex implementation of those solutions and the opportunity for an endless array of specific adaptations to different tasks (from XSL to SOAP). Such standards allow keystones to create significant functionality to support them, and make it possible for them to add a large number of truly useful platform components to provide this support.

Integrate Tools to Implement Popular Standards into the Platform

These motivations have important consequences. They force keystones to compete on the things they do best: not bundling proprietary instances of general solutions but building effective tools for *implementing* them, packaging and structuring access to them, and identifying and defining meaningful standards that allow them to do this. This sets up a potentially win-win dynamic. Firms such as Amazon.com, Google, or eBay cannot simply rely on their dominant positions to ensure their continued success. They recognize that they need to make their solutions available in a convenient form to the widest possible audience. In doing so they hope to ultimately define the idioms of expression for their respective domains, which means that they must focus on the quality of that language and the capabilities it enables. Google's and Amazon's Web services–based tools and APIs not only extend the reach of these firms' technologies but also define a new arena for competition among different search or retail firms: the quality, breadth, and effectiveness of their platforms and the standards they embody.

Beware of Losing Key Capabilities

Once a standard is selected, organizations need to be constantly aware of an important dynamic set up by standards. To the extent that the standards are complex and powerful, and to the extent that keystones provide useful abstractions that simplify their implementation (both good things for niche players *and* keystones), other players risk losing contact with the details of the standard. The standard becomes a given, which must be supported, but the platform remains the gateway to its actual implementation. Increasingly, for example, developers become expert not in XML per se, but in the platform APIs used to manipulate XML. It is therefore crucial for all players in an ecosystem to invest in an understanding of the structure of the standards they leverage and to understand their implications for the more subtle dependencies they create and for the value of the products on which they focus.

The Connecting Fabric

Fundamentally, platforms and standards serve as the connecting fabric of an ecosystem. They draw the boundaries and define the relationships among its members. They serve as a framework for them to share value and are fundamental to the functioning of the network. Despite the power and pervasiveness of platforms and standards, however, we do not live in a Legolike world. Collaboration between ecosystem members is not frictionless. Major efforts are still needed for the *integration* of different capabilities and components to be effective. This is the topic of the next chapter.

CHAPTER NINE

Integration, Innovation, and Adaptation

Integration is the second foundation for competition in a business ecosystem. Given the dispersed nature of assets and organizations, it is almost tautological to say that integration capability has become essential to innovation. This capability is not only important to ordinary design activities, but also crucial in times characterized by significant innovation and organizational adaptation.

From Empire to Keystone

In April 1999, IBM stunned the computer establishment by announcing a partnership with Red Hat Software, thereby making the Linux operating system integral to IBM strategy. Abandoning its tradition of internal R&D, IBM tied its destiny to an asset developed and maintained by thousands of independent programmers scattered from India to Finland. Linux is completely different from traditional IBM products. Not only is it licensed differently, but it's architected differently, developed differently, sold differently, and maintained differently, and its application follows a different business model. In a stunning reversal, what was once considered to be the quintessential internal R&D empire began to integrate the capabilities of a completely dispersed innovation network.

In December 2000, IBM stunned observers again by announcing it would invest $1 billion in Linux development and in complementary products and services. The investments ramped up IBM's efforts to integrate Linux with its product and service offerings, ensuring its compatibility with a variety of IBM hardware and software platforms. IBM became a keystone for the Linux community. It invested in Linux foundations, worked on tools and complementary technologies, developed a highly effective enterprise sales channel for open source software, and provided robustness to Linux companies by essentially guaranteeing their products.

Since that time, IBM has worked hard to integrate Linux and other open source technologies with its businesses, in areas ranging from telecommunications to retail. It has developed deep connections with the open source community, created processes to collaborate with it and integrate its innovations, shaped architectural decisions around standards, and internalized a variety of capabilities that were previously largely external to the firm.

With these decisions and investments, IBM de facto transformed Linux from an intriguing novelty into the foundation for a leading enterprise IT platform. The strategy has proven quite effective. IBM has shaped and extended an immensely valuable and powerful ecosystem asset. In doing so, it leveraged Linux to sell a variety of integrated products and services, ranging from its WebSphere enterprise software suite to consulting and support offerings. Through this evolution, IBM has rejoined the leadership of the computer industry, providing, along with Microsoft, one of its two leading platforms.

Integration Capability

Integration capability is an organization's capacity to combine the impact of different competencies, both internal and external to the firm. This capacity affects a variety of key business processes, influencing both innovation and day-to-day operations, effectively tying together old and new capabilities. If platforms provide a base on which to construct new products and services, integration provides the glue with which to add new concepts and technologies. We start by discussing the fundamental importance of integration in networks, and go on to discuss the specific nature of integration in business.

Networks and Integration

Business operations are not alone in showcasing the importance of integration in a networked context. The literature on the evolution of complex systems provides a look at some intriguing similarities. Much of this literature examines the ways in which networks of loosely interconnected and often independent entities become increasingly interdependent and integrated over time. From the evolution of social insect "superorganisms" from solitary ancestors to the creation of the cellular machinery of animals and plants from once independent bacterial precursors, this literature highlights the fact that a process of increasingly tight integration creates a powerful, stable core around which new, loosely coupled entities can be built.[1] Indeed, many of the novel capabilities often popularly attributed to distributed networks in general are dependent upon the existence of a tightly integrated and evolving core around which the loosely connected network of agents operates.

The stunning information gathering and processing capabilities of honey bee colonies, for example, are predicated on "integration processes," through which critical information is exchanged in tightly confined spaces using a language that is simple and entirely hardwired.[2] Moreover, the mere fact of cooperation at the level required for such free exchange of information is only possible because of the near genetic identity of the apparently independent agents.[3] The entire notion of "independence" in the sense that we appreciate it is completely absent from almost all natural systems that exhibit "swarm intelligence." The notion of "self" exists only at the level of the centralized invisible forces governing the tight integration of the colony unit that are a prerequisite for the more conspicuous distributed networks of interactions we actually see.

Integration is often an elusive concept. We are generally unaware that a process of progressive integration of previously separate components has led to much of the rich complexity and remarkable capabilities of the natural world. This is largely because once-distinct components are obscured by their current tight integration, so that we often lack even words for describing them as separate entities. The intricately complex machinery of our cells, to cite just one example, is assembled from a huge array of once-independent components over a wide range of scales, from free-living bacteria (our present mitochondria) to self-replicating RNA fragments (the likely precursors of important parts of our genetic machinery).

Despite the difficulty in discussing these as separate components, it is instructive to imagine what the world would be like today—specifically, what biological systems as a whole would be capable of—if the process of integration had been obstructed at some point in the ancient past. Instead of towering trees that store sunlight in chemical bonds, insects that can build arches and farm fungus or build towering perfectly air-conditioned structures, or brains that can execute landings on the moon, life would still be a flat soup of self-replicating chemical fragments. As a whole, then, the evolution literature suggests both that the capacity for creating novel functions is an important measure of system health and, critically, that the process of integration is an important way of achieving such novelty.[4]

Technology Integration

The evolution literature resonates with business literature on technology integration, which highlights the importance of innovation through integration and recombination.[5] Technology integration literature argues that in an ecosystem, products are the combination of a vast variety of technologies, components, or processes. Innovations can therefore not be identified with a single isolated invention, but are instead the integration of a multitude of different inventions with existing product and process components. As with the natural analogies, this process of technological evolution gives rise to tightly integrated combinations of assets, which enable increasingly powerful loosely connected networks of agents.

Take the commercialization of graphical computing, for example. This was not the result of a single technological development, localized within a single organization, but of integrated advances from a large variety of sources. These advances included the invention of the mouse (which dates back to Douglas Engelbart at SRI in the 1960s), the graphical user interface (which has its roots in a variety of projects at Xerox and at SRI), a set of critical application programs (developed at Xerox, Apple, and other companies), and a broad range of advances in semiconductor component technology (dispersed across the industry).[6] These (and many other) individual inventions were combined to form the integrated solution that makes up modern personal computer platforms. The PC in turn has enabled a broad, loosely connected community of organizations (the independent software vendors) to produce a massive number of related innovations, ranging from the financial spreadsheet to flight simulator games.

From software to retail, the process of technology integration provides a critical engine of business evolution, as the capabilities and technological components provided by ecosystem participants are recombined to create constantly improving product and service offerings. The process is critical to dominators, which must constantly integrate new assets into their operations; to keystone organizations, which need to tightly integrate the latest technological developments into the platforms they provide; and to the niche players, which integrate components provided by the keystones and by other technology providers into their own offerings.

When Microsoft made the decision to turn Internet Explorer 3.0 (its first internally developed Internet browser) into components in 1996, the decision was essential to renew its platform and sustain its keystone strategy. In this way, Microsoft ISVs such as Intuit Corporation or AutoDesk could integrate Internet Explorer 3.0 components in order to Web-enable their individual applications, rapidly turning the diffusion of the World Wide Web from a threat to a business opportunity.

Mastering Integration

Integration is not a simple challenge. Many authors have highlighted how difficult it is for established organizations to renew themselves and integrate new, fundamentally different capabilities.[7] History is replete with stories of firms' failure in the face of discontinuous changes in technology and business models. Much of our own research confirms this view. Indeed, in studies of integration capability performed over the last ten years in over a hundred firms, we witnessed dramatic performance differences. We saw projects aimed at very similar integration challenges that were characterized by differences of more than a factor of two in speed and productivity. This variation was critical to the firms. In several cases, the projects that were at the poor end of the performance spectrum caused drastic outcomes, such as industry exit and firm failure.

Although mastering integration is difficult, there is no good alternative for an established firm. Plenty of research has shown that individual, autonomous efforts are not likely to be effective in building large, scalable businesses in a complex setting.[8] Sooner or later, the challenge of integration will have to be confronted. Our research has highlighted several critical drivers of integration capability, which cut across both process and organizational design.

Process

It is a fundamental tenet in management theory that organizations reflect in many ways the systems they create.[9] This implies that tightly integrated organizations will produce tightly integrated systems, and vice versa. In essence, this means that the organizational process for integration should match its architectural constraints. Designing across tightly coupled interfaces will be accomplished best by the use of focused core teams, whereas designing across loosely coupled interfaces may be left to loosely coupled communities.

Although our research has shown that focused core teams can have a great track record in designing integrated products, it is important to emphasize that the process for managing that team should not keep the team isolated from its external environment. The knowledge base necessary to make decisions, even within the core design of a platform, is much broader than the expertise that can be contained by the team itself. This knowledge base is increasingly dispersed among a variety of sources, both internal and external to the firm. An effective integration process thus has its roots in active, broad-based, external scanning to generate needed information and in focused, committed teamwork for execution.

The best news for managers in a networked industry is that the sources of key technologies and operating capabilities are many and readily available. When Walgreens had to build a new Internet retail channel, countless enterprise software companies and systems integrators were available to provide the needed assets and competencies. The company had to build very little from scratch. Even in the more recent technology downturn, the sources of new technology are still many and varied, and established firms are, if anything, in a better bargaining position. Companies therefore have an ever-present need for a strong process for evaluating options offered by technology providers, selecting the most promising ones, and implementing them to evolve their ongoing operations.

This process for technology integration has as its central objective the fusion of knowledge about existing operations with knowledge of new possibilities. This knowledge is typically embedded in people and systems scattered across the ecosystem, ranging from customers to internal experts, and from external consultants to technology suppliers. Despite the broad reach needed, the best processes witnessed in our research were managed by a focused team of players. In businesses as varied as semiconductors and consumer products, the best integration processes were led by a focused team of managers embodying a diverse range of experience, which we have called the "integration group" in past work.[10] Their role is to assemble the required knowledge base, understand how new possibilities will affect the existing operation, design the architecture of the future operation, and drive implementation. Although they need not implement all activities (and should in fact leverage as much external expertise as possible), this integration team should define the architecture of the solution, drive the process, and ensure its coherence over time.

This team is crucial to integration because capabilities scattered across a dispersed ecosystem can offer a variety of interesting options but cannot by themselves design the integrated core of a system. Suppliers cannot define the best IT architecture for Dell or dictate how Walgreens should interface its Internet channel with traditional fulfillment. Even in organizations as diffuse as the open source software community, decision making about the Linux core is focused on a very small group of architects, led by Linus Torvalds. This is not a passive process: This key group of players is central to any major decision and actively shapes the future of the software.

Even at this high level of generality, these ideas about integration processes have fundamental implications for firms. They imply, first of all, that a company (following any of the strategies outlined throughout this book) should not leave key decisions about integration to external players. In turn, this implies that an organization should acquire and retain the people required to make those decisions. All too often, we have witnessed how companies, during ill-fated cost-cutting efforts, have let go of critical talent who were knowledgeable about how their supply chain or retail systems actually functioned. In the words of an executive at the Ford Motor Company, "with past cost cutting efforts, we have let go of so many people that understand our supply chain system that we no longer have the strong capabilities we need to understand how the whole system works."[11] It is thus crucial that companies do not mistakenly destroy critical knowledge of systems and capabilities. As the business environment becomes more distributed, and more external assets can be leveraged, the knowledge of how these assets affect current operations is, if anything, more important and more complex than ever before.

Organization

The need to retain and constantly evolve a base of integrative knowledge has important implications for structuring both innovation and operations. Traditional lore argues that established operations are often fraught with inertia and that innovation typically thrives in autonomous organizations.[12] Following these ideas, managers have found a number of ways to create largely autonomous groups to foster innovation when an established firm is faced with disruptive technological or business threats. One such group is a corporate "spin-off," created by setting up a separate, external corporate entity, often with additional venture capital backing; these were particularly popular during the Internet bubble.

Table 9-1 highlights a continuum of options for an established firm that wishes to design an organization aimed at integrating new capabilities into its established business, and notes some implications for integration. As we go from traditional R&D toward increasingly independent organizational forms, it is crucial not to lose sight of the

TABLE 9-1

A Continuum of Approaches to Managing Major Technological Transitions

Type of Approach	Characteristics of Approach	Examples	Implications for Integration
Independent venture	Only relationship to original firm is investment.	Ventures in Kleiner's Java Fund	Not recommended if integration is the ultimate goal, since capabilities and incentives are totally separated from parent firm.
Joint venture or consortium	Independent but part-owned by initiating firm(s).	Covisint, WorldWide Retail Exchange	Create plans and capabilities for integration at the outset to counteract differences in capabilities and incentives. Prepare to face substantial integration challenges.
Autonomous venture	Autonomous company or wholly owned subsidiary. Although part of the original firm, this venture is designed to maximize independence.	Strategic business unit, CVS.com	Create plans and capabilities for integration at the outset to counteract differences in capabilities and incentives. Prepare to face substantial integration challenges.
Internal venture	Separate business with own P&L responsibility that is encouraged to leverage existing infrastructure when appropriate.	e-Schwab	Seed business with experts on existing assets and capabilities and strong contacts with parent organization. Create early plans and expectations for integration in selective key areas.
Integration team	Although the entire product development team is not separated, it is led by a strong team of dedicated integrators that own the system and pull the product together.	Merrill Lynch, Walgreens	Staff integration team with a combination of experts in new and old capabilities. Push team to innovate out of existing constraints, but also to integrate selectively with key existing assets.
Traditional R&D	Product development effort is conducted strictly within the functions, with at most lightweight coordination between functional subunits.	Bell Laboratories, Xerox PARC	Not recommended. It is usually very challenging for a dispersed R&D organization to focus on major architectural or disruptive changes.

increasingly difficult integration challenges. These challenges can be fatal, as our research shows (see figure 9-1). Of a sample of thirty major spin-offs performed in response to the Internet after 1997, *none* was left as a functioning autonomous unit by 2001. Most of the organizations were reintegrated. Those that could not be integrated with the parent (because of enduring architectural or organizational differences) were shut down.

These considerations leave us with a significant challenge. There is no question that the management of innovation efforts during substantial technological or business discontinuities is difficult, and that the creation of an independent, autonomous organization can aid in execution speed, especially in the early stages of an effort. However, the ultimate goal is almost always the integration of new capabilities with existing assets.

FIGURE 9-1

The Performance of E-Commerce Ventures Launched by Incumbent Firms

Of a sample of thirty external ventures launched by leading bricks-and-mortar firms that we identified by searching through Forrester, ABI/Inform, PROMT, and Dow Jones Interactive databases, 78 percent were subsequently reintegrated (typically with significant integration costs and general turmoil), and the remaining 22 percent were shut down. As of April 2002, none of the ventures in the sample was left standing.

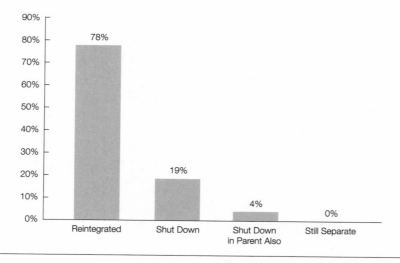

Integration in Action

The following examples highlight some critical lessons in performing this integration well. The Cisco example illustrates an internal effort, whereas the Schwab example depicts a more independent venture.

Integration at Cisco

Cisco Systems has managed sustained growth in an environment fraught with high levels of turbulence and innovation. In spite of being in the middle of one of the world's most technologically sophisticated businesses, Cisco has traditionally de-emphasized internal research and has instead adopted a strategy of integrating innovation from a variety of external sources. These capabilities have enabled the company to sustain its leadership through a variety of discontinuities in technology and business drivers, ranging from the adoption of the World Wide Web to the bursting of the dot-com balloon. Despite getting hurt by the collapse of a large part of its ecosystem, as described in chapter 3, the company has reemerged in a position of leadership.

Cisco has traditionally emphasized integration in both operations and product development. Its operating model leverages the assets of a distributed community of suppliers and channel partners (resembling the Dell model discussed in the previous chapter), enabling it to achieve one of the highest figures of sales per employee in its industry. These organizations are linked through a sophisticated information technology platform that shares market information to sharpen the collective forecasting capabilities of the network.

Cisco also emphasizes integration capability in its acquisition process and in product development. Its process of product development is built on five foundations: a culture of empowerment and execution for small innovation teams; clear decisions on project justification, commitment, and resourcing (known as the "Commit Process"); a clear, flexible process for technology integration and product development (known as "GEM," or Great Engineering Methodologies); a cadre of highly experienced architects and engineers with a track record of multiple product shipments; and an aggressively open approach to partnering for technology development. These foundations enable Cisco to leverage a variety of internal and external technologies to revitalize and expand its product line.

One of the lesser known examples of Cisco's approach to integration is the way it revolutionized the cable equipment industry. The leadership in this effort was provided by Carson Chen, a long-time Cisco engineering manager, previously responsible for developing a number of Cisco's most successful core routers. Upon returning from a sabbatical, Chen was seeking something new to get involved in and was offered the opportunity to lead a small team that would investigate Cisco's entry into the cable equipment business. The team launched an investigation of the current market, which was dominated by Motorola, with over 70 percent market share. At the time, the equipment market was vertically integrated, with proprietary standards between the cable modem termination system (CMTS) installed at cable service provider sites and the cable modem deployed in consumer households. Chen's team sensed that an open protocol between the CMTS and cable modems could revolutionize the industry. An open protocol between the CMTS and modems would decouple the two systems and enable a range of different modems to interoperate with the same CMTS, which would open up the possibilities for dramatic cost reduction and performance improvement, as well as create an opportunity for Cisco to become the dominant platform. In essence, this architectural innovation had an effect similar to the shift in computing model from a mainframe with dedicated software and terminals to a personal computer with an open interface that enabled a wide variety of hardware to interoperate with a wide variety of software.

Chen's team gathered steam and was greatly influenced by a white paper, sponsored by the cable industry standards association, that described how a standard interface could be designed. It immediately went after the realization of this idea. Still not satisfied with their approach, however, the team lined up meetings with every major service provider's chief technical officer (CTO) in the cable industry. The CTOs further validated the idea and provided a wealth of feedback on Cisco's proposed implementation.

To maximize the speed and efficiency of the effort, Chen's team integrated a number of traditional Cisco technologies and components in the design of the new product, basically starting by stripping down a conventional Cisco router system and leveraging microprocessor cards, interface cards, and software, which dramatically increased the speed of the design effort. However, Cisco had no capabilities or experience in the design of radio frequency components, critical to enabling a cable service provider network, so it immediately went after partnerships with other organizations. After going through an exhaustive partner evaluation, Chen committed to a close partnering relationship with Broadcom and ESP. After resolving the usual initial debates regarding intellectual property ownership, the collaboration took off, and Chen's team met weekly with its Broadcom and ESP counterparts during the entire length of the effort.

After six months of intense development efforts, Chen's team created a prototype that was shown to the same group of CTOs that had originally been queried. Again, a wealth of feedback was received, and the design of the system evolved further. Six months after that, the system was shipped to a variety of cable service providers, as Cisco ramped up its dedicated sales force in this vertical market. Cisco's sales machine went to work, and three quarters later the company had shipped hundreds of millions of dollars of product and obtained over 65 percent market share. This not only established Cisco as the leader in a space in which it previously had no presence, but also integrated these offerings with Cisco's traditional businesses, which created enormous opportunities for new products and services.

Integration at Schwab

The story of Charles Schwab's foray into online trading is well known. To provide focus and promote aggressive growth in the new business, e-Schwab was set up as an independent unit that reported directly to Schwab co-CEO David Pottruck. This allowed e-Schwab total focus on fierce competition with E*trade and Ameritrade, even if this meant taking customers away from Schwab's traditional retail brokerage.

What isn't well known is that e-Schwab leveraged a variety of traditional Schwab expertise, capabilities, and systems to maximize integration while retaining flexibility.[13] Executives at e-Schwab used a simple rule: Deviate from the offline version only where it's absolutely essential to ensure the required focus. Thus, e-Schwab was led by a highly respected senior executive from Schwab's traditional retail organization, and staffed with experienced Schwab managers and IT architects, working side by side with new hires and consultants. Its back-office technology platform was designed to integrate with Schwab's traditional IT systems. Internet trading essentially became a different front end for the firm's legacy trading system, and integrated with other existing online channels and PC-based applications (such as Intuit, MSN, and Schwab's own Streetsmart). Furthermore, as e-Schwab evolved, the team made sure not to alienate people from the traditional retail business. Managers from e-Schwab met regularly with their colleagues in the traditional organization to resolve issues. They could do this because they already knew and liked each other, having worked together in Schwab's traditional business for many years.

These integration decisions had deep implications for e-Schwab, including restrictions on pricing models and system architecture. But they allowed e-Schwab to immediately leverage the company's traditional assets (e.g., back-end trading system, brand) and capabilities (e.g., scalable IT architecture, trading system design) to trump the competition. This strategy was successful, and by early January 1998, e-Schwab was the most successful online broker in the United States, with 1.2 million online accounts (three and a half times more than the next largest competitor in the industry).

Implementing an Effective Integration Process

We have just discussed two different firms in environments as distant as telecommunications equipment and financial services. Despite the differences, the integration processes of these companies share important similarities with each other, and with many other examples examined in our research.

The Impact of Leadership

Countless practitioners and academics have emphasized the essential role of leadership and leadership teams in the success of innovation efforts.[14] Many have shown that a strong leadership team that brings together a diversity of perspectives and experience is critical in managing technological innovation. As the examples indicate, leadership is also crucial at the level of the individual innovation team to inspire, protect, and focus the team that is managing through the complex challenges posed by organizational inertia.

Leverage Deep Knowledge of Internal and External Domains

The effectiveness of integration processes hinges on the quality of information about the technology, market, and customer domains that an organization manages to acquire. We saw how in the Cisco project, Chen put enormous emphasis on eliciting rich and frequent contacts with his emerging customer community. The project was in many ways a shared effort between Cisco and its future domains of customers and suppliers. The team obtained frequent, high-quality feedback from customers and suppliers during many iterations of the development cycle. Development engineers were also expected to perform extensive competitive analysis and be up-to-date on the functions and features of all the competitors they were attacking. The extensive internal feedback was then combined with more carefully staged external beta releases in order to organize market feedback and limit the risk that imperfections in early product releases would damage the company's reputation.

Overlap Conceptualization and Implementation, but Don't Sacrifice Architecture

To be effective, customer and market knowledge must be rapidly translated into decisions about technology, product, and operating requirements. Projects at both Cisco and Schwab responded frequently and rapidly to changes within the development cycle. There is little point in waiting to begin execution until all the major design issues are resolved—they will never be resolved completely. Projects should therefore expect a significant amount of design work to evolve during the course of a project. Despite the overlapping of design with execution, it is important to carefully define a strong architectural framework before execution gains too much momentum. Defining the interfaces around the product core and designing the architecture of the core itself to minimize the impact of uncertainty over the life of the project are essential to the project's success.

Both the Cisco and Schwab projects illustrate this point well. The early stages of the projects included time spent evaluating technology options and making critical architectural design decisions. Once true implementation began, the organizations worked within the established architectural frameworks and responded to many changes demanded by fluctuations in market requirements and the technology base.

Merge Experimentation and Experience

Good decision making is built on knowledge—which is generated through experimentation and accumulated largely through experience. In most current industrial environments, significant turbulence causes the rapid obsolescence of knowledge and makes experimentation the centerpiece of all integration efforts. Reflecting this idea, we see an emphasis on building a working system model or prototype early in each of the projects examined. This helps define and refine the context and features of the system, ensuring a much better match between the two. It is a critical milestone because it sets priorities for detailed development, creates a vehicle for user feedback, and allows some of the most important trade-offs to be addressed. Although the prototype does not have to be fully functional, it must reflect the essence of the product in terms of how users interact with it.

Over the last ten years, sophisticated prototyping and experimentation capability has gone from a differentiator to a must-have in many product development environments. However, in implementing operational changes, many organizations still approach prototyping as an afterthought. Operating managers must understand that designing the evolution of an operation, a new retail platform, or an improved supply chain system will involve as much uncertainty and complexity as many product development breakthroughs. Prototyping and experimentation should be front and center in the effort.[15]

As the pulse of the project, prototypes punctuate the effort by integrating technology into a physical (or at least simulated) package. They are essential to discovering interactions among various parts of the system. Once its basic features have been tested, the prototype provides a baseline for the addition of new features or refinements.

Experimentation cannot resolve all issues, however. When we asked managers in countless companies about the ingredients most critical to a successful integration project, they consistently pointed to the *experience* of software engineers and managers. Their experience was deemed crucial to guiding the experiments, navigating them through the complexity of the company's operating environment and its external ecosystem. This is as true for hundred-year-old firms such as Li & Fung as for more recent operations such as Yahoo! As a Yahoo! manager put it, "Experience is essential. It is the only thing that lets you see how the whole system works. It is critical to make the right tradeoffs as the project evolves."[16]

Integration and Adaptation

Ultimately, integration is important because it represents the quintessential opportunity for the renewal of an established organization, as shown earlier in the chapter in the example of IBM and Linux. We now present two additional examples, drawn from banking and appliances, that further illustrate this concept. The examples show that the crucial challenge in innovation is not in managing a research laboratory, but in acquiring new capabilities from across the ecosystem and using them to change the firm.

Merrill Lynch: Integration and Adaptation

When the Internet exploded, many perceived the advent of online trading to be a serious challenge to Merrill Lynch.[17] The reasons were many—not least among them being that Merrill's traditional formula for success in the private client brokerage business was embedded in its 14,000 paid financial consultants, whose access to and knowledge of customers (reaching over 5 million households) made up a central asset for the company. These consultants earned 65 percent of their salaries from commissions on trades, and there were plenty of concerns about how their compensation would change if online trading took off. More broadly, online trading was perceived to be highly disruptive to Merrill, changing both its business model and technology architecture.

In mid-1998, Launny Steffens, Merrill's vice chairman and head of the Private Client Group, assembled two task forces to examine this problem. After a brief period of intense analysis and debate, which leveraged the input of traditional Merrill clients and outside consultants, the task forces issued a unanimous recommendation: Merrill had to change its IT infrastructure and its business model. Both technology foundations and pricing structure had to change, and do so in a drastic way.

Despite being a critical asset to the company, the financial consulting model had always been problematic for Merrill, causing many incentive problems, but it had traditionally been very difficult to change. When organizations such as E*Trade and Charles Schwab seriously threatened Merrill's business, however, management had an opportunity to make deep-rooted changes. The problem was figuring out *how* these changes should be made. Some suggested that changing the existing organization was simply too challenging and pushed hard to set up a highly autonomous, external online venture that would compete directly with its traditional trading business. Others argued that an autonomous venture would not scale, and that Merrill's core organization should evolve: The change should thus be approached within its traditional trading business.

The arguments were resolved by late 1998, with Steffens committing to changing the existing organization. Merrill thus decided to take the problems on directly. It launched an online channel within the existing business, and used the changes as an opportunity to fundamentally rework the organization. To do this, it leveraged a variety of external consultants, who helped with crafting strategy and redesigning compensation systems. Additionally, Merrill leveraged critical external technology assets, including Microsoft's platforms and programming components, which became instrumental to redesigning the architecture of Merrill's IT infrastructure.

The efforts paid off, and Merrill announced two products: Unlimited Advantage and the Web-based Merrill Direct. Both products leveraged Merrill's traditional capabilities and customer base and were positioned as offerings that were integrated with the company's existing operations and IT infrastructure. They offered both new and old customers a complete menu of integrated choices for trading and asset management. The products were extremely successful and neutralized the advantages gained by Merrill's upstart competition. Perhaps even more important for the long run, the efforts changed many of Merrill's traditional ways of doing business, including the compensation structure of the typical broker. The strategy, championed passionately by Chairman David Komansky and led by former Internet nonbeliever Launny Steffens, worked brilliantly. By using its deep integration across services and product lines, Merrill has outsold its online competitors every month since the fourth quarter of 1999. Merrill embraced the Internet and new operating principles at its very core, and caused one of its most traditional business operations to evolve.

Merrill's story illustrates that effectiveness in managing technological change should be judged by impact, not speed. Merrill could have acted faster by bypassing its traditional capabilities, but the decision would have dramatically decreased the impact of its innovations. Impact, for an established firm, is typically best achieved by integrating new capabilities with traditional ones, and external assets with internal ones. Despite the turbulence of modern industrial environments, the reality is that no innovation will be so revolutionary as to make all existing assets irrelevant. Incumbents can sell new innovative products through existing channels, sell old products through newly enabled channels, manufacture disruptive products on existing lines, leverage existing supply chain relationships in novel lines of business, use new channels to reach old customers, and use existing service networks for new customers. Even with a change in technology infrastructure and business model, Merrill's traditional assets still had enormous value.

Even in a turbulent context, innovation in a business ecosystem is, in its essence, about integration and adaptation. Integration capabilities can pull together new and old competencies, internal and external assets, and constantly evolve and extend a firm's role in its ecosystem by tying together previously disconnected elements. Firms that do not (or cannot) integrate new technologies with existing assets are at a tremendous disadvantage. Not only will they take longer in translating new technologies into sizable businesses, but they will also miss out on critical opportunities to renew themselves.

Adapting existing organizations to leverage new technology and business models is not an easy process, but as long as the right set of integration capabilities exists, technological changes can give rise to dramatic organizational evolution. The best incumbents work with their partners to embrace new technologies, internalize them, and use them to transform the way they do business, just as firms such as Merrill, Walgreens, Schwab, and Li & Fung each used the Internet "threat" to revitalize their traditional operations. In doing so, such firms leverage their financial strength, operational capabilities, technological skills, and marketing relationships to overpower start-ups and other competitors.

Merloni: Evolution Through Networked Innovation

Threats can be a convenient motivator, but are not a prerequisite for incumbent evolution. Nestled among the rolling hills and valleys of the Marche region of Italy, the beautiful medieval town of Fabriano showcases the headquarters of Merloni Eldo, a $5 billion manufacturer of home appliances. Merloni ships over 20 million major appliances every year under a variety of different brands, and ranks among the top three appliance manufacturers in Europe by revenue. In some ways, Merloni can be thought of as a traditional company. Many of its managers have been with the company for many years, and most wear jackets and ties to work and exhibit great reverence and respect for the president, Vittorio Merloni. Vittorio is the son of the company founder, Aristide, who started the company in the mid-1960s.

Under the leadership of Vittorio Merloni and Andrea Guerra, the company's thirty-five-year-old CEO, Merloni has enjoyed impressive growth over the last five years, becoming the most profitable company in Europe in its entire sector, and more than doubling its market capitalization during the recent market downturn. Merloni's secret is innovation. Smack in the center of a very traditional and mature industry, Merloni has made a killing by figuring out how to make the best of its internal creativity and focused understanding of appliances by leveraging the capabilities of its innovation network.

During the mid-1990s, Merloni reinvented its approach to innovation. It started by redesigning its development and production processes. It ignored advice to set up a centralized R&D center and instead energized a small number of focused product development teams to create a flexible product platform in each of its four business areas: washers, dishwashers, refrigerators, and cookers. Their mandate was to reduce the complexity of product lines and production processes and create a framework for integrating technology from selected key global suppliers. They scoured the world for interesting technology partners, from creative design firms such as IDEO to electronics suppliers such as Motorola and NEC. Working with other world-class innovators energized the creativity of Merloni engineers, who began to formulate a number of intriguing new approaches to the design and production of their products.

This process introduced a steady stream of successful new products. Among many innovations, Merloni was the first appliance company outside the Far East to introduce washers with "fuzzy logic" controls, which enabled the design of very simple but powerful customer interfaces that were tremendously successful in the marketplace. It also introduced a variety of exploratory products, ranging from the Leonardo kitchen appliance to appliance networking systems. Beyond focusing on innovative customer features, Merloni leveraged its emergent electronics expertise to introduce dramatic cost reductions in its production and service processes. By 2004 it was the first company in its sector to be deploying a standard operating system–based software platform across the bulk of its products, creating enormous reductions in purchasing, manufacturing, and service costs. The year before, more than *half* of its SKUs were made up of new products. Not bad for a company in an old-fashioned sector that had been cautioned about how the emergent digitalization of appliances would threaten its traditional business.

Merloni's example shows how an organization can promote ongoing organizational evolution and continually sharpen differentiation.

Despite its substantial size, Merloni competes as a nimble niche player and differentiates itself by continually pushing the envelope on consumer value, technology, and product and service innovation in its domain. To do this, it has built an engine of innovation that leverages a variety of external assets, ranging from software platforms to consulting services.

Networked innovation strategies like Merloni's are founded on integrating platforms and other complementary assets provided by different ecosystem participants. In a healthy ecosystem, platforms will continue to evolve and offer increasing functionality over time. This continually expands the range of possibilities for other firms, providing new opportunities for innovation and differentiation. New and established firms in turn can fulfill these opportunities by integrating the platforms' assets with internal, focused capabilities.

The strategies can be a powerful renewal mechanism. Merloni leverages a variety of platforms provided by a number of external players, ranging from Motorola to Solectron, which evolve and provide constant opportunities for innovation. The rapidly decreasing costs of microprocessor and memory platforms, for example, have provided the opportunity for major innovations in areas as different as appliance user interfaces and appliance service networks.

Naturally, networked innovation strategies are not without risks. The biggest challenge for a niche player is to find itself in an ecosystem characterized by weak platforms or in an environment in which its platforms become in some way endangered. When the platform is threatened, the niche player typically gets hurt. When Hitachi spun off its microcontroller group, Merloni found itself threatened and had to implement a costly partner switch. In a different setting, Sun Microsystems' current financial weakness has become a real threat to the large number of technology companies, IT departments, ISVs, resellers, and technology providers that depend on the Java programming frameworks that Sun controls.

Organizations executing networked innovation strategies should therefore closely monitor the health of the platforms they leverage and work hard to reduce dependencies. Whenever possible, they should entertain using multiple platforms, or at least design their offerings so that the cost and time of switching platforms is minimized. In recent years, for example, Intuit has developed sophisticated internal methodologies to ensure that the applications it creates can work seamlessly on multiple platforms. Whenever possible, the company leverages a variety of external tools and programming frameworks, but it also makes sure that its product offerings are designed to rapidly migrate from platform to platform.

The Great Equalizer

Although mastery of integration capability is challenging, the ecosystem provides a great equalizer: Any firm, whether it is located in Fabriano, Italy, or Armonk, New York, has access to enormous markets of intellectual and physical assets. These assets can and should be used to constantly renew organizational capabilities. The ultimate implications are quite important for the established firm. In essence, they reshape the challenge of innovation: Innovation is not about fundamental discovery, but about the art of leveraging the ecosystem to integrate established capabilities with new opportunities. Doing this well is a function of architecture and integration, and also of market design and operation, the subject of the next chapter.

CHAPTER TEN

Market Design, Operation, and Competition

The emergence of business ecosystems implies that a large and increasing part of our economy is being driven by market-based transactions. The design and management of complex marketplaces has therefore become a crucial operational challenge for all firms, and the third foundation for competition in a networked setting.

Market Failures

Although it is impossible to get an accurate number, it is likely that hundreds of thousands of new Web-based marketplaces—trading private jets, dog-walking services, and everything in between—were created between 1996 and 2000. Launched by organizations as different as Pets.com and General Motors, many of these enterprises were Wall Street darlings. But by January 2003, a minuscule fraction remained as healthy, functioning entities. It seems almost redundant to point out that despite markets' central role in a business ecosystem, their elusive dynamics are often poorly understood.

Markets and Operational Complexity

Going beyond the trading of simple goods and services, firms in industries ranging from software to media and from banking to energy are increasingly using markets to organize *operating* tasks in areas as different as innovation and distribution. Some actually look like conventional marketplaces, such as the commodity trading operations that Bunge Ltd. uses in managing its extensive agribusiness supply chain. Others do not. Microsoft's operating systems effectively form complex marketplaces that coordinate transactions between the many complementary domains in their ecosystems—most significantly the consumers, developers, technology providers, and systems integrators. The existence of a healthy diversity of applications and hardware configurations to satisfy user needs is dependent on the effective management of these market relationships.

Most firms in a business ecosystem depend on a variety of increasingly complex markets as a fundamental operating necessity. Most keystone strategies involve the design and operation of one or more such marketplaces, and most niche players leverage a variety of marketplaces as an integral part of their operating environment. Merloni is leveraging an open source platform for all its advanced electronics— understanding the complex market mechanisms that determine the existence of the hardware and software components necessary for the design of its products has become a critical competitive necessity.

Understanding the dynamics of complex marketplaces can thus no longer be delegated to the finance and marketing arms of the corporation. Managing markets is crucial to almost all operating activities, ranging from supply chain to distribution and from research to product design. Designing and managing *effective* marketplaces, however, has proved elusive for a wide variety of organizations, both large and small. Although the emergence of distributed information technology has created more opportunities for organizing large communities, many of the principles behind the operation of complex markets have roots in traditional, established businesses ranging from dating services to credit cards and from apparel distribution to securities trading. It is essential to spend some time understanding the lessons learned. The implications are important whether the company operates marketplaces or is simply dependent on them for its operating activities.

This chapter therefore focuses on the dynamics of these complex markets and on the principles behind the use of technologies, processes, and institutions for their effective design and management. It draws on insights from new and old organizations and from economics and operations management. In studying industries as different as software operating systems and energy trading, and companies as different as Enron and eBay, we found many examples of both great successes and dramatic failures. We investigated a number of critical factors, from the pricing strategies necessary to attract the different communities of participants, to the technologies and operational capabilities needed to manage them.

N-Sided Markets

The markets that coordinate domains in a business ecosystem are typically more complex than traditional examples. A traditional marketplace is relatively simple because it only connects two domains—a domain of buyers and a domain of sellers. A traditional vegetable market connects the domain of vegetable producers to the domain of vegetable consumers. Microsoft, eBay, American Express, and Enron are instead examples of organizations that manage what economists have recently started to call "*N*-sided" markets, which are markets that connect two or more disparate groups of customers to sellers.[1] Visa is the classic example: Its credit cards connect communities of retailers, banks, and consumers to each other in a market that works only if each group of customers is present and has enough critical mass to buy or provide the services required by the integrated system. Unlike a traditional market that adds value incrementally for each additional customer, Visa would provide no value to retailers without a critical mass of cardholders. Similarly, Visa would have no value to cardholders if too few retailers participated in the system.

N-sided markets are vast and pervasive, including energy trading systems, financial trading environments, and business-to-business marketplaces (see table 10-1). They also include IT platforms, such as the ones sold by IBM, Microsoft, Palm, and Sun. These systems form *N*-sided markets in the sense that they need to attract thousands of application and technology providers in order to present a meaningful product to users. Much like in the credit card example, different communities need to be present in critical mass for the system to function properly.

TABLE 10-1

Examples of *N*-Sided Markets, Indicating Sources of Revenue and Asymmetries in Charging

Industry	Platform	Side 1	Side 2	Side That Gets Charged Little	Sources of Revenue
Real estate	Residential property brokerage	Buyer	Seller	Side 1	Real estate brokers derive income principally from sales commissions.
Real estate	Apartment brokerage	Renter	Owner/Landlord	Typically side 1	Apartment consultants and locater services generally receive all of their revenue from the apartment lessors once they have successfully found tenants for the landlord.
Media	Newspapers and magazines	Reader	Advertiser	Side 1	Approximately 80 percent of newspaper revenue comes from advertisers.
Media	Network television	Viewer	Advertiser	Side 1	For example, Fox earns half of its revenues from advertisers.
Media	Portals and Web pages	Web surfer	Advertiser	Side 1	The average portal gets slightly over half of its revenues from advertisements. All other Web pages generally receive about a tenth of their revenue from advertisements.
Software	Operating system	Application user	Application developer	Side 2	For example, Microsoft earns at least 67 percent of its revenues from licensing packaged software to end users.
Software	Video game console	Game player	Game developer	Neither—both sides are significant sources of platform revenue	Both game sales to end users and licensing to third-party developers are significant sources of revenue for console manufacturers.
Payment card system	Credit card	Cardholder	Merchant	Side 1	For example, in 2001, American Express earned 82 percent of its revenues from merchants.

N-sided markets even include trading companies such as Li & Fung, which attracts multiple seller and buyer communities (aggregating more than 8,000 companies and 1,000,000 employees) in order to provide the sorts of comprehensive supply chain services that large apparel retailers like the Gap now require. N-sided markets are almost ubiquitous in business ecosystems, since each business typically depends on multiple other businesses in different domains for operational tasks.

N-sided markets are more complex than conventional market systems. Organizations that manage multisided markets master unique challenges involved in attracting and retaining the simultaneous participation of multiple different communities. For Linux to take off in the corporate environment, interested technology providers, application developers, service providers, systems integrators, and corporate information technology departments all needed to reach critical mass simultaneously. This would not have happened without IBM's early commitment, clever strategy, and broad-based investment. For Linux to continue to succeed, each of these communities needs to be retained and nurtured.

Unlike the expectations of many business practitioners and entrepreneurs, the experience of the last few years shows that these kinds of complex marketplaces are not simple to launch and scale: Simple network effects are not sufficient to automatically drive them to success. Their effectiveness is the result of continued investments and deeprooted operational capabilities. These markets are not well characterized as simple, passive hubs like trading pits at the Chicago Board of Trade but should instead be viewed as real business operations. By this we mean markets comprise the comprehensive combination of technologies, business processes, and organizational institutions that coordinates the activities of the multiple customer domains involved in the market.

Market Operations

In the early days of network economics and the IT bubble, academics and practitioners often adopted a faith that once markets were created, the rest would take care of itself. In this view, the key to defining opportunities for new markets was in identifying industry-level inefficiencies, often created by industry fragmentation or by the existence of old-fashioned intermediaries. But history has proved that finding inefficiency is the least difficult part of the challenge. This mistake was made not only by Internet start-ups, but also by a broad variety of organizations across a wide spectrum of industries.

As our discussion of Enron (see chapter 6) clearly illustrates, finding inefficiencies is not enough, and complex markets can only sustain themselves if they create value. In a networked setting, in which markets connect large numbers of organizations, markets very often exhibit so-called network or positive-feedback effects by which the value created increases with the number of participants. This sharply increasing value curve motivated the early optimism of many entrepreneurs, who believed that if the market could only get started, the value created would rapidly take off.

Unfortunately, a successful business model is dependent not only on value creation, but also on cost. Costs can include customer acquisition costs, customer retention costs, customer service costs, integration costs, and others. In a networked environment, a cost curve can rise as fast as or even faster than the value curve, making the business model unsustainable.

Abundant examples of this problem can be found in a variety of Internet bubble ventures, ranging from enterprise software application companies such as Ariba and CommerceOne (where the multisided market is formed by the application providers, the systems integrator community, and the enterprise customers) to B2B marketplaces such as Chemdex and Petrocosm. In each of these cases the margins of the market organizations decreased sharply (and became significantly negative) as the revenues increased. The cost curve was rising faster than the value curve. This is not a new problem. The early entrants into credit cards in the 1950s, such as Bank of America and Chase Manhattan, incurred significant losses. Chase Manhattan discontinued its card program, whereas Bank of America got its costs under control and evolved into Visa USA.

Designing and Operating Markets

Markets should be designed so that the value curve quickly exceeds the cost curve. The cost curve needs to be designed so that the losses generated before the market reaches critical mass are manageable. The most successful markets—eBay's trading operations or Microsoft's operating systems—have value curves that not only exceed the cost curve but rise much more rapidly.

Pricing Mechanisms

Pricing strategies are essential to customer acquisition and retention and are thus very important to the design and management of market operations. In a multisided environment, optimal pricing will not track the incremental costs on each side of the market. Look at American Express, which makes most of its card revenues from merchants.

In an N-sided market, price should be set so that the right communities are attracted to the market in the appropriate combination and balance. A good pricing strategy can go a long way to ensure the success of an N-sided market. Setting up the right pricing and incentive structure means that less effort needs to be expended in operations to attract and sustain the needed market communities. Pricing strategies can thus have a fundamental impact on the cost curve of the market operation.

In some cases, enough is known about asset value and opportunity costs that good analytical models can be developed to help discover the right pricing structure. Examples of sophisticated pricing mechanisms can be found in the electricity sector, where the price of using a given transmission line changes in real time to reflect the congestion patterns in the entire network (the bottlenecks will shift from hour to hour, depending on the geographic consumption pattern). The dynamic pricing strategies employed greatly improve network efficiencies, lowering operating costs and decreasing investment in expensive generating and transmission equipment. These strategies (known in the trade as locational marginal cost pricing) define the local price by calculating the full, *systemwide* opportunity cost of the resources used. In other words, rather than pricing each transmission line independently, the whole electricity grid is treated as a single, giant, N-sided market, and the price of each network link is dependent on what is happening in all the other links.

The essence of the argument is that in an N-sided market, the value obtained by each type of customer depends on the presence of the other types of customers. Pricing should reflect all systemwide inter-actions, opportunity costs, and shared costs, such as the cost of achieving and maintaining critical mass in all market components. Because of these costs, the price will not reflect marginal cost in any individual market side, even in a competitive environment. For exam-ple, in software operating systems, pricing is set so that most of the cost burden is carried by end users, not developers, because develop-ers provide critical value to the system by creating third-party applica-tions. Palm could charge developers significantly more for the soft-ware tools and information necessary for writing applications for the Palm OS, but it chooses not to because fewer developers would write fewer applications and would thereby decrease the value of the Palm OS to end users.

Operating Processes

Despite the best pricing policies, it takes real capabilities to manage market operation and make sure transactions actually clear. A complex market requires careful design of its operating processes to work prop-erly, attracting the appropriate communities of buyers and sellers, sup-porting their efforts to buy and sell, keeping each above critical mass, and ensuring that the value that the market generates is greater than the costs required for its operation. Designing market operations should focus on both internal and external processes. The failure of many B2B exchanges provides a plethora of examples of ineffective market design.

SupplierMarket, a B2B exchange for direct materials, never mastered an effective process framework for its internal operations—the basic activities that are necessary to make market transactions clear. Despite attracting thousands of users to its site and listing a large number of transactions, the marketplace never became truly liquid. Why didn't the transactions close? Part of the answer is found in the design of its internal operations. Behind the façade provided by the Web applica-tion, the operation of the market was entirely manual. SupplierMarket had hired more than 40 market makers, who spent their time on the phone calling potential buyers and sellers, attracting listings, and mak-ing large transactions close. With this operating framework, a single transaction typically would take many weeks and lots of manual effort to clear, costing considerably more than the transaction fees charged to the market participants. The cost structure was out of control, the system could not scale, and the marketplace failed. This kind of challenge was shared by many of Enron's troubled marketplaces.

The internal operations of the Chemdex B2B exchange were more streamlined than SupplierMarket. However, the marketplace never effectively integrated into the processes of its participants. The Chemdex market application had been designed to enable customers to shop but could not integrate with other enterprise software systems. Thus, Chemdex could function as a traditional market, but not as the hub of a distributed operation. Not surprising, most of its customers found it impossible to leverage Chemdex as an integral part of their supply chains, since they depended on internal enterprise applications for procurement and account management. Therefore, despite a fast initial ramp-up, Chemdex was not sustainable because users reverted to their tried and true applications for managing procurement. Chemdex was shut down in the summer of 2000.

Successful market operations look very different: Their operating strategy defines clear, scalable frameworks for core operations, integration, and coordination. Take Yahoo! Personals as an example. Yahoo! Personals boasts a continually updated software application with a sophisticated matching algorithm to automate internal business processes and maximize the operating efficiency (and "liquidity") of the site. This application easily manages enormous user volume with a minimum of computing capacity. Furthermore, it integrates closely with other Yahoo! properties such as My Yahoo! to maximize synergies between the different businesses. Finally, it links to a cleverly defined advertising and promotion strategy to coordinate the behavior of different communities to make sure that each reaches critical mass in a balanced fashion. Despite starting later than its competitors, Yahoo! Personals is highly successful and adds substantially to Yahoo!'s revenue and profits.

Credit cards provide a more traditional example of the organizational challenges of creating a scalable market. Bank of America originally created a franchise system to expand from a California-based card to a national card (in the days of interstate banking restrictions).

This did not work well, because other banks did not like promoting Bank of America even though it wasn't a direct competitor. Additionally, Bank of America had not thought out the rules for managing transactions between the members of the system. Chaos and inefficiency resulted.

Recognizing the potential value of the system, but cognizant of the requirements for creating an effective market, the franchisees finally persuaded Bank of America to sell its property to a cooperative of banks. The cooperative developed a clear system of rules and procedures upon formation. These included a scalable voting and ownership structure that has accommodated a dramatically changing and growing membership, an agreement to exchange transactions between the merchant's bank and the cardholder's bank at a fixed and uniform fee, and rules on the risk borne by each of the parties to the payment card transaction (the cardholder and his or her bank, the merchant and its bank, and the system). This created a balanced market that could manage, integrate, and coordinate the contributions of a broad variety of consumers and institutions. The operation grew rapidly, while costs declined and quality of service improved.

Technology

Market operations are increasingly shaped by the technology decisions made in their design. Chemdex's inability to integrate with enterprise applications was determined by architecture decisions made early in its existence (contrast its architecture with the Dell example in chapter 8). The effectiveness of Yahoo! Personals is dependent on the efficiency of the matching algorithms it embodies. A market's technology is thus critical to its effectiveness.

Naturally, market technology will vary widely from application to application. In software operating systems, the core technology serves to enable the fundamental functions performed by a computer (and to make sure that a diversity of third-party applications will run on it), whereas in bond trading the core technology is aimed at risk management, and in corporate charge cards the core technology focuses on information management. Despite the diversity in focus, in all cases deep technical and operational expertise is required to make market-places function properly. It is very difficult to develop this kind of expertise in many unrelated markets at the same time, as Enron was attempting to do.

The operation of a market can also include integration technologies such as application programming interfaces (APIs) that enable third-party participants to connect to the market hub or develop value-added applications on top of it. This adds to the market's created value, its scalability, and its sustainability. Such technology integration strategies are increasingly critical not only to software operating systems such as Windows but also to trading systems such as eBay or supply chain platforms such as Dell and Li & Fung. In eBay's case, the company introduced third-party APIs two years ago, which enabled the creation of applications that now drive over 30 percent of the site's revenue volume. In Li & Fung's case, Microsoft's .NET technology is being used to link manufacturing organizations around the world to jointly provide services to its customer base. Li & Fung (along with other major supply chain platforms such as Wal-Mart and Dell) provides suppliers and customers what amounts to supply chain APIs that they can use to link into internal enterprise applications for procurement and channel management. In many cases, Li & Fung (along with Wal-Mart and Dell) will even fund the creation of the integration interface for its most critical market participants.

Finally, an effective market will invest significant time and money to ensure that its standards and interfaces are well communicated to its community of market participants, effectively coordinating the efforts of buyers and sellers. For example, when Intel introduced MMX technology in its line of Pentium processors, it began to instruct its community of third-party developers about the technology *two years* before it was actually introduced, effectively coordinating industry-wide development efforts. In electricity deregulation, the operators of the electric power pools of New York and Pennsylvania–New Jersey–Maryland assembled working groups from all market participants to jointly specify the new market design. This coordinated the activities of all market participants years before the new markets were launched.

Managing Markets

It is useful to distill some of the observed best practices in complex marketplaces into a set of distinct tactics, which we believe can help managers steer around the many challenges involved in the design of market operations. These tactics are useful for crafting both keystone and niche strategies.

Achieve Liquidity First

We define *liquidity* as the condition in which a market is able to process buyer–seller transactions efficiently, in an acceptable amount of time. Achieving liquidity at a reasonable operating cost may be the most challenging aspect of multisided market management. We found that a common failed strategy consisted of making large investments in technology and operations early in the life of a market, long before liquidity was achieved.[2] The strategy would seem to make sense and is almost mandated by adherents of the network economics literature— investment in the right technology and operations infrastructure should help achieve liquidity over time. In fact, however, it does not.

The problem is that it is very difficult to know in *what* technology and operating infrastructure the money should be invested. The most successful markets in our study were cautious. They achieved liquidity first, tweaking their market designs with minimal investment in technology and operating infrastructure, and *then* scaled up. Both Microsoft and eBay were cash-flow positive from the start. Both became pervasive in small communities (microcomputer software developers in 1978 and Pez package collectors in 1996, respectively) before any significant investment had been made. Both achieved liquidity first, and then scaled up. The birth of credit cards provides a similar example. Diners Club started its charge card on an experimental basis with restaurants and their patrons in Manhattan and then Los Angeles. Only after being locally successful, on a very small scale, did it scale up to offer its card beyond restaurants and in other geographic areas.

A deeper examination reveals that the liquidity-first strategy makes good sense. Given the vast complexity of reaching broad user bases and capturing complex multisided markets in most of the spaces we studied, no investment in technology and operations, no matter how large, can ensure scalability and sustainability if the market is not properly designed. The ecosystem a typical market needs to reach is simply too large and dispersed. Liquidity needs to be a self-sustaining process, and if you don't achieve this in a contained fashion at a smaller scale before committing to large investments, it is likely you will never achieve it at scale. This implies that the best strategy for scaling up a market is to first achieve liquidity when the market is small and easily manageable. Once the right balance in the communities is achieved, and once the operations and technology strategies have proved themselves, the market can gradually be ramped up.[3]

Price to Balance Communities

In our study, many of the more effective marketplaces employed sophisticated pricing strategies. In contrast with most of the failed B2B exchanges, in which the pricing policies were trivial (e.g., 5 percent of transaction value for all transactions, paid by the sellers), effective markets used complex and evolving pricing policies to maintain the appropriate balance of customer and seller communities.

Pricing is possibly the most effective mechanism for achieving and maintaining liquidity in a multisided market. We argued previously that pricing should reflect systemwide value and costs. The challenge is that these are frequently difficult to forecast, or even to estimate once a market is operational—how do you quantify the value provided by an additional Windows application? Pricing for a complex market is therefore often a function of experimentation and experience. This implies that to be effective, markets need significant pricing freedom and should invest in the capability to continue to evolve and reoptimize pricing policies.

Design a Flexible Market

The strategy of achieving early market liquidity has significant consequences for market design. It implies that a market operation will need to undergo enormous change as it scales up after reaching liquidity.

Visa, for example, has migrated through three generations of payment processing technology, and eBay has gone through five major transitions in the technology that powers its Web sites.

Practice Experimental Market Adoption

Enron encouraged entrepreneurs to analyze and select markets, raise money, and make essentially irreversible commitments in chosen areas. eBay watched where its user communities were going and simply reinforced the markets that were already functioning well. Enron created a culture and incentive structures that reinforced managing to committed targets. eBay encouraged its employees to be flexible and alert to where its customers were going. In the words of an eBay manager, "[W]e got interested in B2B vertical markets when we started to get calls from companies that already found their own products on sale at e-Bay and wanted to gain some control over that process."[4] eBay's B2B vertical markets generated $300 million of transaction volume and were highly profitable before they were announced to the investment community.

In a way that is representative of other successful market operations, eBay's selection process for new markets is completely evolutionary. Its architecture is designed to adopt new markets in an opportunistic way, following its user base in a variety of areas. No commitment is made until the areas are proved to have a strong business model.[5] Although it flies against traditional top-down strategic analysis, this model appears very sensible when one considers the enormous uncertainties and complexities underlying the functioning of any new market.

The difficulty of expanding into new market segments is illustrated by American Express's botched introduction of its first credit card. Its failure came despite having operated a highly profitable and efficient charge card operation for almost 30 years. It thought all it had to do was put credit cards in the hands of its charge card customers. But without reimbursement from their companies—many of the customers had had corporate cards—these customers had higher rates of delinquency than American Express expected. After a very challenging introductory period, American Express significantly scaled down its initial credit card operations.

Leverage the Ecosystem

To maximize scalability and adaptability, market operations should leverage the operational capabilities of their participants. A well-designed market should minimize the internal effort needed to make sure that transactions clear. As discussed at length earlier, this does not mean that the technology and operations strategies of a market are irrelevant. They are critical, but should be defined so that market transactions can be accomplished with minimal and decreasing *internal* effort and, therefore, manageable costs and a maximum of scalability.

This highlights the importance of tool design as part of the market. In organizations ranging from eBay to Microsoft, the design of comprehensive, easy-to-use toolkits that enabled participants to participate in market operations (say, by creating eBay listings or designing Windows applications) was essential to their success. Similarly, Visa created very effective, easy-to-use tools for credit checking and transaction processing that enabled a vast community of retailers to use the Visa system with minimal oversight.[6]

In this view, the much maligned "beta software" phenomenon (in which unfinished and often buggy versions of products are widely distributed) is not so much a consequence of the speed of product development as it is an expected component of a strategy that leverages external communities.[7] Similarly, the seemingly endless sequence of new versions and "patches" to software programs is not necessarily a consequence of poor product development, but is an element of a strategy that views a product's interactions with external communities in the ecosystem as part of an open-ended product development process that incorporates feedback from the experiences of these communities with the product.

Minimize Internal Market Positions

Because of potential conflicts and massive risk exposure, market-making organizations should be extremely careful in taking part in the trading activities performed in the markets they manage. Enron sharply exacerbated its troubles by taking direct positions in many of the marketplaces it created. This dramatically increased its risk exposure, further exacerbating the company's position. In sharp contrast with Enron, eBay never takes substantial positions in the markets it creates. The volume of transaction flow in many of these markets at scale is truly gigantic. Thus, taking positions could add dramatically to company revenues but is likely to entail almost unbearable risk exposure unless extremely conservative policies and sophisticated analysis tools are developed. This is a lesson that financial institutions learned the hard way during the Depression and that now needs to be internalized by organizations across a much broader variety of industries.

Create and Manage Trust

Trust is fundamental to the development and sustainability of a market. In its early days, eBay ensured that customers and sellers trusted each other by using direct e-mail exchanges between customers and the company's founders. The founders would personally track sellers, interact with them in chat rooms, and develop an informal trust rating. Today, eBay handles millions of transactions every day. Its trust management system is still a fundamental part of its market design, although a distributed rating system has naturally taken the place of the founders' e-mails. Trust is essential to good market operation because ultimately it decreases operating costs and risk exposure. A well-trusted marketplace will need to spend less in attracting customers and in managing their interactions, which means that it will be much easier to scale.

Define a Clear Market Governance Structure

There is significant variety in market governance structures. Some successful markets (e.g., eBay, American Express, or Yahoo!) are highly profitable and independent publicly traded companies, whereas others (e.g., the New York Power Pool or Visa) are nonprofit cooperatives. Although both extremes work, what seem not to work are intermediate models. During the heyday of B2B exchanges, most adopted unusual governance structures—many were consortia owned by a portion of the targeted participants, such as Covisint, Petrocosm, or

ProvisionX. These organizations had uncertain charters, with some members aiming at a quick IPO while others were focused on much more conservative objectives. The result was a set of organizations with mixed strategies and often conflicting incentives, which created significant problems any time major strategic decisions had to be considered.

The governance structure of the market should be clearly defined. For-profit models have worked well, but what appears to be required here is a clean, clear structure that is independent of market participants—eBay provides a great example. To make cooperatives work well, it appears crucial to think through governance systems and objectives very carefully and to ensure completely balanced participation by all market members. Take the PJM Interconnection in electricity as an example: Board participation and voting rights are allocated based on precise estimates of transaction volume shares on an annual basis. The MasterCard and Visa cooperatives are organized on the same principle.

New Market Challenges

As we write about these ideas, the pendulum may be swinging back too far. The failure of Enron's trading operations has caused a large number of organizations to shut down their own specialized trading operations, which in turn has caused a liquidity crunch in energy markets. The failure of a vast variety of B2B consortia has put in question the whole idea of interenterprise applications, which in turn has caused the failure of many software firms, regardless of the value provided. Organizations in a variety of industries may be overreacting to the lessons of recent years.

As the world economy repositions itself for growth, it is essential to reflect on the lessons learned through the many failures of recent years in order to distill the good ideas from the poor ones. Developing a deeper understanding of markets, particularly their design and operation, is crucial to this task, because they possibly provide the most common coordinating mechanism in a network economy.

CHAPTER ELEVEN

Business Ecology: Managing Disruption, Evolution, and Sustainability

At the dawn of the twentieth century, established firms invented the R&D laboratory to keep themselves safe from technological threats. Companies such as IBM and AT&T invested in internal research and development in virtually all relevant fields of science and technology to make sure that they remained on top of any likely innovation. They developed and provided everything that was needed for their products, from raw materials to software applications. They built huge, vertically integrated operating infrastructures that took care of every aspect of a customer's needs.

But at the dawn of the twenty-first century, the world has become too complex for this approach to innovation and operations, and even giants like IBM and AT&T cannot come close to covering all capabilities in important fields. The range of players in related industry domains has grown, and the diversity of companies focused on the introduction of state-of-the-art technologies has exploded. We have seen how in the computer industry alone, the limited environment of the 1960s, encompassing IBM and its seven vertically integrated competitors (the "seven dwarfs"), has grown into a complex ecosystem populated by thousands of firms in dozens of major domains providing everything from state-of-the-art semiconductor design modules to interenterprise software. Innovation and operations have become networked phenomena.

This massive, dispersed activity created a number of new threats for firms as traditional players braced themselves for attack by a variety of challengers from a much broader industry base. The impact reached well beyond the traditional "technology" industries to threaten established business models in traditional sectors such as banking and appliances. It is therefore not surprising that countless academics and practitioners predicted that this era of technological ferment would pose virtually insurmountable challenges for established firms. With so many new companies and so many technological dislocations, how could old giants mired in technological legacy and organizational inertia survive?

Along with the threats, however, business ecosystems also created a massive number of new opportunities. Thousands of firms, new and old, emerged to provide solutions to established firms, in areas ranging from software applications to technology platforms, and from systems integration to business consulting services. Opportunities for integrating novel external technologies and adopting new business models soared. To the surprise of many, most of the incumbents survived, many of them emerging much stronger than when they started. They took their old, traditional, established organizations and changed them. They integrated new technologies with old capabilities, and emerged with organizations that were stronger because of the combination.

This completely changes the game. Traditionally, technological innovation had been confined to the small number of firms with deep R&D traditions. Bell Labs represented innovation, not Merrill Lynch; Xerox was "innovative," not Merloni. Now, however, the huge number of new technology providers ensures that it is easier for a firm to have access to the latest technologies in areas as different as semiconductor production equipment, pharmaceutical targets, Internet software applications, or wireless chips. Thus, as long as the capability to integrate technology is there, established firms can leverage their ecosystems and adapt to and even drive major technological changes. This is true from the hills of central Italy to the crowds of Wall Street, far from traditional R&D laboratories, and even far from Silicon Valley. The firms that succeed are not those with the best labs but those that have the best processes for leveraging their business ecosystems, integrating new technologies, and using them to evolve their existing businesses.

In this way, the massive technological changes of the 1990s may have had an unexpected outcome. Rather than heralding the death of the incumbent organization, they may have enabled it to find the passion to leverage its business networks to fix old problems, strengthen traditional capabilities, and emerge stronger than ever before.

Despite the many dire predictions by academics and practitioners of incumbent failure caused by the "disruptive," "radical," or "architectural" innovations of the World Wide Web, biotechnology, Internet retailing, and online trading, it is now clear that these technological transitions were survived by the overwhelming majority of incumbent firms. Indeed IBM, Microsoft, Novartis, Wal-Mart, and Merrill Lynch are in many ways stronger than before. Each now enjoys greater revenues, revitalized organizations, and new, innovative businesses in those very same areas that appeared almost hopelessly threatened. Just as Microsoft and IBM are leading in the introduction of Web services, Novartis has become an important player in biotechnology, Wal-Mart leverages Internet technology for new customer channels and supply chain management, and Merrill has a superb online trading operation.

The preponderance of evidence argues that the scary predictions of the late twentieth century foreseeing disruption and marginalization for many traditional firms were an overreaction. Figure 11-1 depicts the pervasive survival of incumbents in the software ecosystem through a variety of disruptive and discontinuous transitions. The firms that really were disrupted were not the incumbents but the ones that were supposed to be doing the disrupting—start-ups, spin-offs, and joint ventures.

Of course, not all incumbent firms fared as well as Wal-Mart and Microsoft. But the failed firms of the last few years, from WorldCom to Enron, appear, if anything, to have overestimated the disruptive impact of technological change. Just as Enron's profitability and risk profile suffered as it moved into new areas such as bandwidth trading and online operations ahead of its competitors, so WorldCom dived into bankruptcy by overinvesting in new optical networks.

In previous generations, corporations were often criticized by experts for failing to respond to new technology—for example, moving too slowly, not doing enough, or not dedicating resources to new

FIGURE 11-1

The Remarkable Stability of the Computing Industry in the Face of Waves of Significant Change

The figure depicts the survival rate for software firms over the last ten years. The data were assembled by gathering the complete sample of public software firms. The survival rate in any year is quite high, even during the periods of greatest turbulence. Moreover, there is no correlation at all between any decrease in survival rate and the timing of major technological or business model transitions, also depicted in the figure. The rate only dips below 90 percent during 2001 and 2002. These years do not represent any major new disruption in technology, architecture, or business model. They instead correlate quite well with the overall collapse of the computing ecosystem described in chapter 3. Note that the only time that a significant drop in firm survival is observed is during a period of general economic downturn. The kinds of technological and business model shocks traditionally viewed as causing firm death have little effect by comparison.

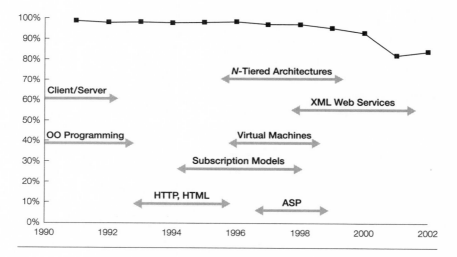

projects. But in the current generation of managers the challenge appears instead to be understanding precisely *when* and *how* to respond. Everyone knows that new technology is an important priority for a firm. Incumbents are all too aware that they need to understand the impact of new technology and do something about it. What is often not quite as clear, particularly after the many mistakes made in the last few years, is *what* to do about it—whether the technology is a threat or an opportunity, whether it is better matched to the capabilities of a small or a large organization, and whether it should be developed internally or by leveraging the capabilities of external partners. The biggest problem faced by many organizations in managing the Internet was not a lack of reaction, or even a slow reaction, but the *wrong* reaction.

The establishment of business ecosystems has changed the range of options open to firms, the nature of their markets, and the key capabilities and assets needed to compete. Perhaps most critically, it has provided opportunities to revitalize aging firms and open the world of innovation to a much broader range of players. This new ecology of innovation can do wonders to promote evolution in established firms. Those that develop the capabilities and understanding required to do well in the new system can achieve new levels of competitiveness and sustainability.

The Nature of Business Evolution

Because most critical assets are now outside firms' boundaries, it should come as no surprise that managing organizational evolution is largely dependent on an organization's connection with its ecosystem. In traditional views, incumbent organizations are dinosaurs doomed to extinction, lumbering along until the next shock drives them out of existence. What we argue here is quite different—that incumbents endure and adapt. That, in fact, the networks of which they are a part, and the nature of the process they use to leverage and maintain those networks, should ensure their continued existence. This might seem a strange conclusion for a framework inspired by a biological view of business networks. After all, much of what is axiomatic about the established views of competition, firm survival, and technological evolution takes its inspiration from biology: the notion that established and entrenched species are eventually doomed to extinction and replacement and hence that sustained success eventually leads to complacency and vulnerability. Therefore, like the dinosaurs, a long, abundant, and successful reign is seen as mere pride before the fall. In this view incumbency leads to firms becoming "hopelessly outmoded or unwieldy" and sets them up for being wiped out by some unforeseen external shock.[1]

Like many metaphors taken from biology, however, this view misses an important point. It fails to ask the important question about just *what* survives. Species come and go and whole lineages can be wiped out, but not only is this a rare event, but also something—something significant—at some level *always* survives. The "extinction" of the dinosaurs, to be sure, represented the elimination of some of the most spectacularly successful creatures on earth, but a huge range of things persisted, from specific features to "body plans," fundamental metabolic processes, and (of course) the genetic code and its apparatus for expression and implementation. What is significant about the loss of so many species of dinosaurs is not that these dinosaurs had no descendants, but that the enduring plan for vertebrates embodied in these dinosaurs survived *despite these losses*. The loss of dinosaurs represents nothing more than a shaping and pruning of this plan: not so large, better insulation, perhaps smarter and more active, at least on land. The pruning of individuals or even branches of lineages does not mean the end of the entire tree, or even all or most of the shared characteristics of that tree, it is simply the way evolution channels and directs the course that a tree takes.

This refocusing of the biological metaphor points to our first implication for business strategy: Because something always survives, the first critical decision for incumbents is to identify and leverage the range of assets and capabilities that are likely to survive. The challenge is not the trivial one of simply placing a good bet on a product that is likely to experience sustained popularity or a technology that seems unlikely to be easily displaced by foreseeable innovation. Indeed, such an approach would represent the kind of "old" thinking about innovation that we are attempting to change here—the view that the only ways for an incumbent to survive disruptions are to avoid them or attack them with a separate venture. Instead, the search for what will survive has a very different goal: to identify the specific assets that are likely to endure and thrive in the face of those inevitable changes and to integrate new capabilities with them.

The task of achieving this goal has many facets, but two are fundamental. First, firms must identify enduring architectures with a capacity to adapt and integrate. Like the insect body plan or the genetic code, these are the foundations that have the capacity to sustain experimentation and variety and have a capacity to evolve over time. Many of the issues related to identifying, building, and evolving such platforms have been already been discussed in chapter 8. But the key points to keep in mind here are that for keystones, this means defining and growing the platform architecture with a constant eye to what provides flexibility and adaptability—to what is likely to endure in new contexts, new markets, and new business realities. For others in a network, it means evaluating potential alternative platforms based on their capacity to provide these attributes. What matters is not which platform architecture is optimal, or cheaper, or most stable, or even which is currently the most capable—what matters is which platform has the largest installed base, is most adaptable, and is thus most likely to endure. This is a critical shift in perspective. For example, it is less important whether Linux is marginally cheaper than Microsoft's platform technologies for certain applications. What really matters is which platform is more likely to endure in the face of shocks and transitions, which is more able to evolve, and which embodies a greater capacity for integration.

The second fundamental aspect of achieving the goal of establishing an enduring architecture and linking to it is to build and sustain a network around the platform. As we have discussed in earlier chapters, this is the collaborative work of keystones and their partners. Keystones must create opportunities for leveraging and must define the platform in a way that encourages partnership, cooperation, and use. Niche players need to adopt a mind-set that focuses on taking advantage of these opportunities. Together this symbiosis creates a set of relationships, not just among firms, but among their technologies and products, that facilitates integration and joint evolution. Like ancient varieties of bacteria that once lived in close proximity and consumed each other's metabolic products, this intimate association creates the possibility for absorption and integration; extending the platform to encompass new elements enhances its internal capabilities and, through the sharing enabled by the platform, ends up enhancing and evolving the capabilities of the whole network. What matters is not only evolving the platform and its parent organization, but the whole ecosystem of partners that depends on it.

The consequences of this process of business evolution are dramatic. The combination of an adaptable architecture and a dynamic network of technologies connected to it distinguishes healthy networked industries from the brittle monolithic business models that shape existing views of disruption and displacement. Healthy networked industries have a strong capacity for evolution through integration. All network members should benefit from this capacity. Niche players can gain insulation from minor shocks, opportunities to be buoyed by the growth of the architecture, and the power of leverage (as we have discussed in earlier chapters). Keystones benefit uniquely, which is ultimately the source of the incumbent's advantage in a networked environment based on an adaptable platform: The incumbent can use the network to respond to potentially disruptive changes, as we saw in the cases of Merrill and Merloni in chapter 9.

Holistic Technology Strategy

Much of the technology strategy tradition is focused on studying how firms tackle a single, identifiable technology transition. Whether it is the transition from wind and animal exertion to steam as the source of power or the transition from 5.25-inch to 3.5-inch disk drives, strategists have traditionally advised firms how to marshal internal resources and respond to *individual* threats and opportunities. We are instead advocating a more holistic approach to managing technology, a way to understand, systematically, how to make the best of the myriad of threats and opportunities that confront today's executive every year. The focus for innovation leaders should be on understanding the overall health of their business ecosystems and on responding to and influencing their ecosystems' evolution. Panic about individual threats should be replaced by broader, systematic consideration of ecosystem health and by deep-rooted capabilities in technology selection, architecture, and integration. Combined with strong and diverse leadership, this is much more likely to give rise to a proactive, holistic way of crafting technology strategy.

Good ecosystem health is essential. If a business ecosystem is productive, robust, and continues to create niches, plenty of opportunities for innovation will be created. But if a firm shares its fate with an unhealthy ecosystem domain, its future well-being will be uncertain.

The threat for Microsoft is not in any individual technological transition, but in a potential decrease in the health of its ISV community or in that community's gradual transition to a new platform. Wal-Mart will be threatened not by new technology or new channels, but by changes in the dynamics of its ecosystem that would cause its suppliers or technology providers to switch away from it or go out of business.

The implications for niche players are also fundamental. When the ecosystem is healthy, leveraging centralized industry platforms such as Microsoft or Li & Fung is a source of great advantage. These platforms nowadays frequently offer solutions that are superior to those available through internal R&D. The availability of superior external technology does not mean that firms need no internal capabilities for managing technological change. However, it does mean that the capabilities that they need are fundamentally different. Rather than the capacity to perform autonomous innovation, they need the capability to architect and integrate external technology. This will enable them not only to manage individual transitions more effectively, but also to put in place the kind of capability to manage the large variety of different technological changes the typical firm now faces simultaneously.

Implementing this approach requires more than a shift in outlook. Simply monitoring ecosystem health is not enough: Firms must take an active role in responding to and shaping ecosystem health in ways that promote and facilitate the leveraging of an enduring and evolving core. Niche players should assess their ecosystems for changes in the ease with which the ecosystem enables them to respond to emerging challenges: Are new technologies or business models made available through the ecosystem with a minimum of upheaval and cost? Do the platforms on which they rely encapsulate the implications of these changes in ways that are useful rather than disruptive? They should also proactively develop options in case the keystones and networks they rely on become less healthy or change strategy, or simply fail to reliably meet these important requirements. Conversely, firms that sit at significant hubs in their business networks should do all they can to ensure that these requirements are met. They should focus on managing the enormous impact they will have on the health of their ecosystems and of neighboring domains.

This is the price that keystones must pay for their privileged position at the hub of a business network and as the owners of enduring assets: Keystones *must* manage the health of their ecosystems as a key business priority. They must meet the dual challenges of focusing on what endures in a platform in the face of major changes while at the same time exploiting novelty by incorporating solutions from around their network and then sharing those solutions with the network. At the heart of this process is the proactive management of transitions—the explicit recognition of opportunities for change, and the active guidance of the ecosystem through those changes via a process of platform evolution.

Microsoft may provide the quintessential example of the way in which a keystone manages these processes. Although Microsoft's ecosystem has witnessed dramatic shifts in technology, the number of firms in that ecosystem has grown consistently, and their productivity has remained remarkably stable (see figure 11-2). Through each of these transitions, Microsoft has provided a series of new technology platforms to its community of partners to help them respond to the dramatic changes in their environments. The company provided key building blocks for organizations in its ecosystem to effect needed evolutions in technology, infrastructure, and business model. These were leveraged by thousands of firms, ranging in size from giants such as AOL to small start-ups such as Groove Networks.

Each of these transitions is complex and involves many parallel efforts. In each the central task is to respond with an evolutionary approach: to view each "threat" as a potential new avenue for the evolution of the platform. This requires not only mapping out a forward-looking strategy that incorporates the changes enabled by the new development, but also a careful process of redefining of the core platform—a process of identifying and defining what endures. This is the crux of platform durability: When effectively managed, platforms consistently reinterpret changes that in their raw form might destabilize individual firms and express them in terms of an enduring set of shared solutions. This enables incumbents to adapt and to leverage past investments, and allows the ecosystem as a whole to preserve much of its structure and dynamics. Rather than being disrupted, the system *evolves*.

FIGURE 11-2

Managing Stability Through Transitions in the Microsoft Ecosystem

Despite significant shifts in the technologies upon which the majority of applications are built (several are indicated with approximate dates of initial impact), Microsoft's ecosystem has remained remarkably stable. Through each of these waves, productivity (measured as millions of dollars of revenue per employee for public firms with between 50 and 50,000 employees) and firm numbers (both total numbers and numbers of public firms) in this ecosystem (defined as software firms that produce products targeting the Windows platform) have grown steadily.

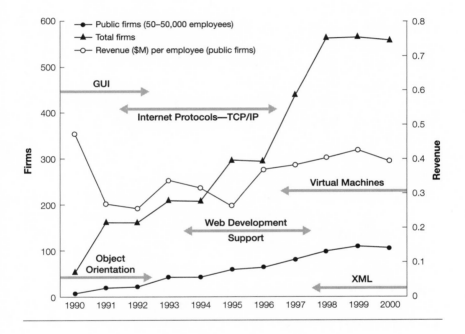

Business Ecology and Sustainability

The evolution of business ecosystems, their ubiquity, and the reliance by organizations on other organizations to accomplish all but the simplest tasks have changed the nature of business. From a world of vertical integration, internal capabilities, internal R&D, internal projects, and internal infrastructure, we have come to a world of mutual dependencies, distributed innovation, technology integration, trading collaboration, and on-demand capabilities. Leveraging the distributed assets of an extended network of business partners has opened the way to unprecedented innovation and operational flexibility. At the same time, it has introduced massive and complex dependencies that are increasingly dominating firm performance. This increasingly ingrained web of dependencies in modern business has broader implications for the ecological analogies drawn in this book.

We are bound together by the nature of the relationships among products, technologies, markets, and innovation. Leveraging these relationships is critical to enhance firm productivity, to protect organizations from disruption, and to enhance their ability to innovate, evolve, and adapt. This means that no firm, product, or technology can be an island: No firm can afford to act alone, and no products can be designed in isolation. We are not just talking about technology networks that connect different information systems to make business processes more efficient. We are talking about interconnected communities of people and organizations that truly share in collective success and failure.

The dynamics of an ecosystem change our perspective about the sustainability of business strategies. Because collective effects are crucial to firm performance, sustainability is a function of the health of the whole ecosystem, not just of individual firm's capabilities. This demands a new look at notions of competition. Two different species in the same ecosystem may compete for food, but both will thrive if their ecosystem is healthy. Each will be hurt if their ecosystem suffers (for example, if it becomes polluted). In a similar fashion, different technology firms, although they may compete on multiple fronts, share a collective interest in the health of the technology sector. Despite perhaps competing on individual product lines, each will benefit from collective accomplishments such as the establishment of common standards and integrative platforms. All too often, however, we have seen that companies and communities will still abandon the common perspective when facing critical business decisions.

Even when executives embrace the idea of an ecosystem on the surface level, they often will stop short of making decisions that go beyond the optimization of individual business performance. They will often insist on arguing that "their" ecosystem is better than their competitors, ignoring the fact that both ecosystems are effectively one and the same. Moreover, we have seen how considerations of long-term ecosystem health are consistently ignored in order to maximize individual short-term profits. Enron and WorldCom came close to destroying their respective industries in short-sighted efforts to maximize individual wealth. Linux and Windows would both be better (and their customers better off) if their respective champions stopped fighting and found ways to integrate with each other more effectively.

If we take the concept of an ecosystem seriously, the analogy should carry us beyond traditional notions of competition to a more progressive understanding of interfirm dynamics. We have outlined in previous chapters how individual organizations should move to better leverage and shape their surrounding ecosystems. We have discussed key assets and capabilities, and defined a number of strategies for deploying them. But to reach the full potential of these ideas, we feel that a deeper philosophical shift is needed. The emergent philosophy should emphasize that individual firms will live and die by the health of their ecosystems, and should thus take these fundamental considerations deeply into account when making business decisions.

The greatest part of this burden will fall on the small number of firms that occupy business network hubs. Companies such as Microsoft, Wal-Mart, Li & Fung, and eBay have performed an enormously important role in our society, with a very large impact on large sectors of our economy. It is almost incredible to think that a few thousand people at Microsoft and eBay have shaped the destiny of the 7 million developers that program for the Windows platform, or of the 70 million members of the eBay community. As part of effective keystone strategies, these organizations have promoted the health of their ecosystems, and have benefited as a result. Crucially, what started as an opportunity, and continued as a clever and effective strategy, has now in a sense become a responsibility. Society would suffer deeply if these organizations stopped playing their respective roles (or if competition or regulation somehow prevented them from doing so).

We believe that it is essential for the health and vigor of our economy that the crucial roles played by these organizations be safeguarded and reinforced. These considerations should influence future thinking regarding policy and regulation. We hope that the ideas in this book will spur a new look at antitrust economics, balancing the potential threat of monopolistic behavior with the value that can be created by an effective keystone strategy. At the same time, we also believe that executives would benefit from a deeper understanding of the enormous impact that their organizations have on their ecosystem and on society at large. It was sobering to us to discover how often in the past ten years careless mistakes were made that had an impact that was far broader than predicted. All too often executives in organizations ranging from AOL to Enron simply had no understanding of how some immediate decision they had to make could have an impact on companies they did not even know existed.

The implosion of the dot-com and telecommunications industries has generated rampant uncertainty and strong concerns about the future strength and stability of the technology sector, or even of our economy at large. Polarizing arguments have ensued among communities of academics, policy makers, analysts, and practitioners that challenge basic notions of innovation, intellectual property, and competition. We suggest that much of the disruptive confusion regarding these subjects may have been prompted by the fundamental changes discussed here, and caused by the frequently surprising collective behavior of distributed networks of organizations. We hope that the frameworks presented in this book will generate new, structured analysis and debates on the dynamics of business ecosystems. We believe this would have important implications for a wide range of domains, from product architecture and operations to business strategy and policy.

Notes

Chapter One

1. Our work builds on the work of a variety of other authors who have shaped this field, most importantly, James F. Moore, who pioneered the application of biological ecosystems to the business context. See James F. Moore, "Predators and Prey: A New Ecology of Competition," *Harvard Business Review,* May–June 1993; James F. Moore, *The Death of Competition: Leadership and Strategy in the Age of Business Ecosystems* (New York: HarperBusiness, 1996).

2. For a conflicting viewpoint on the value of ecology as a metaphor for industries, see "Business as a Living System: The Value of Industrial Ecology. A Roundtable Discussion," *California Management Review* 43 (Spring 2001): 16–25.

Chapter Two

1. Robert Gavin, "Regional Report: States Join to Prepare for Disasters," *Wall Street Journal,* 12 December 2001, B11.

2. Jeff D. Opdyke and Karen Damato, "Accessing Money Proves Difficult in These Trying Times," *Wall Street Journal,* 14 September 2001, C1.

3. Quentin Hardy, "The Killer Ad Machine," *Forbes,* 11 December 2000.

4. See J. D. Nason, E. A. Herre, and J. L. Hamrick, "The Breeding Structure of a Tropical Keystone Plant Resource," *Nature* 391 (12 February 1998): 685–687; F. R. Lambert and A. G. Marshall, "Keystone Characteristics of Bird-Dispersed Ficus in a Malaysian Lowland Rain Forest," *Journal of Ecology* 79 (1991): 793–809; and T. G. O'Brien et al., "What's So Special About Figs?" *Nature* 392 (16 April 1998): 668.

5. This vivid image is from E. O. Wilson, quoted in *Harvard* magazine, March–April 2003.

6. See C. Y. Baldwin and K. B. Clark, *Design Rules* (Cambridge, MA: MIT Press, 2000) and E. M. Pugh, *Memories That Shaped an Industry* (Cambridge, MA: MIT Press, 1984).

7. Moreover, this distribution of innovative activity brings the opportunity to innovate closer to the loci of innovative thinking and problem solving, thus

enhancing the quality and relevance of innovations. See, for example, Eric Von Hippel, "The Impact of 'Sticky Data' on Innovation and Problem Solving," *Management Science* 40, no. 4 (1994): 429–439; and Eric Von Hippel and Stephan Thomke, "Customers as Innovators: A New Way to Create Value," *Harvard Business Review*, April 2002, 74–81.

8. See, for example, James F. Moore, *The Death of Competition: Leadership and Strategy in the Age of Business Ecosystems* (New York: HarperBusiness, 1996).

9. Examples include automobiles (see Moore, *Death of Competition*), construction (see R. G. Eccles, "The Quasifirm in the Construction Industry," *Journal of Economic Behavior and Organization* 2 [1981]: 335–357), and biotechnology (see W. W. Powell, K. W. Koput, and L. Smith-Doerr, "Interorganizational Collaboration and the Locus of Innovation: Networks of Learning in Biotechnology," *Administrative Science Quarterly* 41 [March 1996]: 116–145).

10. This section on apparel draws from F. Warren McFarlan and Fred Young, "Li & Fung (A): Internet Issues," Case 9-301-009 (Boston: Harvard Business School, 2001).

11. Janice H. Hammond and Maura G. Kelly, "Quick Response in the Apparel Industry," Case 9-690-038 (Boston: Harvard Business School, 1991).

12. Dennis K. Berman et al., "Leading the News: Telecom Sector's Crash Shows Signs of Deepening" *Wall Street Journal,* 23 April 2002.

13. Yochi J. Dreazen, "Behind the Fiber Glut: Telecom Carriers Were Driven by Wildly Optimistic Data on Internet's Growth Rate," *Wall Street Journal,* 26 September 2002.

14. Ibid.

15. Rebecca Blumenstein and Gregory Zuckerman, "Domino Effect: Telecom's Troubles Spread from Upstarts to Sector's Leaders," *Wall Street Journal,* 13 March 2002.

16. Steven Rosenbush et al., "Inside the Telecom Game," *BusinessWeek,* 5 August 2002; Dreazen et al., "Behind the Fiber Glut."

17. Blumenstein and Zuckerman, "Domino Effect." Prices have also declined. Price wars have "brought down long-distance per-minute prices to as low as a penny a minute." "Prices for data transport among the many fiber-optic companies have declined as much as 50 percent a year." Wireless prices have also fallen. A *BusinessWeek* review of the industry sees harder times ahead, before any meaningful transformation of the industry can take place: "The first stage, happening now, is managing the glut. This involves slashing costs and struggling to come to terms with massive debt. This period, which should last another two years, will continue to drive many companies to the brink of insolvency or beyond. But relief won't arrive until stage two, consolidation. That's not likely to come until mid-decade, when the surviving companies have

cleaned up their balance sheets and can afford to snap up rivals who have been driven to rock-bottom prices—pennies on the dollar." (Steve Rosenbush et al., "When Will the Telecom Depression End?" *BusinessWeek,* 7 October 2002.)

18. See Baldwin and Clark, *Design Rules;* M. L. Tushman and P. Anderson, "Technological Discontinuities and Organizational Environments," *Administrative Science Quarterly* 31 (1986): 439–465; and M. Iansiti and T. Khanna, "Technological Evolution, System Architecture and the Obsolescence of Firm Capabilities," *Industrial and Corporate Change* 4, no. 2 (1995): 333–361.

19. This important insight is drawn from Baldwin and Clark's *Design Rules,* which discusses it in depth.

20. Von Hippel and Thomke, "Customers as Innovators."

21. See Baldwin and Clark, *Design Rules.* Also see Carver Meade and Lynn Conway, *Introduction to VLSI Systems* (Reading, MA: Addison-Wesley, 1980).

22. Interestingly, it was the early but smaller-scale success of the Apple II and the TRS-80 that caused IBM to introduce the PC in the first place, and the strong time-to-market pressure generated by the perceived threat of these platforms was a major contributing factor in shaping the architecture of the PC.

23. See, for example, Frank P. Coyle, *XML, Web Services, and the Data Revolution* (Reading, MA: Addison-Wesley, 2002). For a look at loosely coupled organizations, see J. D. Orton and K. E. Weick, "Loosely Coupled Systems: A Reconceptualization," *Academy of Management Review* 15 (1990): 203–223; and J. W. Rivkin, "Reproducing Knowledge: Replication Without Imitation at Moderate Complexity," *Organization Science* 12, no. 3 (May–June 2001): 274–293.

24. J. I. Cash and B. R. Koszynsky, "IS Redraws Competitive Boundaries," *Harvard Business Review,* March–April 1985, 134–142.

25. EDI involved the translation of each common business document, such as a purchase order, purchase order acknowledgment, or sales order, into a very specific, relatively rigid format.

26. For example, see M. Hammer, "The Superefficient Company," *Harvard Business Review,* September 2001, 82–91.

27. McFarlan and Young, "Li & Fung (A)," 6.

28. Ibid.

29. "Li & Fung, Microsoft Tie Up for SCM," <http://www.microsoft.com/hk/enterprise/lifung.htm> (accessed 12 March 2003). "Microsoft represents the industry standard," said Fung. He added that although the U.S. software giant had yet to prove as venerable as his own 100-year-old company, "We're confident that [Microsoft] will be here 100 years from now."

30. See Stanley Wasserman and Katherine Faust, *Social Network Analysis* (Cambridge, UK: Cambridge University Press, 1994).

Chapter Three

1. See R. D. Dewar and J. E. Dutton, "The Adoption of Radical and Incremental Innovations: An Empirical Analysis," *Management Science* 32, no. 11 (1986): 1422–1433; M. L. Tushman and P. Anderson, "Technological Discontinuities and Organizational Environments," *Administrative Science Quarterly* 31 (1986): 439–465; R. M. Henderson and K. B. Clark, "Architectural Innovation: The Reconfiguration of Existing Product Technologies and the Failure of Established Firms," *Administrative Science Quarterly* 35 (1990): 9–30; and Clayton M. Christensen, *The Innovator's Dilemma: When New Technologies Cause Great Firms to Fail* (Boston: Harvard Business School Press, 1997).

2. Part of this is made possible by the way that the Windows APIs have evolved. For example, the APIs that were used for accessing files on floppies and drives have been expanded to deal with each new storage medium (from CD-ROMS to DVDs and digital cameras) as it has been introduced.

3. Interestingly, this continuity may lead to an underappreciation of the extent to which an ecosystem is responding constructively to potentially threatening innovations. The assimilation of digital photography as a core part of both the Windows and Macintosh platforms over the last few years has occurred with little remark, partly because of the continuity with which it has been achieved. This contrasts with more noticeable failures to achieve similar integration, such as the incorporation of Memory Stick slots into most recent Sony televisions.

4. The case of figs is again instructive (see J. D. Nason, E. A. Herre, and J. L. Hamrick, "The Breeding Structure of a Tropical Keystone Plant Resource," *Nature* 391 [12 February 1998]: 685–687).

5. C. Y. Baldwin and K. B. Clark, in their book *Design Rules* (Cambridge, MA: MIT Press, 2000), provide an interesting classification of different "modular operators" that carve out products to provide new technological configurations.

6. It is important to note, however, that these features by no means define network health in any general sense. A wide variety of networks exist, designed to achieve a wide variety of goals, and these goals may be quite different from those of productive, stable, and creative business networks. One need only think of the dramatic counterexample of terrorist networks such as Al Qaeda. Such networks are neither interested in creativity nor productivity, but are focused primarily on survivability and invisibility. Moreover, although survivability is superficially a kind of "robustness," it is precisely the opposite of the kind we believe is important for business networks: Terror networks are most concerned with being invulnerable to targeted malicious attacks, and so avoid the presence of hubs altogether. Such networks would have a very different set of network health measures.

See chapter 5 for an elaboration of the health measures discussed in this book as applied to Microsoft's effect on the computing ecosystem.

Chapter Four

1. See Michael Porter, *Competitive Advantage: Creating and Sustaining Superior Performance* (New York: Free Press, 1985) and Pankaj Gemawat, *Commitment: The Dynamic of Strategy* (New York: Free Press, 1991), among many others. For the classic view of "operating strategy," see R. H. Hayes and S. C. Wheelwright, *Restoring Our Competitive Edge: Competing Through Manufacturing* (New York: John Wiley & Sons, 1984) and R. H. Hayes, S. C. Wheelwright, and K. B. Clark, *Dynamic Manufacturing: Creating the Learning Organization* (New York: Free Press, 1988).

2. See, for example, D. Garvin, "Quality Problems, Policies, and Attitudes in the United States and Japan: An Exploratory Study," *Academy of Management Journal* 29 (1986): 653–673; and K. B. Clark and T. Fujimoto, *Product Development Performance: Strategy, Organization, and Management in the World Auto Industry* (Boston: Harvard Business School Press, 1991).

3. See, for example, A. D. Chandler Jr., *Scale and Scope: The Dynamics of Industrial Capitalism* (Cambridge, MA: Belknap Press, 1990) and W. Lazonic, *Competitive Advantage on the Shop Floor* (Cambridge, MA: Harvard University Press, 1990).

4. See D. J. Teece, "Towards an Economic Theory of the Multiproduct Firm," *Journal of Economic Behavior and Organization* 3 (1982): 39–63; R. Nelson and S. Winter, *An Evolutionary Theory of Economic Change* (Cambridge, MA: Belknap Press, 1982); C. K. Prahalad and G. Hamel, "The Core Competence of the Corporation," *Harvard Business Review,* May–June 1990, 79–91; D. Leonard-Barton, "Core Capabilities and Core Rigidities: A Paradox in Managing New Product Development," *Strategic Management Journal* 13 (1992): 111–125; and Jan Rivkin, "Imitation of Complex Strategies," *Management Science* 46 (2000): 824–844.

5. See M. Iansiti and K. B. Clark, "Integration and Dynamic Capability: Evidence from Product Development in Automobiles and Mainframe Computers," *Industrial and Corporate Change* 3, no. 3 (1994): 557–605; M. L. Tushman and C. O'Reilly, *Winning Through Innovation: A Practical Guide to Leading Organizational Change and Renewal* (Boston: Harvard Business School Press, 1997); and K. M. Eisenhardt and D. Sull, "Strategy as Simple Rules," *Harvard Business Review,* January–February 2001, 106–116.

6. See, for example, Clark and Fujimoto, *Product Development Performance,* and E. von Hippel, *The Sources of Innovation* (New York: Oxford University Press, 1988).

7. Much of the literature on supply chains is based on the field of operations research, which is focused more on problems such as production forecasting and capacity optimization than on the more general managerial implications of network interactions and network structure.

8. The work of Charles Fine, captured in his book *Clockspeed: Winning Industry Control in the Age of Temporary Advantage* (New York: Perseus Books, 1998), provides a notable exception. Additionally, the work of Ananth Raman, Nicole DeHoratius, and Zeynep Tom provides fascinating accounts and analysis of real, imperfect supply chain networks, targeting problems caused by asymmetric incentive structures or bad data.

9. Among this literature, one can sample W. J. Abernathy and J. M. Utterback, "Patterns of Industrial Innovation," *Technology Review* 50 (1978); M. L. Tushman and P. Anderson, "Technological Discontinuities and Organizational Environments," *Administrative Science Quarterly* 31 (1986): 439–465; R. M. Henderson and K. B. Clark, "Architectural Innovation: The Reconfiguration of Existing Product Technologies and the Failure of Established Firms," *Administrative Sciences Quarterly* 35 (1990): 9–3; and Clayton M. Christensen, *The Innovator's Dilemma: When New Technologies Cause Great Firms to Fail* (Boston: Harvard Business School Press, 1997).

10. Baldwin and Clark, *Design Rules;* Carl Shapiro and Hal Varian, *Information Rules: A Strategic Guide to the Network Economy* (Boston: Harvard Business School Press, 1998); Annabelle Gawer and Michael Cusumano, *Platform Leadership: How Intel, Microsoft, and Cisco Drive Industry Innovation* (Boston: Harvard Business School Press, 2002).

11. Shapiro and Varian, *Information Rules.*

12. Examples in nature are food webs (see Richard J. Williams and Neo D. Martinez, "Simple Rules Yield Complex Food Webs," *Nature* 404 [2000]: 180–183) and ecosystems (see Gary A. Polis, "Ecology: Stability Is Woven by Complex Webs," *Nature* 395 [1998]: 744–745). For examples in the man-made world, see Brian W. Arthur, "Why Do Things Become More Complex?" *Scientific American,* May 1993, 144.

13. For the forest fire example and many others, see Richard Sole and Brian Goodwin, *Signs of Life: How Complexity Pervades Biology* (New York: Basic Books, 2002).

14. Dirk Helbing and Martin Treiber, "Jams, Waves, and Clusters," *Science* 282 (1998): 2001–2003; L. D. Henley, "The RMA After the Next," *Parameters* (Winter 1999–2000): 46–57; James Dao and Andrew C. Revkin, "A Revolution in Warfare," *New York Times,* 16 April 2002; Ann Grimes, "Looking Backward, Moving Forward," *Wall Street Journal,* 20 June 2002; Eric Bonabeau, Marco Dorigo, and Guy Thereaulaz, *Swarm Intelligence: From Natural to Artificial Systems* (Cambridge, UK: Oxford University Press, 1999).

15. B. A. Huberman, *The Laws of the Web: Patterns in the Ecology of Information* (Cambridge, MA: MIT Press, 2001); S. A. Kauffman, *The Origins of Order: Self-Organization and Selection in Evolution* (Cambridge, UK: Oxford University Press, 1993).

16. See, for example, Reka Albert and Albert-Laszlo Barabási, "Emergence of Scaling in Random Networks," *Science* 286 (1999): 509–512; David Cohen, "All the World's a Net," *New Scientist* 174, no. 2338 (2002): 24–29; M. E. J. Newman, "The Structure of Scientific Collaboration Networks," *Proceedings of the National Academy of Sciences* 98 (2001): 404–409; and Albert-Laszlo Barabási, *Linked: The New Science of Networks* (New York: Perseus, 2002), 64.

17. "The Oracle of Bacon at Virginia," University of Virginia, Department of Computer Science Web page, <http://www.cs.virginia.edu/oracle/> (accessed 5 May 2002).

18. Huberman, *Laws of the Web*.

19. For Web hubs, see Bernardo Huberman and Lada A. Adamic, "Growth Dynamics of the World-Wide Web," *Nature* 401 (1999): 131. For the "bow-tie" structure of the Web, see Andrei Broder et al., "Graph Structure in the Web," IBM Almaden Research Center Web site, May 2000, <http://www.almaden.ibm.com/cs/k53/www9.final> (accessed 1 March 2004).

20. Reuven Cohen, Keren Erez, Daniel ben-Avraham, and Schlomo Havlin, "Resilience of the Internet to Random Breakdowns," *Physical Review Letters* 85, no. 21 (2000): 4626–4628.

21. See references above and reviews in Barabási, *Linked,* and Duncan J. Watts, *Small Worlds: The Dynamics of Networks Between Order and Randomness* (Princeton: Princeton University Press, 2002).

22. See Y. Tu, "How Robust Is the Internet?" *Nature* 406 (2000): 353–354.

23. The ecological literature contains many conflicting definitions of the term *keystone,* and some debate the extent of its relevance. See, for example, L. S. Mills, M. E. Soulé, and D. F. Doak, "The Keystone-Species Concept in Ecology and Conservation," *BioScience* 4 (1993): 219–224. Its original use was quite narrow (see R. T. Paine, "Food-Web Analysis Through Field Measurement of Per Capita Interaction Strength," *Nature* 355, no. 6355 [1992]: 73–75), but current usage sometimes ranges to the indiscriminate. Here we use the term in its most neutral and least technical form: A keystone is simply a species that governs important ecosystem health, often without being a significant portion of the ecosystem itself. Other analogies can be found in social network theory. J. F. Padgett and C. K. Ansell, in "Robust Action and the Rise of the Medici, 1400–1434," *American Journal of Sociology* 98, no. 6 (1993): 1259–1319, analyze the ways in which the Medici manipulated the social networks of which they were the center to effectively consolidate a stable modern state around them.

24. Indeed, this relationship between keystone species and their ecosystem is an element of the criteria used in the Endangered Species Act to evaluate the ecological value of species. Dramatic examples of the loss of nonkeystone species include the passenger pigeon and American chestnut. See Richard B. Primack, *Essentials of Conservation Biology* (Sunderland, MA: Sinauer Associates, 2000).

25. See, for example, D. Tilman and J. A. Downing, "Biodiversity and Stability in Grasslands," *Nature* 367 (1994): 363–365.

26. See Paine, "Food-Web Analysis."

27. J. A. Estes and J. F. Palmisano, "Sea Otters: Their Role in Structuring Nearshore Communities," *Science* 185 (1974): 1058–1060.

28. G. R. Van Blaricom and J. A. Estes, eds., *The Community Ecology of Sea Otters, Ecological Studies* 65 (New York: Springer-Verlag, 1988); J. A. Estes and D. O. Duggins, "Sea Otters and Kelp Forests in Alaska: Generality and Variation in a Community Ecological Paradigm," *Ecological Monographs* 65 (1995): 75–100.

29. Although sea otters are among the smallest marine mammals, they lack a thick layer of blubber and depend on high metabolic rates to maintain body heat, which requires that they consume up to one-third of their weight in food a day.

30. R. T. Paine, "Food-Web Analysis"; M. E. Power et al., "Challenges in the Quest for Keystones," *Bioscience* 46 (1996): 609–620.

31. S. L. Collins et al., "Modulation of Diversity by Grazing and Mowing in Native Tallgrass Prairie," *Science* 280 (1998): 745–747. In fact, simply simulating grazing (e.g., by mowing) has much the same diversity-enhancing effect.

32. J. H. Brown et al., "Complex Species Interactions and the Dynamics of Ecological Systems: Long-Term Experiments," *Science* 293 (2001): 643–650.

33. Domination of ecosystems is a major theme of the literature on conservation ecology. Threats to many native ecosystems from non-native invaders often take the form of domination of the ecosystem by the invader. See, for example, J. A. Drake et al., eds. *Biological Invasions: A Global Perspective* (Chichester, UK: Wiley, 1989).

34. Daniel Q. Thompson, Ronald L. Stuckey, and Edith B. Thompson, "Spread, Impact, and Control of Purple Loosestrife *(Lythrum salicaria)* in North American Wetlands," U.S. Fish and Wildlife Service, *Fish and Wildlife Research* 2 (1987).

35. Estes and Duggins, "Sea Otters and Kelp Forests."

36. See, for example, Noah Schactman, "A War of Robots, All Chattering on the Western Front," *New York Times,* 11 July 2002, E5.

Chapter Five

1. Corporate Technology Information Services (CorpTech, since acquired by OneSource Information Services) collects annual data on high-technology companies. The CorpTech data contain observations for more than 11,000 software firms based in the United States in 2000.

2. EDC publishes two surveys that are relevant. The North American Developers (NAD) survey consists of a panel that includes both corporate and ISV developers. About 50 percent of respondents develop software for use primarily inside the company. The other half design custom or commercial software for sale to clients or customers outside the company. The survey includes developers working for companies of all sizes in a wide variety of industries. The survey considers two important questions. First, it asks respondents for "the operating system that they run primarily on the computer they use to do most of their programming." In total, 77 percent of respondents said that they primarily used a Windows operating system (95, 98, NT, or 2000) to develop software applications. Second, the survey asks, "Which target OS best describes the type of apps you work on most often?" About 72 percent of respondents said they were primarily targeting Windows operating systems. The percentage of developers who said that they would primarily target a Windows operating system in 2001 was 69.1, with a big shift in focus from Windows NT to Windows 2000. About half of developers said they would begin to target Windows 2000 in the next 12 months, and another 17 percent said it would take them more than a year to begin developing applications for Windows 2000.

Data regarding IT managers come from the Enterprise Development Management Issues (EDMI) survey, which consists of interviews with 400 senior IT managers employed at corporate enterprises with 2,000 or more employees. The survey instrument is similar to the one used for the NAD survey. About 72 percent of respondents to the EDMI survey said that they used a Windows platform (NT, 9x, 2000) to do most of their programming. This represents a slight increase from the 2000 survey, in which 66 percent said they primarily used a Windows platform. About 69 percent of respondents say that they are targeting "most" of their applications to Windows platforms, a decline from 74 percent in early 2001. Moreover, 77 percent of respondents say that they intend to develop applications for Windows XP at some point in the future.

3. For example, Microsoft has hired an outside market research firm to conduct surveys of developers, including independent software developers (20 percent of respondents), corporate MIS departments (40 percent of respondents), and third-party software consulting firms (about 40 percent of respondents). The results of the most recent study, conducted in October 2001, are consistent

with the CorpTech and Evans data. They show that a majority of developers target their software development to multiple platforms, but that Windows remains the primary target operating system. Fifty-nine percent responded with multiple answers when asked, "For which of the following computer operating systems do you currently target applications?" Ninety-one percent responded with at least one version of Windows when asked, "For which of the following computer operating systems do you currently target applications?" Seventy-five percent responded with some version of Windows when asked, "Which is the *primary* operating system to which you target applications?"

4. Prepared text of remarks by Craig Mundie, Microsoft senior vice president, "The Commercial Software Model," New York University Stern School of Business, 3 May 2001. Available at <http://www.microsoft.com/presspass/exec/craig/05-03sharedsource.asp>.

5. IDC, *Worldwide Software Review and Forecast, 2001–2005,* Report no. 25569, 2001. This percentage pales in comparison with similar revenue share numbers by IBM during the 1960s. See Charles H. Ferguson and Charles R. Morris, *Computer Wars: The Fall of IBM and the Future of Global Technology* (New York: Times Books, 1994).

6. See <http://www.asp.net/webmatrix/>.

7. See, for example, Microsoft Corporation, *Real Stories from Real Customers Building Real Applications* (Redmond: Microsoft Corporation Visual Studio.NET Launch, February 2002).

8. See Microsoft Developer's Network Web site: <http://msdn.microsoft.com/library/default.asp?url=/library/en-us/dnbda/html/psimp.asp>.

9. IDC tracks three broad categories of software: applications development and deployment software (ADD), applications software, and systems infrastructure software.

10. IDC, *Worldwide Software Review,* Table 18.

11. Findings of Fact, *United States of America v. Microsoft,* Civil Action no. 98-1232 (5 November 1999): III.2.1.40.

12. Mundie, "The Commercial Software Model."

13. Direct testimony of Paul Maritz, *United States v. Microsoft,* Civil Action no. 98-1232 (20 January 1999): III.A.2.136.

14. Ana Volpi and Carol Monaco, *Developing Developers: Developer Support Program Dynamics and the Strategic Role of Developer Support,* International Data Corporation Report no. 23966 (March 2001).

15. Steve Lohr, "Microsoft Puts Its Muscle Behind Web Programming Tools," *New York Times,* 13 February 2002, C1.

16. In more formal terms, the value curve should increase with N with an exponent that is larger than 1. This does not have to be the case for the entire

value curve, since the value of the assets may eventually saturate, but should indeed be the case for the region in which the organization that makes up the platform hub operates.

17. Ann Zimmerman and Emily Nelson, "In Hour of Peril, Americans Bought Guns, TV Sets," *Wall Street Journal,* 18 September 2001, B1.

18. "Distribution Network Slated for Expansion," *Mass Market Retailers* 17, no. 8 (2000): 67.

19. Amy Tsao, "Where Retailers Shop for Savings," *BusinessWeek Online* (15 April 2002), <http://www.business.week.com/technology/content/apr2002/tc20020415_6269.htm>.

20. "Hicks with Bags of Tricks," *The Australian,* 14 December 2001, 34.

21. "Chicago Summit Retail Systems '97: Demand-Side Economics," *Chain Store Age,* 1 October 1997, 19B.

22. Ibid.

23. Bradford C. Johnson, "Retail: The Wal-Mart Effect," *McKinsey Quarterly,* no. 1 (2002): 40–43.

Chapter Six

1. Frank Gibney Jr., "Enron Plays the Pipes," *Time,* 28 August 2000.

2. David Campbell and Ron Hulme, "The Winner-Takes-All Economy" *McKinsey Quarterly,* no. 1 (2001).

3. Robert Preston and Mike Koller, "Enron Feels the Power," *InternetWeek,* 30 October 2000. "In the natural gas sector, for instance, the company now sells about 20 times its pipeline capacity (and it owns 5,000 fewer miles of pipeline than it did in 1985)."

4. Ibid.

5. William H. Miller, "Vision Vanquisher," *Industry Week,* 18 May 1998.

6. Julian E. Barnes, Megan Barnett, Christopher H. Schmidt, and Marianne Lavell, "How a Titan Came Undone," *U.S. News and World Report,* 18 March 2002.

7. Suzanne Kapner, "A Rush to Hire Enron Employees," *New York Times,* 8 March 2002.

8. Letter from Joseph I. Lieberman, Chairman of the Senate Governmental Affairs Committee, to Pat Wood, III, Chairman of the Federal Energy Regulatory Commission, 14 May 12002, <http://www.senate.gov/~gov_affairs/051502 woodletter.htm> (accessed 22 January 2003).

9. Harry Hurt III, "Power Players," *Fortune,* 5 August 1996.

10. Julia King and Gary H. Anthes, "Enron Hits the Gas," *Computerworld, Inc.,* 20 November 2000.

11. Malcolm Gladwell, "The Talent Myth," *New Yorker,* 22 July 2002, 30.

12. Loren Fox, *Enron: The Rise and Fall* (Hoboken, NJ: John Wiley & Sons, 2003), 208–210.

13. Chris Taylor, "California Scheming," *Time,* 20 May 2002, <http://cgi.cnn.com/ALLPOLITICS/time/2002/05/20/scheming.html> (accessed 5 March 2003).

14. Fox, *Enron,* 208–210.

15. Taylor, "California Scheming."

16. Ibid.

17. Erick Schonfeld, "What Goes Around Comes Around," *Business 2.0,* 21 July 2000, <http://www.business2.com/articles/web/0,1653,6923,FF.html> (accessed March 5, 2003).

18. See, for example, R. M. Henderson and K. B. Clark, "Architectural Innovation: The Reconfiguration of Existing Product Technologies and the Failure of Established Firms," *Administrative Science Quarterly* 35 (1990): 9–3; Clayton M. Christensen, *The Innovator's Dilemma: When New Technologies Cause Great Firms to Fail* (Boston: Harvard Business School Press, 1997); and M. L. Tushman and P. Anderson, "Technological Discontinuities and Organizational Environments," *Administrative Science Quarterly* 31 (1986): 439–465.

19. Indeed, as we have mentioned elsewhere, the relationship between stability and diversity in biological ecosystems is complex and poorly understood, and there are cases where lower diversity enhances stability.

Chapter Seven

1. Iris Origo, *The Merchant of Prato* (Boston: D.R. Godine, 1986), 113.

2. Naturally, significant precision can be added to the definitions of "typical" and "relationship." For the first, one can assume a certain distribution of relationships for certain classes of ecosystems, and define a precise level below which organizations are defined as niche players. For the second, one can track various types of business relationships, such as formal or informal partnerships, buyer–customer linkages, and so forth.

3. Interview with Gerry Mooney, IBM VP of Strategy, 28 January 2003.

4. "About deNovis," <http://www.denovis.com/about/overview/> (accessed 21 January 2003).

5. Examples cited by Ralf Brown, CTO, include things such as "threading models" that other platforms, such as IBM's WebSphere, do not "hide" effectively. Interview with Ralph Brown, 23 April 2001.

6. An important corollary of the role of keystones in driving the continued expansion of the platform is that this process also drives all firms in the ecosystem "outward" toward new functionality and new niches at the edge of the eco-

system. Many firms that fail to (or choose not to) follow this path in domains that are not durable as distinct segments may find themselves in a high-risk (but also potentially high-stakes) game for which they may be unprepared.

The situation of having a niche encroached on can also arise when a firm simply stakes out a niche that is "too close" to the frontier of the platform. Netscape and Real are examples of firms that, famously, have set up shop too close to the advancing frontier of the Microsoft platform.

7. Vermeer Technologies, the source of Microsoft's FrontPage technology, is an example of a firm that chose to use its "platform frontier" position effectively by striking a lucrative deal with Microsoft that contributed to overall ecosystem health and ensured the continued survival of the firm's products and technologies (in much the same way that a single bacterial cell, by being absorbed into the "eukaryotic platform," ensured its position as the ancestor of every mitochondrion on Earth). It is worth noting that in following this path, firms must resist the desire to preserve a clear identity for themselves. This creates an important dynamic in growing ecosystems that pits inertial forces of firm identity against the free flow of components among products, most notably into the platform.

8. A lack of direct competition is not the whole story. It is easy for a keystone, given its powerful, hublike position in a network, to extract an excessive amount of value from the ecosystem and thereby damage its health. This is particularly threatening in environments in which switching costs for niche players are high.

9. NVIDIA SEC 10-K filing for fiscal year ended 27 January 2002.

10. Chris Malachowsky, interview by author, August 2002.

11. Bruce Einhorn, Frederik Balfour, Cliff Edwards, and Pete Engardio, "Betting Big on Chips: Why TSMC Boss Morris Chang Is Spending Billions Despite the Tech Slump," *BusinessWeek,* 30 April 2001, 18.

12. Charles Bickers, "Technology: Fab Innovator," *Far Eastern Economic Review,* 14 October 1999, 10.

13. Ibid.

14. Ibid.

15. Keith Katcher (director of product and test engineering, NVIDIA), "The Virtues of Virtual Test for Fabless IC Developers: A Fabless Company's Case Study," *Integrated Measurement Systems, Public Relations,* 9 March 1999.

16. Ibid.

17. NVIDIA SEC 10-K filing for fiscal year ended 27 January 2002.

18. Application programming interfaces play a crucial role here on both Windows and Linux platforms. On Windows, this role is played by Microsoft's Direct3D API; on Linux, by SGI's OpenGL API.

19. For example, see R. M. Henderson and K. B. Clark, "Architectural Innovation: The Reconfiguration of Existing Product Technologies and the Failure of Established Firms," *Administrative Science Quarterly* 35 (1990): 9–30; and Clayton M. Christensen, *The Innovator's Dilemma: When New Technologies Cause Great Firms to Fail* (Boston: Harvard Business School Press, 1997).

20. NVIDIA Channel Partner Web site, <http://www.nvidia.com/view.asp? PAGE=channel> (accessed 3 March 2002).

21. NVIDIA Developer Web site, <http://developer.nvidia.com/> (accessed 3 March 2002).

Chapter Eight

1. Data from Visa USA; *The Nilson Report,* no. 780 (January 2003); *The Nilson Report,* no. 756 (January 2002); *The Nilson Report,* no. 759 (March 2002); *The Nilson Report,* no. 760 (March 2002); U.S. Census Bureau, <http://www. census.gov/hhes/income/histinc/h05.html> (accessed 12 December 2002); "The Trick Is Managing Money," *BusinessWeek,* 6 June 1970; and Irwin Ross, "The Credit Card's Painful Coming-of-Age," *Fortune,* October 1971.

2. David Evans, "More Than Money: The Development of a Competitive Electronic Payments Industry in the United States," National Economic Research Associates Working Paper, January 2003, 7.

3. Ibid., 7–8.

4. "Carte Blanche Offering Its Credit Card System to Banks on Franchise," *Wall Street Journal,* 7 July 1966; "American Express, Like Rivals, Will Offer Franchises to Banks for Its Credit Cards," *Wall Street Journal,* 15 July 1966.

5. Evans, "More Than Money," 11.

6. Joseph Nocera, *A Piece of the Action: How the Middle Class Joined the Money Class* (New York: Simon & Schuster, 1994), 68.

7. National BankAmericard 1973 Annual Report, 4.

8. Dave Pogue, "Survival of the Fittest for Small Software Companies," *New York Times,* 19 September 2002.

9. Indeed, the early history of both money and abstract number systems suggests the difficulty presented by this abstraction for people who had until its introduction used concrete iconic tokens to serve their functions (the ancient use of distinct clay tokens for cattle, beer, etc., is an example of a kind of standard that lacked the abstractness and generality that makes standards powerful). This has interesting parallels in the comparison of purpose-specific file formats with generally more abstract—but "insubstantial"—standards such as XML.

10. Numerous excellent sources of information on XML are available online. See, for example, <http://www.xml.com>.

11. Conversions between formats are especially powerful because they often result in an ability to interoperate *over time:* Documents and data can age without becoming inaccessible as long as it is possible to perform a conversion from an older format to a current one.

12. Actually, it resulted in a lose-lose-*lose* situation because users ended up with data that couldn't be exchanged among applications.

13. In Microsoft's current platform, for example, XML is pervasive: from integral support in Office XP to the large set of XML-related APIs (not only in the namespaces that explicitly support XML, but also throughout the platform, where it is woven into the fabric of already-existing APIs supporting everything from databases to Web form controls). Almost everywhere that structured information could be of use, support is provided for representing it as XML.

Chapter Nine

1. For the evolution of social insects, see, for example, E. O. Wilson, *The Insect Societies* (Cambridge, MA: Harvard University Press, 1971). For the evolution of cells, see C. De Duv, "The Birth of Complex Cells" *Scientific American,* April 1996, 50–57.

2. T. D. Seeley, *The Wisdom of the Hive* (Cambridge, MA: Belknap Press, 1996).

3. E. O. Wilson, *Consilience* (New York: Knopf, 1998).

4. In fact, some authors argue that the process of integration may be an important and underappreciated *driver* of biological evolution—at least as important as mutation. See Lynn Margulis and Dorion Sagan, *Acquiring Genomes: A Theory of the Origins of Species* (New York: Basic Books, 2002). This line of thinking has intriguing parallels with our arguments here about the relative importance of integration and innovation in business contexts.

5. See, for example M. Iansiti, *Technology Integration: Making Critical Choices in a Dynamic World* (Boston: Harvard Business School Press, 1998); R. M. Henderson and K. B. Clark, "Architectural Innovation: The Reconfiguration of Existing Product Technologies and the Failure of Established Firms," *Administrative Science Quarterly* 35 (1990): 9–30; and Clayton M. Christensen and Richard Rosenbloom, "Explaining the Attacker's Advantage: Technological Paradigms, Organizational Dynamics, and the Value Network," *Research Policy* 24 (1995): 233–257.

6. SRI International, "The Beginning of the Global Computer Revolution," SRI Timeline Web page, <http://www.sri.com/technology/mouse.html> (2002); Xerox PARC, "PARC's Legacy," Xerox PARC Web page, <http://www.parc. xerox.com/history.html>; Apple Corporation, "Apple History," <http://www. apple-history.com/history.html> (accessed 1 April 2002).

7. For example, see Henderson and Clark, "Architectural Innovation."

8. See, for example, George Westerman, "Innovating While Integrating" (Ph.D. diss., Harvard Business School, 2002).

9. Henderson and Clark, "Architectural Innovation"; Iansiti, *Technology Integration.*

10. Iansiti, *Technology Integration.*

11. Interview with Joe Hinrichs, Director of Logistics, Ford Motor Company, 5 March 2003.

12. See, for example, Clayton M. Christensen, *The Innovator's Dilemma: When New Technologies Cause Great Firms to Fail* (Boston: Harvard Business School Press, 1997).

13. See Westerman, "Innovating While Integrating."

14. See, for example, M. L. Tushman and C. O'Reilly, *Winning Through Innovation: A Practical Guide to Leading Organizational Change and Renewal* (Boston: Harvard Business School Press, 1997).

15. Stefan Thomke's *Experimentation Matters: Unlocking the Potential of New Technologies for Innovation* (Boston: Harvard Business School Press, 2002) discusses this important topic in great detail.

16. Interview with Tim Brady, Chief Product Officer, Yahoo!, 15 March 1997.

17. This example is drawn with much gratitude from Warren McFarlan's work. See, for example "Merrill Lynch: Integrated Choice (Abridged)," Case 9-301-081 (Boston: Harvard Business School, 2003); and M. Iansiti, F. M. McFarlan, and G. Westerman, "The Incumbent's Advantage," *MIT Sloan Management Review* 44, no. 4 (2003): 58–64.

Chapter Ten

1. See J. C. Rochet and J. Tirole, "Cooperation Among Competitors: The Economics of Payment Card Associations," *Rand Journal of Economics* 33, no. 4 (2002): 1–22; and D. Evans, "The Antitrust Economics of Two-Sided Markets" (mimeograph, AEI-Brookings Joint Center, 2002).

Although not usually covered in the economics literature on this subject, the idea can also be extended to markets that link two or more groups of sellers to buyers, which follow similar principles.

2. In the case of Chemdex and its parent company Ventro, investments in technology and operation totaled hundreds of millions of dollars.

3. Amazon is an often-noted "counterexample" to this simple guideline. Amazon did indeed scale up, but took a long time to achieve cash flow–positive status. Despite lack of overall profitability, however, Amazon was liquid very early, particularly in its core business, books. Amazon then worked hard to move its community of buyers to other domains, ranging from toys to auctions.

Amazon's largest investments were not in designing its original market, but in scaling it up rapidly once it was liquid and in moving its impact to a broad variety of other products, which delayed the time for reaching overall positive cash flow.

4. Interview with Patrick Jabal, Manager, B2B markets, eBay, 12 December 2002.

5. Interestingly, an effective pursuit of experimental market adoption places keystones in the surprising position of being aggressive followers rather than leaders. Microsoft, for example, is notable for being a fast and formidable "second mover" in a variety of domains, with Web browsers being a recent and contentious example. But this approach is entirely consistent with the way one would expect platforms (see chapter 8) to evolve: Keystones continuously monitor the experimentation going on at the frontier of their platform, watching for markets that prove successful and adopting them (and incorporating them into the platform) only once they have proved themselves sufficiently.

6. The lightweight standards embodied in XML-based Web services are an important tool for precisely this kind of leveraging of the ecosystem. These take affiliate programs such as those offered by eBay or Amazon.com to a new level: Web service–based APIs such as those now provided by Google or Amazon allow external communities to literally weave Google or Amazon into the fabric of their products and services, creating a wide range of opportunities for experimentation in novel uses of these firms' technologies.

7. This strategy includes not only explicit beta releases (which are expected to have limitations) but also versions of software that contain incomplete or experimental features.

Chapter Eleven

1. From the definition of *dinosaur* in *The American Heritage Dictionary of the English Language,* 4th ed. (Boston: Houghton Mifflin, 2000).

Index

About the Authors

Marco Iansiti is the David Sarnoff Professor of Business Administration at the Harvard Business School, where he joined the Technology & Operations Management faculty in 1989. Since then, he has performed research on more than one hundred major firms, in industries ranging from software to semiconductors and from automobiles to pharmaceuticals. He is the creator of two courses, Managing Product Development and Starting New Ventures, and has taught extensively in both the M.B.A. and executive programs. Iansiti has authored dozens of papers and cases, including four *Harvard Business Review* articles. His previous book, *Technology Integration: Making Critical Choices in a Dynamic World,* was published by Harvard Business School Press in 1997.

Iansiti is an authority in technology strategy and in the management of innovation and product development. He has worked with a large number of leading organizations, including IBM, Hewlett-Packard, AT&T, Fidelity Investments, Microsoft, General Electric, Unilever, and Sony, along many others. He is Founder and Chairman of the Board of Keystone Strategy Inc., a consulting firm focused on defining and implementing technology and operations strategy for *Fortune* 1000 firms.

Roy Levien's professional career has been almost exclusively in technology, though he was trained as a biologist. His career includes a seven-year tenure at Microsoft, where he served as a program manager and technology architect working on many of the firm's foundational products. His interests range widely, covering everything from game design to product architecture, and from the evolution of complexity to the relationship between technology and society. He is currently pursuing the latter interests in two related books: *Resistance is Futile,* which extends many of the themes introduced in *The Keystone Advantage,* tracing the increasing integration and parallel loss of sovereignty that have characterized human cultural and social evolution; and *Exodus II,* a work of fiction on the same topic.

Levien is Principal and Manager of Keystone Advantage LLC, a consulting firm specializing in the implications of networks, especially for firms and the architectures of their products. He also runs Aldaron, small board game company, and serves as an inventor at Invention Science Laboratories.